Anne around the World

# Anne around the World

## L.M. MONTGOMERY AND HER CLASSIC

Edited by Jane Ledwell and Jean Mitchell

McGill-Queen's University Press
Montreal & Kingston · London · Ithaca

© McGill-Queen's University Press 2013

"Uncertainties Surrounding the Death of L.M. Montgomery"
© Mary Henley Rubio

ISBN 978-0-7735-4139-9 (cloth)
ISBN 978-0-7735-4140-5 (paper)
ISBN 978-0-7735-8858-5 (ePDF)
ISBN 978-0-7735-8859-2 (ePUB)

Legal deposit second quarter 2013
Bibliothèque nationale du Québec

Printed in Canada on acid-free paper that is 100% ancient forest free
(100% post-consumer recycled), processed chlorine free

This book has been published with the help of a grant from the
Canadian Federation for the Humanities and Social Sciences,
through the Awards to Scholarly Publications Program, using funds
provided by the Social Sciences and Humanities Research Council of
Canada.

McGill-Queen's University Press acknowledges the support of the
Canada Council for the Arts for our publishing program. We also
acknowledge the financial support of the Government of Canada
through the Canada Book Fund for our publishing activities.


Library and Archives Canada Cataloguing in Publication

Anne around the world : L.M. Montgomery and her classic / edited
by Jane Ledwell and Jean Mitchell.

Includes bibliographical references and index.
ISBN 978-0-7735-4139-9 (bound). – ISBN 978-0-7735-4140-5 (pbk.)
ISBN 978-0-7735-8858-5 (PDF). – ISBN 978-0-7735-8859-2 (EPUB)

1. Montgomery, L. M. (Lucy Maud), 1874–1942. Anne of Green
Gables.   2. Montgomery, L. M. (Lucy Maud), 1874–1942 – Criticism
and interpretation.   3. Montgomery, L. M. (Lucy Maud), 1874–1942
– Influence.   I. Ledwell, Jane, 1972–   II. Mitchell, Jean, 1953–

PS8526.O55Z5193 2013      C813'.52      C2013-900094-1


Set in 10.4/13.5 Warnock Pro with Nexa
Book design & typesetting by Garet Markvoort, zijn digital

# Contents

# Acknowledgments

The origin of this collection of essays was the Eighth Biennial International L.M. Montgomery Conference, held in 2008 by the L.M. Montgomery Institute at the University of Prince Edward Island, Canada. The conference, "L.M. Montgomery, *Anne of Green Gables* and the Idea of 'Classic,'" inspired a variety of fascinating investigations, and the scholarly discussion continued after the conference. This volume includes papers based on presentations to the conference and is amplified with specially requested and selected submissions that follow upon and extend the discussion. We acknowledge the Social Sciences and Humanities Research Council for its support of the conference and thank the eminent conference co-chairs Elizabeth Epperly, Mary Rubio, and Elizabeth Waterston, as well as conference organizer, Elizabeth DeBlois.

We are grateful for assistance in preparing this volume. Dolores LeVangie was a dedicated partner at every stage of its preparation; we could not have done it without her. Suna Houghton was a perceptive and encouraging reader. Wendy Henderson was an unflagging technical support. We are also grateful to fellow members of the L.M. Montgomery Institute at the University of Prince Edward Island, especially Mark Leggott and Simon Lloyd, and other colleagues at the University of Prince Edward Island and the PEI Advisory Council on the Status of Women.

Material written by L.M. Montgomery is excerpted with the permission of Heirs of L.M. Montgomery Inc. Excerpts from *The Selected Journals of L.M. Montgomery*, Volumes I, II, III, and IV (copyright 1985, 1987, 1992, and 1998, University of Guelph), edited by Mary Rubio and Elizabeth Waterston, and published by Oxford University Press, Canada, are reproduced with the permission of Mary Rubio, Elizabeth Waterston, and the University of Guelph, courtesy of the L.M. Montgomery Collection, Archival and Special Collections, University of Guelph

Library. The manuscript of *Anne of Green Gables* is excerpted courtesy of the Confederation Centre of the Arts, Charlottetown, Prince Edward Island. "L.M. Montgomery," *Emily of New Moon*, *The Story Girl*, and *The Blue Castle* are trademarks of Heirs of L.M. Montgomery Inc. and are used with permission. *Anne of Green Gables* and other indicia of "Anne" are trademarks and/or Canadian official marks of the Anne of Green Gables Licensing Authority Inc. and are used with permission. We are particularly grateful to Sally Keefe Cohen for help in obtaining permission to use this material.

The lengthy preparation of this volume was punctuated by births and critical illnesses. We are thankful for support from the team at McGill-Queen's University Press, particularly from the erudite and gentlemanly Mr Mark Abley and from perspicacious editor Jane McWhinney. We are grateful to the contributors for their steadfast commitment to seeing the volume into print and, most of all, to our families for their love and support, with special thanks to Jim Rodd, Marian Mitchell, Stephen MacInnis, and Anna and Samuel Ledwell MacInnis.

We dedicate this volume to Melanie Dale Scott and the memory of Patti MacKenna.

Anne around the World

# Introduction

JANE LEDWELL AND JEAN MITCHELL

More than a hundred years ago, a curious and often lonely young woman from the north shore of Prince Edward Island published her first novel, *Anne of Green Gables*. It became the first Canadian international best-seller and has now sold over fifty million copies and been translated into more than thirty languages and numerous media, including illustrations, silent film, film series, animated series, plays, musical plays, heritage sites, and Web sites. This book has powerfully influenced generations of readers and helped shape the identities not only of Montgomery's readers around the world but also of her beloved Prince Edward Island and the fictional worlds of childhood.

Lucy Maud Montgomery's childhood was not unusual; nor was it typical. She had lost her mother to tuberculosis and her father to migration west, and was raised by her grandparents and other relatives. When she wrote the story of Anne, she was unmarried and had no children. She lived on a handsome but small island on the eastern coast of a still-new country whose society and traditions were mostly unaccounted for; and yet these were entirely a part of the colonial, imperial projects of global politics. Neither was the Anne character that Montgomery imagined a typical child – an eleven-year-old orphan who survived many tragedies and yet remained hopeful, a child unaccountably odd and remarkable, and yet a clear manifestation of literary tropes and imaginative flights of romance.

It seemed unlikely that this author and this heroine, who on the surface seemed to yoke the ordinary with the conventional, would find a place in print, let alone a lasting place on the bookshelves of several generations in many locales around the globe. And yet readers of different ages and eras and diverse cultures have read beyond literary conventions and the conventionalities of literary genre, style, and culture.

As Montgomery scholar Elizabeth Waterston has said, "Biography does not explain the alchemy of art."[1] In the character and experience of Anne Shirley, readers have discovered experiences they relate to, identify with, and are moved by. This girl-child heroine, born of L.M. Montgomery's imagination and inflected with aspects of her experience, has been adopted as an icon of childhood across time and across cultures.

First termed a "classic" in Canada as early as 1924,[2] *Anne of Green Gables* was a contentious addition to any then-emergent Canadian canon. And yet, a century after its publication, *Anne of Green Gables* continues to attract new audiences, and its complex author continues to intrigue an international community of readers. Intergenerational and intertextual readings of *Anne of Green Gables* reveal a range of specific but broadly extending associations through many eras, texts, and tales – originating, as Irene Gammel traces in her book *Looking for Anne: How Lucy Maud Montgomery Dreamed Up a Literary Classic*, "not merely in the turbulent nature of Prince Edward Island's north shore and the timeless romance of apple blossoms, but also in the popular cosmopolitan magazines of New York."[3] *Anne*'s continuing life has remained cosmopolitan. Celebratory and critical writings have reframed *Anne*'s place in the literary canon and opened the text's singular heroine and author to multiple interpretations. The chapters in this volume are from contemporary scholars and readers engaging with Montgomery's work across disciplines, critical stances, and temporal moments.

Now that *Anne of Green Gables* has been in the world more than a century, it is possible to reflect on what has made possible this fulmination of thought about Anne and her author. To mark her centenary in 2008, international conferences took place in Charlottetown, Prince Edward Island; Guelph, Ontario; and Uppsala, Sweden, where a 2009 conference marked the centenary of the first Swedish translation. Similarly, to mark the singular occasion, numerous volumes of scholarship were published; all of them take as a given that *Anne of Green Gables* is a classic. Elizabeth Waterston's *Magic Island: The Fictions of L.M. Montgomery* finely investigates Montgomery's craft, concluding, "The total sequence of [Montgomery's] books constitutes a fluctuating complex commentary on life and art," and noting that "behind the complexity stands a mysterious creator, a mature craftsman [sic] absorbedly at work."[4] Elizabeth Epperly's *Imagining Anne: The Island Scrapbooks of L.M. Montgomery* engages with imagery, photography, and paratextual sources to relate a narrative of the visual imagination. Mary Rubio's *Lucy Maud Montgomery: The Gift of Wings* provides an authoritative account of Montgomery's life, alongside Montgomery's own journals, of which a first complete and not selected volume has now been released, *The Complete Journals of L.M. Montgomery: The PEI Years, 1889–1900*, edited by Mary Henley Rubio and Elizabeth Waterston. As noted above, Gammel's *Looking for Anne: How Lucy Maud Montgomery Dreamed Up a Literary Classic* traces Anne's origins through the gaps and silences in Montgomery's journals and through the evidence in the book, finding Anne's presumptive precursors in popular, and especially American, precedents. *Storm and Dissonance: L.M. Montgomery and Conflict*, edited by Jean Mitchell, contributes to Montgomery scholarship a collection of papers that engages with conflict and its avoidance – and shades in the darker side of Montgomery's writing in personal and political spaces. Another collection of essays, *100 Years of Anne with an "e": The Centennial Study of "Anne of Green Gables,"* edited by Holly Blackford, examines changing ideas of childhood within Anne's narrative, describing the ways in which Anne is on the crest of larger social changes that are taking place, in addition to registering those changes. The collection assesses "the classic value of *Anne* by placing a novel in its original historical and literary context as well as by investigating the continuing aesthetic and cultural life of the novel in other times, places, and media."[5] Finally, *Anne's World: A New Century of Anne of Green Gables*, edited by Irene Gammel and Benjamin Lefebvre, looks ahead (rather than back) to the multiple readings and interpretations that we can anticipate in the twenty-first century as this twentieth-century "classic" text lives its afterlife.[6]

It is not surprising that the hyperverbal Anne inspires such conversation; the garrulous girl from her first appearance on the page engages ideas of self and other, private and public, and reveals the porousness of divisions among reality, imagination, and identities, be they literal, fictive, or adopted. It is a particular gift of *Anne of Green Gables*, the novel, and Anne of Green Gables, the character, to have been adopted by generation after generation over a century. Anne engages scholarly reading, children's reading, teachers' choices, translators' voices, and adults' re-reading. In her essay in this volume, Cynthia Sugars lists a multiplicity of readings specific to *Anne*: "Anne's reading of Avonlea; Anne's reading of works of literature; other characters' readings of

Anne's stories; other characters' readings of Anne herself; our reading of Anne; our reading of Anne reading Avonlea; our reading of *Anne of Green Gables*; [and] the narrator's reading of the story she is relaying." What this collection captures is the intimacy of these readings and the way that reading *Anne* animates the aesthetics of reading and of the everyday. A recurring theme in the essays that follow is the particular memory of reading the novel and the physical and emotional, not to mention geographical, circumstances of reading. Åsa Warnqvist has recorded over three hundred "reading experiences" from Swedish readers, and provides many moving images of reading *Anne*, including a richly evoked experience of one girl reading with her back against the stove. Other authors give us a girl in Uruguay reading by the fireplace and dreaming of ice cream; girls in Iran responding enthusiastically to the performative text by acting out its parts; women in Japan creating multi-media homages in Anne-centred exhibitions; a writer in Canada writing her own novel in response to *Anne*, in a cottage facing the sea as the months slip into autumn, imagining her surroundings taking on the aspect of a boat as she writes by hand. Such images, and others in this book, enlarge what we think *Anne* is capable of achieving.

Scholarship on *Anne of Green Gables* is now also markedly intergenerational. A special feature of this volume is its collection of essays offered by a handful of women scholars who have shaped the international understanding of *Anne of Green Gables* and of L.M. Montgomery. Their contributions represent distillations of their thought about *Anne of Green Gables* over a generation of scholarship and conversation among scholars and enthusiasts. Equally special to this volume is the focus on the intertextuality that illuminates the novel's impact. This book introduces a chorus of new voices to Montgomery scholarship: in addition to literary scholars who have never previously approached Montgomery, the volume includes responses to *Anne* from scholars from academic disciplines other than English literature, children's authors, and teachers from other countries. The field of Montgomery scholarship has been expanding rapidly, and the diversity of writers engaging with Montgomery's work is a sign of its maturation.

Elizabeth Epperly, founder of the L.M. Montgomery Institute at the University of Prince Edward Island, first conceptualized the establishment of the institute after attending Wordsworth and Tennyson conferences in England.[7] She was guided by the idea of mixing audiences who love an author's works and those that analyse or write about the works. Epperly offered us a clue to the development of this volume: that "sleuthing and analyzing will be done by academics and fans together in new forms of scholarship,"[8] another kind of intertexuality and engagement. As Gammel has said, "Today, the field of Montgomery Studies has matured and become remarkably diverse, so that the novel is no longer discussed exclusively in proto-feminist terms."[9] To signal this diversity and maturation, the essays that follow engage discussions from varied points of view (such as the international, comparative, and [auto]biographical), including provocative and contentious readings of gender, class, colonialism, and religion. A variety of critical frameworks inform the authors' readings. The maturation parallels and announces the gradual emergence of *Anne of Green Gables* as a classic text, a status the essays in this volume explore in multiple facets.

## SITUATING MONTGOMERY AND HER CLASSIC

When it was first published, *Anne of Green Gables* was not critically embraced as a "classic" of literature. Helen Siourbas has traced the "fluid position of L.M. Montgomery within the canons of Canadian literature and Canadian children's literature," which, she suggests, tells us something about the nature of the Canadian canon.[10] Montgomery's currency as a writer waxed and waned, and during her lifetime she encountered the indifference and patronizing attitude of male writers "who were," as Waterston says in this volume, "shoving her aside, mocking her work, and excluding her from professional rewards." In the volume *Anne's World*, Carole Gerson skillfully maps the trajectory of Anne from fictional character to Canadian icon and commodity, naming seven milestones in the creation of a classic: the book's publication by L.C. Page; Anne entering Hollywood; the intervention of government and Canada's National Parks; Anne's travel to Japan; the advent of *Anne of Green Gables: The Musical*, the emergence of the miniseries for television, and the publication of the *Selected Journals*; the launch of L.M. Montgomery Studies; and, finally, centennial commemoration.[11] In considering Montgomery's writing career and her literary legacy with the benefit of more than a hundred years of "milestones," the essays in this first section show that the idea of the classic is enmeshed in processes of cultural signification that are historical and hierarchical.

As Elizabeth Waterston and Mary Rubio demonstrated in their selections for the five volumes of Montgomery's *Selected Journals*, Montgomery's fiction-writing and life writing together reveal the act of writing as a deep chronicle of one human spirit and its possibilities. In her contribution to this volume, Waterston is intrigued by the essential elements of Montgomery's creativity, as manifest in *Anne of Green Gables*. She distills Montgomery's writing to its essential elements: "facts," "focus," "flash," "frenzy," and "fix." Waterston elaborates on these elements by selecting novels written over Montgomery's lifetime to underline the author's "life-long openness to creative inspiration combined with readiness to change." Waterston reminds us how prolific Montgomery was after the success of *Anne* in 1908: twenty-one volumes of fiction over thirty years written "in the interstices of an incredibly busy life" and written for changing styles, genres, audiences, and markets between 1909 and 1939. She wrote for a living, and perhaps for her survival; writing is the one necessary act of Montgomery's existence.

Like Waterston, Elizabeth Epperly is fascinated by what is essential in Montgomery. Epperly illuminates the mystery of how Montgomery's picture-making in text creates the visible world and imprints a vision on readers' metaphor-hungry minds. Epperly historicizes readings of Montgomery's work in selecting the recurring iconic images of "the bend, the arch, and the circle," which "act as a kind of aesthetic shorthand" in the literal and emotional landscape of Montgomery's age. Epperly's essay flashes forward to the way imagery constructs the contemporary imagination in our visually saturated culture. Epperly argues that the way in which Montgomery constructs the visual, and visualizes processes of memory and imagination, is a clue to the remarkable translations Anne has undergone into movies, animations, exhibitions, illustrations, and other media. In her inspiring opening essay, Epperly explains that as a rich source of metaphor, Montgomery's writing, and especially Anne, tells us "about creativity itself and possibilities for the human spirit."

Life-giving possibilities take on poignant meaning in Mary Rubio's reflection on the last surviving writing from Montgomery's life, a contentious "suicide note" that Rubio problematizes as a textual bookend to the writer's life. She provides a fascinating gloss on the idea of "surviving in print." In 1981 Montgomery's son Stuart Macdonald gave Mary Rubio a note he believed to be his mother's suicide note. Having stored it away safely for a quarter of a century, Rubio reread the note in 2006 after her many years of work on Montgomery's journals and just before the publication of her biography of Montgomery. Rubio was "astonished" to find that her reading of the note was now entirely different from that of twenty-five years earlier. As Rubio says, "Understanding how Maud wrote, as well as aspects of her complex personality and the dynamics of the Macdonald family" are all key to an interpretation of the "so-called suicide note." This note is tantalizingly connected to the *Anne of Green Gables* saga, since the uncertainty about Montgomery's last days is bound up with the uncertain status of her last manuscript, another chapter in Anne's story, *The Blythes Are Quoted.*[12]

Concluding this section on "Situating the Classic," Barbara Carman Garner provides an astute overview of early critical response to *Anne of Green Gables*, assiduously arguing that readers and reviewers were, from the beginning, as interested in Montgomery's life and her Island home as they were in her wildly successful novel. Now a feature of modern life, interest in Montgomery's personal and private life began in her lifetime and continues unabated. And yet, Garner notes how Montgomery's "auto-discourses" reveal gaps and elisions in the critical response, using the example of the theme of religion in *Anne of Green Gables* to suggest how this sub-theme has consistently slipped from reviewers' grasp, if not their gaze.

Together, these initial chapters situate the richness and variety of substance for critical engagement with the "classic" text: the strata of images and metaphors, the evident appeal of themes over time, the interplay of person and process, the mystery and ambiguity of text that opens it to re-readings, and the nature and historical context of readings and re-readings over time.

## THE TERRAIN OF THE CLASSIC: ALLUSIONS AND INTERTEXTS

As many of the contributors argue, the intertextuality of *Anne of Green Gables* underscores the porous nature of boundaries between texts and among readers, between the classical and the popular. As Theodore Sheckels states of *Anne* and Montgomery, "Intertexts, then, stem from an author's linguistic and cultural context."[13] A number of chapters in this section point to Montgomery's often playful, self-conscious, and self-reflexive use of allusions. In her 1989 inventory of quotations and allusions in the *Anne* books, Rea Wilmshurst says that through these intextextual linkages, "we can watch the fascinating interplay between conscious character creation and unconscious self-revelation."[14] Cecily Devereux argues in her 2004 Introduction to *Anne of Green Gables* that "Montgomery's writing in *Anne of Green Gables* is highly and almost constantly allusive, both in direct quotations and less overt references," as "Montgomery refers to the texts of her own childhood and adolescence because her story is about a girl's education in the same context, and most of the references thus function primarily as didactic markers and part of the moral work of the narrative as a whole."[15]

For Margaret Doody, co-editor of the annotated edition of *Anne of Green Gables*, Montgomery's education, the richness of the oral and rhetorical culture of her time, and her window into the history of literature position Montgomery for literary play rather than for earnestness. Doody argues that Montgomery's first novel is full of ambiguity, but that intertextual exploration finds joy at the centre of Anne's "tragical" experience. As Doody and Wendy Barry explained earlier in *The Annotated Anne of Green Gables*, "The pattern of allusions woven into *Anne* seems quite deliberate," and because "many of the original sources" are rather obscure, "identifying allusions to them uncovers ... other imaginary lands in the world of literature."[16] Doody says in this volume that Montgomery pays attention to the "interior content of classical literature" and treats classics as material to be played with, including a comic play upon a scene in Virgil's *Aeneid*: as Doody reflected in *The Annotated Anne*, embedded quotations are frequently self-reflexive examples of intertextuality which aim to generate humorous effects.[17] Doody does not believe that Montgomery was "overthrown by the challenges of the 'classic' or of 'literature.'" Rather, Doody argues, "Throughout her writing Lucy Maud Montgomery ... appears to relish the ambiguity of literary positioning, begging the distinction between the 'popular' and the 'classic' or 'literary.'"

Doody grants Montgomery sufficient "mastery" of classical allusion to permit play; by contrast, critic Cecily Devereux contends that "Anne's allusions, with their emphasis on prescribed texts, also function as indices of location, situating the novel in relation to [Prince Edward Island] and to the English-Canadian and Anglo-imperial curriculum."[18] Drawing on specific intertext and allusion between *Anne of Green Gables* and Elizabeth Barrett Browning's Victorian "classic" verse-novel *Aurora*

*Leigh*, Paul Keen's chapter draws our attention to the ways in which a classic is always localized. While there may be a universal appeal or value in the classic, Keen proposes, there are "opposite impulses" driving the novel *Anne of Green Gables* and the character Anne. On the one hand the novel is concerned with the local and intensely lived daily life of a small rural locale, and, on the other hand, romantic Anne "yearns for escape into the fictional world of imagined landscapes and distant literary worlds." Keen suggests that Anne is a *bricoleur*, improvising, appropriating, and cobbling together bits and pieces of literary sources and materials to create her world of discourses. Montgomery is acutely aware of the tension between the commonplace and the romantic, and it is this fusion of the classic and the parochial that makes *Anne* so interesting. "The novel's endless allusiveness," argues Keen, "embeds its account of provincial life within a broader literary world that stretches back across the Atlantic and south of the border."

As an avid and excellent reader, Anne Shirley has a stake in the broader literary world. According to Cynthia Sugars, Anne Shirley's reading list, revealed in her allusions, "might suggest that a literary classic is one that combines ... scope for (romantic) imagination *and* an element of homegrown or intuitive mimetic truth." With precision and wit, Sugars relates in her essay how Anne teaches Marilla to be a sympathetic reader too. In her chapter, Doody contends that there is a "hidden acknowledgment" that Montgomery's *Anne* is a classic; Sugars similarly argues that a reading of *Anne* as literary classic is encrypted in the novel and that Montgomery "instructs us in how to read *Anne [of Green Gables]* itself *as* a classic, with its heroine functioning as a kind of metonym for the text itself." By extension, *Anne* and Anne exist in their own ambiguous terrain between the semiotic poles that Sugars describes in Miss Stacy's sympathetic things-as-they-are realism and Matthew's empathetic things-as-they-might-be "schools" of literary criticism.

Looking to distinctly Canadian terrain for literary criticism, Wendy Shilton's lyrically critical chapter offers an understanding of Northrop Frye's ideas of "centre" and "circumference" as he applied them to well-known Canadian writing of his day, when he famously stated, "There is no Canadian writer of whom we can say what we can say of the world's major writers, that their readers can grow up inside their work without ever being aware of a circumference."[19] As Shilton and this volume as a whole together demonstrate, the terrain of the classic has expanded immeasurably (just as the critical and theoretical conversation has extended beyond Frye's universalist assumptions and untroubled certainty about formulations such as "centre" and "circumference"). Holding *Anne of Green Gables* and poems by Emily Dickinson in inspiring equipoise, Shilton describes the emotional force that disrupts and orphans the certainties of both centre and circumference, ideas whose territory is ceded to the powerful "core human needs" of which readers of Montgomery and Dickinson evince so strong a recognition and so close an identification. These needs, once expressed in poetic and literary form, and received by readers, demand an expansion of the canon and the "classic."

## PROVOKING THE CLASSIC: CLASS, COLONIALISM, AND CHRISTIANITY

People read the text of *Anne of Green Gables* from many different perspectives. Shilton points to the expanded terrain for literary criticism since Frye as encompassing "emergent, intersecting lenses of postmodernism, Marxism, feminism, postcolonialism, neurolinguistics, multimodal literacies," and other readings. The idea of the "centre" or of the "frontier" has shifted no less than spatial configurations have really changed. Provoking essentialist terms is crucial to interrogating the production of difference. Different lenses, applied to Montgomery's classic *Anne of Green Gables*, provoke and problematize the book and its author, uncovering the ways in which both are inured to ideologies of class, colonialism, postcolonialism, and evangelical Christianity. Imputations of "classic" status suggesting ahistorical timelessness and transcendence of place find their counterbalance in historicizing and politically charged readings in this section.

In her chapter, Caroline Jones argues, "Stories that reflect our sense of social propriety, that 'sound like us,' that do not challenge our collective sense of the status quo, are more likely to fulfill our expectations of 'classic' texts: resonant, clear, and unchanging." Do novels become classic because they comply with social conventions and political processes that endorse the dominant cultures' hold over the powerless or the marginalization of others? Jones problematizes the perception of the classic *Anne of Green Gables* as a progressive text that fully transcends its own place and time, arguing instead that "Montgomery's conflicted depictions of class in *Anne of Green Gables* ... provide rich material for analysis, particularly emphasizing how Montgomery reinscribes popular perceptions of the 'natural' social order, and exploring how those reinscriptions solidify the novel's status as 'classic.'" Jones locates the social and linguistic boundaries that inform *Anne of Green Gables*, arguing that language, while key to characterization and narrative development, also functions as a strong signifier of social status. In *Anne* Montgomery uses diction and dialect to mark class – the idea of which encompasses markers of economics, culture, language, and national or ethnic identity.

Meanwhile, Jean Mitchell looks at the ways in which colonial Presbyterian missionary activities linked Cavendish and New London, Prince Edward Island, and New Hebrides (Vanuatu) in the Pacific, adding to "our cultural mapping of Cavendish and suggest[ing] a certain kind of cosmopolitanism (however narrow) that was fuelled by restlessness, imagination, and the power of words," and thereby yielding yet another fresh reading of Montgomery's work. Mitchell argues that the powerful and deeply rooted entanglements of evangelizing Presbyterianism and missionary endeavours emanating from Cavendish are also encoded in *Anne of Green Gables*, and that the relationship between the colonial and the postcolonial is central to Mitchell's reading of intertextuality in Montgomery.

In another reading that provokes the tension between colonial and postcolonial intertexts, Brooke Collins-Gearing's critical gaze on *Anne of Green Gables* from Australia privileges the point of view of the colonized indigenous other. Her reading of the *Anne* novel elucidates the violence of absence and the effects of erasure of the indigenous peoples displaced by nation-building. Collins-Gearing examines the novel's colonial roots and depicts Anne as the child of imperialism who renames and transforms the landscape, erasing indigenous presence and claims. Collins-Gearing's location resonates as a double reading of settler colonialism and its "middle-class, Anglo-Celtic" child heroine[20] from an aboriginal perspective.

While these provocative essays argue that Montgomery's classic is linked to the establishment and endorsement of an orderly Protestant bourgeois domesticity, echoing Devereux's reminder that while the agency of Anne is much lauded (by, for example, Temma Berg[21] or Gammel[22]), "Anne's whole story is rooted in an early twentieth-century imperial notion of progress achieved through the advancement of women

... as mothers" in white and Anglo Saxon contexts.[23] At the same time, the contributors to this volume show that the book undermines this construction through affinities to nature, imaginative musings, and acts of agency that unravel the neat texture of everyday life imposed by rigorous rules of conduct. There is a doubleness in *Anne of Green Gables* that both embraces order and precipitates disorder; that both affirms and questions social structures.

In the course of a hundred years of continuous publication, readers have found that *Anne* the novel provides insight into the processes of modernity through its depiction of tradition, its evocation of the past, and the nostalgia it generates in the hyper urban, mobile, and modern spaces we humans occupy around the world. The next group of essays in this volume looks at the novel's circulation over time, in changing social circumstances and, indeed, in societies physically situated far away from Montgomery's Cavendish home.

## *ANNE* AND AFTER: THE LOCAL AND GLOBAL CIRCULATION OF THE CLASSIC TEXT

Several chapters in this volume place us in sympathy with readers of *Anne* around the world. Even during her lifetime, Montgomery was well aware of the international status of *Anne*. Sometimes she brought letters to her public readings and speeches, and, for example, on one occasion in the 1930s read fan mail from a Christian in North America, a Buddhist monk in Tibet, a Muslim student from India, and a Catholic nun in Australia, all of whom found "something" deeply meaningful in Anne.[24] The contribution of *Anne of Green Gables* to discourses of nationhood in Canada has been considered by a number of authors, most particularly Laura Robinson[25] and others in Gammel and Epperly's *L.M. Montgomery and Canadian Culture*. Historical and critical accounts describe the history of the book as an export.[26]

The contributors to this volume add intimate experiential reading to intertextual engagement – Anne's paths mingling in imagination with Persian poet Omar Khayyam, Uruguayan modernist Armonìa Somers, American Willa Cather (by way of a Turkish classroom), Japanese translators and animators, and Swedish publishers of "classics" for youth and adults. Considering the status of *Anne of Green Gables* as a "national icon" and "commodity export" in the context of Canadian nationalism,

Devereux suggests that *Anne* is popular in other national and nationalist contexts "not because it is Canadian, but because it is itself a nationalist narrative"[27] that "has been 'domesticated' in a range of cultural contexts." Anne the character has become "globalized, her local specificity and original nationalism transposed and re-shaped in every location, her function as icon and value as commodity shifting endlessly between cultural and economic, local and global."[28] Margaret Steffler analyzed Anne's postcolonial circuits to trace "the ways in which readings of Montgomery's novel evoke nostalgic ideas and ideals of home in the context of the growing fluidity and nomadism of nation and homeplace in the [twenty-first] century."[29]

The commodification of *Anne* and export of Anne have long been read as contributing to an understanding of being Canadian or Canadianness. In *L.M. Montgomery and Canadian Culture*, the "first systematic effort to investigate the question of the Canadianness of Montgomery's writing," Gammel and Epperly argue that Montgomery "strategically inscribes the signifiers of Canadian distinctness even while appealing to a broad, international readership."[30] More recently, Poushali Bhadury "gesture[s] towards specific ways in which extra-textual commodification ventures in the case of Anne promote within a global context certain 'much-contested' visions of a quintessential, 'authentic' 'Canadianness' as embodied in cultural products."[31] As the local and global circulation of *Anne*'s classic text may demonstrate – and as many of the intimate readings in this volume attest – the local now is embedded within the global. Their arguments cause us to scrutinize the question of whether this constitutes a bypassing or reconfiguring of the national.

In places and lives, both tranquil and traumatic, Montgomery's *Anne* novels have flourished among readers. "L.M. Montgomery's writing changes people's lives," writes Epperly in her landmark monograph *The Fragrance of Sweetgrass*, and people are "inspired by Montgomery's characters, descriptions, and romanticized realism."[32] In sympathy with the mutability of personal response, Janice Fiamengo has described the "portable landscapes" Montgomery created in *Anne*, saying, "Montgomery's emphasis on the ecstatic response of the sympathetic viewer meant that Avonlea, unlike Cavendish, became a portable landscape, one whose enchanting details could be adapted to many regions of the world."[33] Countries engaged in or ravaged by war have looked to the *Anne* novels for "romanticized interconnections between self and home" which are "the essence of Montgomery's appeal."[34] As Waterston notes in this volume, Montgomery's story of the orphan meshed with her early life in her grandparents' house as an orphan story as a motherless child.

If *Anne of Green Gables* was a balm to war-torn nations in the era after the World Wars, it should not be surprising that, as Gholamreza Samigorganroodi illustrates, the novel continues to be a solace to young women in contemporary Iran. He describes how young Iranian women, themselves orphaned and displaced by war, respond to the young orphaned heroine. The trope of orphanhood also speaks to the experience of dispossession among people who continue to be vulnerable in the face of violent geo-political events. And yet, Samigorganroodi's chapter tells us that reading *Anne of Green Gables* generates joy above all. He locates translated poetic language as a source of "fellow-feeling" between Anne's English-speaking and Persian-speaking audiences: "Poetic language is also characteristic of the Persian language and literature, which are often loaded with figures of speech and tropes," and, he continues, "My students ... dramatize the story and act it out in class, translate it into Persian, write poems about it, relate it to their own lives and situations, and read it to replicate themselves." This, too, is *surviving in print*.

*Anne* in the classroom is a theme in several chapters in this volume. Indeed, Anne found her way to Doreley Coll in Montevideo, Uruguay, through the school curriculum, where she was introduced thanks to the fiery imagination of an activist educator and writer. Coll recalls reading *Anne* in Montevideo on "cold south-Atlantic nights." She says, "I would cuddle under thick quilts with my book to be transported," and would dream of Prince Edward Island picnics "as the ice pellets tapped on the window panes." Within women's literary tradition, Coll in her chapter locates intertextuality in Uruguayan culture, where Armonía Somers's love of Montgomery's Anne permeates her highly charged representations of volatile redheads in novels that created a furor over their mysterious authorship and provocative content.

Tanfer Emin Tunc reflects on teaching *Anne* from her point of view as a professor of American Literature at Hacettepe University, Ankara, where young Turkish women have embraced Anne's forthright and outspoken personality as emblematic of feminist girlhood. Tunc analyzes *Anne of Green Gables* in tandem with Willa Cather's *My Antonia* to locate the ways in which feminist voices resonate in both novels. Tunc identifies "the formation of a subversive space in which both characters are able to form their own independent identities," but adds that this space "allows student readers to enter Anne and Antonia's relatively unsupervised worlds by inserting themselves into their permeable landscapes."

Tunc also reminds us that Cather and Montgomery converge in their belief that children have an integral part in building nations[35] or the "imagined communities" that Benedict Anderson suggested were forged as much by language and literacy and the effects of the printed word as by changes wrought by commerce and economics.[36] By linking Antonia and Anne, Tunc adds another reading of settler societies and the violence of frontiers.

Speaking from Japan, Yoshiko Akamatsu explains in an interview with the editors the new ways in which Anne is read in Japan, where the novel was introduced on a large scale after the Second World War and still has a presence in contemporary Japan, despite a declining book culture. An "animation of *Anne of Green Gables* made Anne a recognizable icon in Japan to a whole new generation of young people," and Anne-centred exhibitions have given Japanese people a chance to encounter Anne "first-hand." Akamatsu suggests this hyper-modernity means new ways of experiencing, consuming, embodying, and "seeing" Anne and the products, Web sites, media, and storefront windows and tourist venues that this fictional character generates – attracting them backward, Akamatsu hopes, into the book text itself. The commodified vision of Anne obscures her complexity, limiting the possibilities for multiple readings, and it is in these rich possibilities that Akamatsu and the other authors in this book locate Anne's classic status.

The rewards of reading the book text are vividly and poignantly captured in Åsa Warnqvist's collection of three hundred readers' experiences of reading *Anne* in Sweden over the past century. As one woman Warnqvist canvassed recalls: "I experienced a light." The light from childhood reading extends into adult lives of women readers, who return again and again to read Montgomery's novels. In foregrounding the fascinating details behind the first Swedish translation of *Anne of Green Gables*, Warnqvist discusses the minute adaptations that are inevitably implicated in readers' reception of the book. The Swedish translator Jensen "let the people of Avonlea have coffee with their breakfast (as was customary in Sweden) instead of tea; she adapted botanical terms and food to the Swedish flora and cuisine and changed literary references." However, her retention of Canadian place names and personal names means that "both the exotic and the familiar are present in the work," satisfying the taste for both.

## PARATEXT AND AFTERTEXTS: FURTHER WORDS ON *ANNE*

Internationally, the act of translation, publication, and circulation in various media has brought the local and global, and the exotic and familiar, into constant correspondence. For many Canadian writers, the "classic" status of *Anne of Green Gables* evinces a need to respond to Anne, whether to rewrite her, reimagine her, or write against her. As Theodore Sheckels observes: "Readers read later fiction through the subcutaneous lens of *Anne* as intertext, just as readers reflect on *Anne* through the lens of this later fiction. Intertexuality informs this interpretative cycle."[37] As it is for readers, so it is for writers, as "recurrent motifs of *Anne* are given new skin and thereby rich, new meaning by subsequent ... writers" in Canada.[38]

A recent collection of essays on new Atlantic Canadian short fiction conjures the inevitable Anne to emphasize contrast: *Anne of Tim Hortons: Globalization and the Reshaping of Atlantic-Canadian Literature*, by Herb Wylie, looks at fictions that rebut ideas of Atlantic Canada's quaintness and picturesque nostalgia: the presumptive hallmarks of the commodified Anne.

The front-cover image on Wylie's study, a head of tousled and tortured red hair, recalls the crucial importance of paratext in *Anne*'s history. MacDonald demonstrates that clothing in *Anne of Green Gables* tells us about community, class, femininity, and the status of women. The sartorial presents a complex reading of aesthetics, and especially of colour. Montgomery's texts, as MacDonald argues, are costumed, replete with clothing-related metaphors. MacDonald suggests that as a heroine, Anne "stands as literary and artistic heir not only to the heroines of nineteenth-century novels but also to those of Greek and Roman mythology, [and] medieval legend seen through Romantic and Victorian poetry."

This emanation of legend is a lot for a contemporary fiction writer to contend with, and the final two chapters in the volume trace intertextuality to engage the meanings of Montgomery's influence on the imaginations of subsequent writers. Susan Meyer's chapter examines the inevitable influence of Montgomery on later Canadian writers of literature for children and young readers. Meyer provides careful readings of works by Bernice Thurman Hunter, Kit Pearson, Tim Wynne-Jones, Jean Little, and Julie Johnston which intersect with Montgomery's writing. She argues that Montgomery cast a long shadow on aspiring and established Canadians writers, who have responded variously by revision, contention, and celebration. As Meyer explains, "interesting tensions and rivalries as well as affirmations can and do exist between women writers, tensions that add an element of vitality and complexity to the women's literary tradition."

Budge Wilson, a much-respected and beloved writer for young audiences, has the final word in this volume. A relative newcomer to writing about, or perhaps more accurately *alongside*, Montgomery, Wilson is the author who was selected to write *Before Green Gables*, the prequel to *Anne of Green Gables*, for the centenary. Wilson tells us something about her own creative process when she received the invitation. Like a number of other famous Canadian women writers, Wilson was an *Emily* aficionado but, as she tells us, when she started to read *Anne* she too became "bewitched." Wilson gives Anne Shirley a life before Green Gables in her prequel, but Anne reciprocates by giving Wilson the memory of a shared past with Montgomery through a college room at Halifax Ladies' College. Wilson's chapter captures that unique meld of magic and imagination – of dogged persistence and practicality that readers recognize in the characters of both Anne and Maud and which is mirrored in the creation of *Before Green Gables*.

For scholars and enthusiasts alike, *Anne of Green Gables* is evidently a generative text. Budge Wilson shares the key question that framed her writing of the prequel: "How was it possible that this eleven-year-old child who had had such an appalling early childhood could step down from the train in Prince Edward Island as a richly formed person who was lively, cheerful, feisty, articulate, and spilling over with an unfettered imagination?" This is a question that has haunted readers and inspired in them remarkable identification with Anne Shirley.

The idea of the literary classic has a genealogy that has informed L.M. Montgomery's reception as a writer over the past century. By situating the classic, exploring the terrain of allusion and intertext, provoking the classic in postcolonial territories, examining the local and global circulation of the global text, and writing responsively to the text and paratext, contributors to this volume celebrate Doody's assertion in her chapter that, like all classics, *Anne of Green Gables* can be "teased, played with, and re-examined." It is this sense of *play* – of joy in reading, interpreting, and transforming the novel and the world – that engages readers and readings of *Anne of Green Gables* by "sleuths" (to use Epperly's term) informed by expertise from scholarship and experience. Waterston concludes: "Montgomery had recognized and relished her gift of transcendence, her ability to lift the curtains of reality and rapturously re-enter a more perfect land. She created characters with a comparable capacity of escape into a world of beauty and accomplishment, comedy and pathos."[39] For while Montgomery's uncanny offerings of joy and sorrow help define her appeal across generations, Montgomery and the magic of her creation remain mysterious. We continue to be drawn to that mystery as our efforts to solve the riddle, crack the codes, decipher the encryptions, and unlock the imaginary continue, with multiple and contradictory readings. It is for these reasons that *Anne of Green Gables* continues to attract readers and to generate so much writing and thought, inexhaustibly intriguing, into a second century of life on the page.

## NOTES

1  Waterston, *Magic Island*, 221.
2  Devereux, "'Canadian Classic' and 'Commodity Export,'" 11, quotes J.D. Logan and Donald French's 1924 volume, *Highways of Canadian Literature*, as already terming *Anne of Green Gables* "a book which may be confidently labelled a 'Canadian classic.'"
3  Gammel, *Looking for Anne*, 16.
4  Waterston, *Magic Island*, 220.
5  Blackford, Introduction, xxx.
6  Lefebvre, "What's in a Name?" 192–211.
7  Elizabeth Epperly, personal communication with the editors. See also Gerson, "Seven Milestones," for a more general published account.
8  Ibid.
9  Gammel, "Reconsidering Anne's World," 7.
10  Siourbas, "L.M. Montgomery: Canon or Cultural Capital?" 131.
11  Gerson, "Seven Milestones," 17–34.

12  A version of Montgomery's *The Blythes Are Quoted*, edited by Benjamin Lefebvre, was published in 2009.
13  Sheckels, "Anne of Green Gables as Intertext," 146.
14  Wilmshurst, "L.M. Montgomery's Use of Quotations," 17.
15  Devereux, Introduction, 34.
16  Doody and Barry, *The Annotated Anne*, 457.
17  Ibid., 459.
18  Devereux, Introduction, 34–5.
19  Frye, "Conclusion," 340–1. Quoted in Shilton in this volume.
20  Bradford, "The Homely Imaginary," 179.
21  Berg, "*Anne of Green Gables*," 153–64.
22  Gammel, "Reconsidering Anne's World," 3–16; "Safe Pleasures for Girls," 114–27.
23  Devereux, "'Not one of those dreadful new women,'" 125.
24  Rubio, *Lucy Maud Montgomery*, 473.
25  Robinson, "'A Born Canadian,'" 19–30. Not coincidentally, discourses of nationhood are prominent in Devereux, "Anatomy of a 'National Icon,'" which recasts a media controversy that arose from Robinson's paper on lesbian desire in *Anne of Green Gables* at one of the L.M. Montgomery Institute's biennial conferences.
26  For historical context, see Peterman, "Bestselling Authors," and for critical engagement, Devereux, "'Canadian Classic' and 'Commodity Export,'" 20.
27  Devereux, "'Canadian Classic' and 'Commodity Export,'" 20.
28  Ibid., 19.
29  Steffler, "Anne in a 'Globalized' World," 153.
30  Gammel and Epperly, "L.M. Montgomery," 5.
31  Bhadury, "Fictional Spaces," 214.
32  Epperly, *The Fragrance of Sweetgrass*, 3.
33  Fiamengo, "Towards a Theory," 228.
34  Epperly, *The Fragrance of Sweetgrass*, 12.
35  For example, see Rubio, "Where Does the Voice Come From," and Devereux, "'Canadian Classic' and 'Commodity Export.'"
36  Anderson, *Imagined Communities*.
37  Sheckels, "Anne of Green Gables as Intertext," 145.
38  Ibid., 144.
39  Waterston, *Magic Island*, 220.

## BIBLIOGRAPHY

Anderson, Benedict. *Imagined Communities: Reflections on the Origin and Spread of Nationalism*. London: Verso Editions, 2006.

Berg, Temma F. "*Anne of Green Gables*: A Girl's Reading." In *Such a Simple Little Tale: Critical Responses to L.M. Montgomery's* Anne of Green Gables. Edited by Mavis Reimer, 153–64. Metuchen, New Jersey: Children's Literature Association and the Scarecrow Press, 1992.

Bhadury, Poushali. "Fictional Spaces, Contested Images: Anne's 'Authentic' Afterlife." *Canadian Children's Literature Association Quarterly*, vol. 36.2 (summer 2011): 214–37.

Blackford, Holly, ed. *100 Years of Anne with an "e": The Centennial Study of "Anne of Green Gables."* Calgary: University of Calgary Press, 2009.

– Introduction to Blackford, *100 Years of Anne with an "e"*, xi–xxxviii.

Bradford, Clare. "The Homely Imaginary: Fantasies of Nationhood in Australian and Canadian Texts." In *Home Words: Discourses of Children's Literature in Canada*, edited by Mavis Reimer, 177–94. Waterloo, Ontario: Wilfrid Laurier University Press, 2008.

Devereux, Cecily. "Anatomy of a 'National Icon': *Anne of Green Gables* and the 'Bosom Friends' Affair." In Gammel, *Making Avonlea*, 32–42.

– "'Canadian Classic' and 'Commodity Export': The Nationalism of 'Our' Anne of Green Gables." *Journal of Canadian Studies*, vol. 36.1 (spring 2001): 11–28.

– Introduction to *Anne of Green Gables*, by L.M. Montgomery. Peterborough, Ontario: Broadview Press, 2004.

– "'Not one of those dreadful new women': Anne Shirley and the Culture of Imperial Motherhood." In Hudson and Cooper, *Windows and Words: A Look at Canadian Children's Literature in English Canada*, 119–30.

Doody, Margaret Anne, and Wendy E. Barry. "Literary Allusion and Quotation in *Anne of Green Gables*." In *The Annotated Anne of Green Gables*, edited by Wendy E. Barry, Margaret Anne Doody, and Mary E. Doody Jones, 457–62. Oxford: Oxford University Press, 1997.

Epperly, Elizabeth Rollins. *The Fragrance of Sweet-Grass: L.M. Montgomery's Heroines and the Pursuit of Romance*. Toronto: University of Toronto Press, 1992.

– *Imagining Anne: The Island Scrapbooks of L.M. Montgomery*. Toronto: Viking, 2008.

Fiamengo, Janice. "Towards a Theory of the Popular Landscape in *Anne of Green Gables*." In Gammel, *Making Avonlea*, 225–37.

Frye, Northrop. "Conclusion." *Literary History of Canada, 1st ed.* General Editor Carl F. Klinck, Toronto: University of Toronto Press, 1965, 1945.

Gammel, Irene. *Looking for Anne: How Lucy Maud Montgomery Dreamed Up a Literary Classic*. Toronto: Key Porter, 2008.

–, ed. *Making Avonlea: L.M. Montgomery and Popular Culture*. Toronto: University of Toronto Press, 2002.

– "Reconsidering Anne's World." In Gammel and Lefebvre, *Anne's World: A New Century of Anne of Green Gables*, 3–16.

- "Safe Pleasures for Girls: L.M. Montgomery's Erotic Landscapes." In Gammel, *Making Avonlea*, 114–27.

Gammel, Irene, and Benjamin Lefebvre, eds. *Anne's World: A New Century of Anne of Green Gables*. Toronto: University of Toronto Press, 2010.

- "L.M. Montgomery and the Shaping of Canadian Culture." In Gammel and Epperly, *L.M. Montgomery and Canadian Culture*, 3–13.

–, and Elizabeth Epperly, eds. *L.M. Montgomery and Canadian Culture*. Toronto: University of Toronto Press, 1999.

Gerson, Carole. "Seven Milestones: How *Anne of Green Gables* Became a Canadian Icon." In Gammel and Lefebvre, *Anne's World*, 17–34.

Hudson, Aïda, and Susan-Ann Cooper, eds. *Windows and Words: A Look at Canadian Children's Literature in English Canada*. Ottawa: University of Ottawa Press, 2003.

Lefebvre, Benjamin. "'What's in a Name?' Towards a Theory of the Anne Brand." In Gammel and Lefebvre, *Anne's World*, 192–211.

Mitchell, Jean, ed. *Storm and Dissonance: L.M. Montgomery and Conflict*. Newcastle, UK: Cambridge Scholars, 2008.

Montgomery, L.M. *The Blythes Are Quoted*, edited and with an afterword by Benjamin Lefebvre. Toronto: Viking, 2009.

- *The Complete Journals of L.M. Montgomery: The PEI Years, 1889–1990*. Edited by Mary Henley Rubio and Elizabeth Waterston. Toronto: Oxford University Press, 2012.

Peterman, Michael. "Bestselling Authors, Magazines, and the International Market." In *The Cambridge History of Canadian Literature*, edited by Coral Ann Howells and Eva-Marie Kröller, 185–203. Cambridge: Cambridge University Press, 2009.

Robinson, Laura M. "'A Born Canadian': The Bonds of Communal Identity in *Anne of Green Gables* and *A Tangled Web*." In Gammel and Epperly, *L.M. Montgomery and Canadian Culture*, 19–30.

Rubio, Mary. "L.M. Montgomery: Where Does the Voice Come From?" In *Canadiana: Studies in Canadian Literature / Études de littérature canadienne: Proceedings of the Canadian Studies Conference*, edited by Jørn Carlsen and Knud Larsen, 109–19. Aarhus, Denmark: Department of English, 1984.

Rubio, Mary Henley. *Lucy Maud Montgomery: The Gift of Wings*. Toronto: Doubleday, 2008.

Sheckels, Theodore. "*Anne of Green Gables* as Intertext in Post-1960 Canadian Women's Fiction." In Blackford, *100 Years of Anne with an "e,"* 143–64.

Siourbas, Helen. "L.M. Montgomery: Canon or Cultural Capital?" In Hudson and Cooper, *Windows and Words*, 131–42.

Steffler, Margaret. "Anne in a 'Globalized' World: Nation, Nostalgia, and Postcolonial Perspectives of Home." In Gammel and Lefebvre, *Anne's World*, 150–65.

Waterston, Elizabeth. *Magic Island: The Fictions of L.M. Montgomery*. Oxford: Oxford University Press, 2008.

Wilmshurst, Rea. "L.M. Montgomery's Use of Quotations and Allusions in the 'Anne' Books." CCL: *Canadian Children's Literature*, vol. 56 (1989): 15–45.

Wylie, Herb. *Anne of Tim Hortons: Globalization and the Reshaping of Atlantic-Canadian Literature*. Waterloo, Ontario: Wilfrid Laurier University Press, 2011.

# Situating Montgomery
## and Her Classic

# Anne of Green Gables – and Afterward

ELIZABETH HILLMAN WATERSTON

Creating fiction involves five elements, all beginning with the letter "F": facts, focus, flash, frenzy, fix. When L.M. Montgomery was brooding up the story that would become *Anne of Green Gables*, she had all of these.

The facts that impinged on her consciousness included a very beautiful natural setting – red earth, green meadows, blue sea and sky, golden sands. But that beauty alternated with a bitter, all-white scenery for half of every year. Another fact she faced was the power of the older generation: a grandmother, repressive and cool, and a now-dead grandfather, still lingering in memory as contemptuous and unresponsive to her needs. Strong in her memory, also, was her father: warm and loving, but always distant – out in the Canadian west, unable to give emotional support in her childhood. Of her own age group, few in Cavendish were able to provide the warmth of a "kindred spirit": both Frede Campbell and Norah Lefurgey had moved out of close range. Books remained as central facts in her life: experiences in the traditional literature of Burns and Scott and Bulwer-Lytton; in the riches of more recent writers, Twain and Kipling and Stevenson; and in the current magazines coming through the mail.

Sometime in 1906 these facts of space and family and books came into sharp focus for Maud Montgomery. She looks out of a photograph of that period with an enigmatic smile. She is wearing a stylish bolero of embroideries, with flowers in her hair and at her breast: she is clearly a lover of beauty. She focuses with the self-assurance gained from years of successful sales of short stories and poetry. Her eyes are heavy-lidded: she is visualizing an inner world even while she enjoys the outer one.

Then comes the flash – the moment of extra-vivid perception that she would later attribute to "Emily." Maud Montgomery picks up a news item: "an elderly couple send for a boy – by mistake a girl is sent." All the insurgent sexual politics that had been fermenting in her late-Victorian youth; all the shift from a farm economy where boys were of course more use than girls (in the eyes of the only people who could vote, or hold office, that is, men) – all that ferment flashed into usefulness as a possible story hinge. She would write the story of an orphan girl sent in lieu of a boy. Orphan stories – *Kim, Huckleberry Finn, Rebecca of Sunnybrook Farm, Daddy-Long-Legs* – were in vogue, and Montgomery was a seasoned writer who kept her eye on the market. And indeed she could recall her own lonely early life in her grandparents' house as an orphan story. The possibility of making something of all these facts flashed into her mind: "I can make something of that!"

Simultaneously she experienced a more personal flash: as she began to write her story of *Anne of Green Gables*, a handsome youngish man came calling – a man who was a minister, in a position to need a wife. Ewan Macdonald's appearance as a possible suitor created not so much a flash as a smoulder, setting the storyteller to work in a very hopeful mood. She would include a tentative romance in the book she had just started to write.

That creative flash stirred her into a writing frenzy. She wrote in the kitchen, in the bedroom, in the orchard, impervious (almost) to the cries for usefulness and productivity (pies, organ music, embroideries). The frenzy lasted until a heap of miscellaneous bits of paper stood ready to be transcribed into a typescript.

So now came the fix. Page after page of the typescript needed to be interlarded with additions, corrections, sharpenings, deletions. The finished manuscript remains as evidence of punctilious craftsmanship, and of inspired second and third thoughts about the way the story could be improved. A few corrections that appear on a single page, for instance – from the crucial scene where young Anne faces a teasing, patronizing boy, and bops him over the head with her slate – show how closely she reworked her materials. Phrases and sentences inserted at a late stage appear in italics in this reproduction of parts of that single page:

With her chin propped on her hands *and her eyes fixed on the blue glimpse of the Lake of Shining Waters that the west window afforded,* she was far away in a gorgeous dreamland.

[...]

Gilbert Blythe wasn't used to putting himself out to make a girl look at him and meeting with failure. *She should look at him, that red-haired Shirley girl with the little pointed chin and the big eyes that weren't like the eyes of any other girl in Avonlea school.* Gilbert reached across the aisle, picked up the end of Anne's long red braid, held it out at arm's length and said in a piercing whisper, "Carrots! Carrots!"

[...]

Avonlea school always enjoyed a scene. This was an especially enjoyable one. *Everybody said, "Oh" in horrified delight. Diana gasped. Ruby Gillis, who was inclined to be hysterical, began to cry. Tommy Sloane let his team of crickets escape him altogether while he stared open-mouthed at the tableau.*

Mr. Phillips stalked down the aisle, ... "Anne Shirley, what does this mean?" he said angrily. Anne returned no answer. *It was asking too much of flesh and blood to expect her to tell before the whole school that she had been called "carrots."* ... "I am sorry to see a pupil of mine displaying such a temper and such a vindictive spirit," he said in a solemn tone, *as if the mere fact of being a pupil of his ought to root out all evil passions from the hearts of small imperfect mortals.* "Anne, go and stand on the platform in front of the blackboard for the rest of the afternoon."[1]

Montgomery had worked to fix the story into its final form, sharpening the sense of the girl's dreams, the boy's interest, the teacher's pomposity, and the comic drama of the schoolchildren's reactions. Every single page of the *Anne of Green Gables* manuscript shows the same crafty sharpening.[2]

Finishing and fixing the manuscript took a year's hard work. Then it found a publisher and went out into the world in 1908, to become one of the longest-lasting and most widely acclaimed books of all fiction.

And then what? L.M. Montgomery settled into a long life of further fictions. She experienced new facts and developed a new focus, as she moved away from Prince Edward Island into marriage, motherhood, and role-playing as mistress of the manse. New flashes came, sometimes from a rival's book or from a new environment or from the news of the day; the coming of war or of the jazz age, the Great Depression, the eruption of a second world war, devastating to a woman now the mother of two military-aged sons. Yet, even in her late years of retirement and illness, she was still open to periods of frenzied composition, writing on her lap in the bedroom, where the once-handsome and happy young man, now in the depths of bipolar mood swings, lay groaning. Always after the creative work came the fixing up. Her last manuscripts are as interlarded as the first one with corrections, elections, and additions. In thirty years, from 1909 until 1939, she published twenty-one more volumes of fiction, in the interstices of an incredibly busy life.

Five novels, chosen as a sampling of these subsequent publications, suggest how her world changed, how she changed, and how the brilliance of her writing and the care of her self-editing persisted even when styles and audiences and markets changed. In each, it is possible to see a fine example of one of the "five F's."

*Kilmeny of the Orchard* clarifies the way in which the "flash" of inspiration that came with the appearance of Ewan Macdonald intensified Montgomery's sense of romance. Under pressure from her publisher to provide "another L.M. Montgomery book" for the 1910 market, she revised "Una of the Garden," a serial published several years earlier, creating a longer and richer novel. In this revision the narrator, a man "from away" becomes a more rounded character, more dazzling to the beautiful Kilmeny, a gifted but repressed young woman. The love story, rewritten during the period of Montgomery's engagement to Ewan Macdonald, is intensified by new stress on the power of love to release an artist into full force. Ewan's coming had perhaps stirred the flash that led to Anne's creation; certainly it led to the rich recreation of "Una" as *Kilmeny*.

The "facts" of Montgomery's life had changed radically when in 1916 she wrote *Anne's House of Dreams*. Leaskdale, deep inland in Ontario, replaced seashore Cavendish; the Leaskdale manse, which was hers to decorate, replaced the Prince Edward Island farmhouse dominated by an old-fashioned grandmother. New intergenerational relations emerged between Maud Montgomery Macdonald and her babies – two of them healthy and energetic, one, sadly, stillborn. A newfound joy in a kindred spirit, Frederica Campbell, with whom she could share secret sorrows, alternated with a sense of being pressured by too many of her husband's parishioners, people not "of the race of Joseph." Far away in Europe, the Great War grew daily more terrifying. With such a twist of new facts in the novelist's consciousness, it is small wonder that *Anne's House of Dreams* emerged as a complex story with sombre shadows. Four houses represent Montgomery's developing multiple personae: Anne's seashell house of dreams – where she and Gilbert must endure the death of their first child; the prim angular home of a gossipy feminist; the vine-hidden house of a woman who endures a terrifying marriage; and the lighthouse where a poetic soul creates stories. The new facts of Montgomery's life are used in *Anne's House of Dreams*, but in symbolic form.

*Rilla of Ingleside* shows much more direct use of primary material. Montgomery's journal record of the events of the First World War provides in manifold detail facts that *could* be transferred directly into the fictional account. The *Rilla* manuscript, however, gives us a powerful insight into the "fix" phase: the work of revision. As with the *Anne of Green Gables* manuscript, virtually every single page shows the additions, deletions, and repositionings that move the story into its final polished form.[3] While she was writing *Rilla of Ingleside*, and after she had finished, Montgomery had second thoughts, and third thoughts, and sixtieth ones – all weaving revisions into the story for more clarity, more vividness of characters, more poignancy, more laughter. Sometimes a revision is written in above the first choice of words; at other times, the original word is struck out and the replacing word follows immediately on the same line – as if the change occurred to her immediately. Sometimes a longer emendation is written on a separate piece of paper, lettered to show on what page in the original writing it should be inserted. The changes wrought on one such page show how the intense work of revision increases the poignancy of the passage. Here, Anne's second son, the poetic Walter, broods about bayonets. (Deletions are indicated in strike-through form. The section set in italics was added from a supplementary note marked "Q2.")

"War isn't a khaki uniform or a drill parade – everything I've read in old histories haunts me." ~~No, don't worry – I'm not going – I've no wish to go."~~ I lie awake at night and <u>see</u> things that have happened – see the blood and filth and misery ~~and~~ of it all. ~~And I can't face it.~~ Q2 *And a bayonet charge! If I could face the other things I ~~couldn't~~ could <u>never</u> face <u>that</u>. It turns me sick to think of it – sicker even to think of giving it than receiving it – to think of*

*thrusting a bayonet through another man." Walter writhed and*
*shuddered. "I think of those things* all *the time – and it doesn't*
*seem to me that Jem and Jerry* ever *think of them.* ~~But thinks it~~ *But*
it maddens me to see ~~Jem and Jerry~~ them in the khaki."[4]

Like the revisions to *Anne of Green Gables*, these emendations make
the book more colourful and vivid to its audience. In *Rilla of Ingleside*,
however, an extra intention was in play as she "fixed" her manuscript:
Montgomery now wove in these additions to clarify her private feelings.
In this case, it was the horror of war that gripped her and forced its
harsh way into the novel. The nature of the "fix" was changing, as well
as the "facts" and the "flash."

Montgomery's account of the writing of *The Blue Castle* in 1924–25
shows comparable change in the "frenzy" of putting pen to paper. On
a rare holiday trip to Ontario cottage country in July 1922, she was inspired to write a modern novel in which a woman escapes from the
trap of convention and propriety to find love and beauty on a Muskoka
island. The inspiration came when she was already planning a third
book about Emily Byrd Starr, of New Moon. Between April 1924, when
she first mentioned *The Blue Castle* as "a book I am trying to write,"
and February 1925, when she wrote in her diary that she had finished
a first draft of the novel, she endured family troubles, battles with her
first publisher, fits of depression that brought "little stabs of anguish,"
and conflict in the church over the possibility of union between Presbyterians and Methodists. Yet in the tragically few hours when she
could write, she "revelled" in "gay and brilliant adventures."[5] She wrote
fiercely, somehow pushing away all her troubles when her pen poured
words onto the pages, and when *The Blue Castle* was finished she could
say, "it seemed a refuge from the cares and worries of my real world."[6]
Perhaps in recognition of the difficulties she had faced in maintaining
the writing mood under contrary circumstances, she had to add, "I shall
have a good bit of work revising it."[7]

By the late 1930s, Montgomery's focus on her world had changed dra-
matically since the *Anne of Green Gables* days. When she wrote *Jane of
Lantern Hill* she was living in a new Toronto suburb, having finally es-
caped from the rigours of "minister's wifing" in a church-owned manse,
and moved into a home of her own. She looks out of a photograph of

the period rather grimly, her eyes shaded by a business-like hat; she cocks her chin up with an air of pride in her pearls and earrings and neatly Marcel-waved hair. She has a look of being in charge. Yet, when she looked at the materials chosen for her new novel, she focused in a surprisingly different way.

*Jane of Lantern Hill* is a story of intergenerational struggles, told from a position that seems to be the opposite of the point of view one would expect Montgomery to assume at this stage of her life. By 1938 she was a grandparent, yet the villain mocked in this story is a snobbish, arrogant grandmother. Though she was now deeply disturbed by her sons' choices in romance, the thrust of the *Jane* story is that the grandmother was wrong to try to break up her daughter's marriage. Montgomery was presumably pleased to be in Toronto, a centre of arts and letters, but the central plot celebrates escape from Toronto by sturdy, no-nonsense Jane. This grandchild of the old horror charms us with her down-to-earth coping with her family problems. She is totally unlike Anne or Emily or Kilmeny – not artistic, not imaginative, but proud instead to bake a good pie and make curtains for her dad, once reunited with him, in spite of Grandmother. Intriguingly, "Dad," the adult male, is the successful, imaginative writer in this book – a surprising plot twist, considering that Montgomery was now furiously battling male writers who were shoving her aside, mocking her work, and excluding her from professional rewards.

*Jane of Lantern Hill* reveals something almost schizophrenic in the ambivalence of her focus, as writer and as aging woman. From the point of view of her enamoured readers, however, a different conclusion can be drawn. Maud Montgomery Macdonald might focus on the distressing facts of her life with increasing acidity in her journals. But L.M. Montgomery could invert that vision. She could escape from the aging matriarch she had become and assume a point of view reaffirming youthful capability and enthusiasm. In *Jane of Lantern Hill*, her long career as a creator of fiction came to an unpredictable but rewarding and reassuring climax.

L.M. Montgomery's lifetime achievement in fiction deserves to be described with yet another word that begins with "F." Her work is fabulous – in both senses of the word. Like a fable from Aesop, it shows energetic leaps and slow-paced persistence. As an illustration of lifelong openness to creative inspiration combined with readiness to change with changing times and places, it is phenomenal, astonishing, and well worthy of the admiration it has been accorded for over a hundred years.

## NOTES

1  Montgomery, manuscript of *Anne of Green Gables*.
2  Ibid.
3  Ibid.
4  Montgomery, manuscript of *Rilla of Ingleside*.
5  Montgomery, *Selected Journals*, 3:205.
6  Ibid., 218.
7  Ibid.

## BIBLIOGRAPHY

Montgomery, L.M. *Anne of Green Gables*. Boston: L.C. Page, 1908.
–  *Anne's House of Dreams*. Toronto: McClelland & Stewart, 1917.
–  *The Blue Castle*. Toronto: McClelland & Stewart, 1926.
–  *Jane of Lantern Hill*. Toronto: McClelland & Stewart, 1937.
–  *Kilmeny of the Orchard*. Boston: L.C. Page, 1910.
–  Manuscript of *Anne of Green Gables*. Archives of the Confederation Centre of the Arts, Charlottetown, PEI.
–  Manuscript of *Rilla of Ingleside*. Archives of the McLaughlin Library, University of Guelph, Guelph, Ontario.
–  *Rilla of Ingleside*. Toronto: McClelland & Stewart, 1921.
–  *The Selected Journals of L.M. Montgomery*. Vol. 3, 1921–1929. Edited by Mary Rubio and Elizabeth Waterston. Toronto: Oxford University Press, 1992.

# Lasting Images of *Anne of Green Gables*

ELIZABETH R. EPPERLY

What makes a story last for a hundred years? L.M. Montgomery was a powerful picture-maker who taught millions how to create better pictures for themselves, pictures of a world they would like to live in and help to flourish. We continue to read and to study Montgomery's images in *Anne of Green Gables* not because they are pretty or sweet but because they touch the profound, teaching us about creativity itself and about possibilities for the human spirit.

Montgomery's highly visual imagination enabled her to conjure what she called "memory pictures" in exquisite detail. All her life she was able to overlay a current scene with an image of how it looked days or years before. She could hold the images simultaneously and could also sustain both nostalgia and the thrill of recall. In *Through Lover's Lane: L.M. Montgomery's Photography and Visual Imagination*, I propose that her heightened ability to think in pictures was combined with a gift for seeing those pictures animated, as though her imagination were photo-graphic and also cinematic. She was also accustomed to reading images on several levels at once, turning them into metaphors in her writing.

Cognitive scientists today suggest that the human brain is wired to think in images and to understand through metaphor. George Lakoff and Mark Johnson define imagination as "metaphoric rationality."[1] To interpret life, we see pictures in our minds and tell ourselves stories about them. To understand situations and to process new information, we create analogies, which are themselves forms of metaphor. "My house is my castle." Suddenly my house is more than a house and yet is not a castle. A third thing is created, something prized and protected – a fortress and a symbol of heritage and ownership. The word "castle" carries a world of associations all on its own and these, too, are extended and re-created by the comparison with "house."

In Montgomery's writing, a house is never just a house; nor is a tree simply a tree. Inanimate objects come alive, and places have responsive spirits. Some of the most profound relationships Montgomery's characters experience are with land and home. Montgomery teaches her readers to perceive levels of meaning in the stories her pictures capture. If we think in images, and if we are the stories we tell, then this power to perceive levels of meaning is a means not only to consciousness but to creative critical thought and to choices about how we live our lives. It is this power of perception that is part of the lasting gift Montgomery offers readers.

*Anne of Green Gables* is filled with passionate and playful pictures rendered in colourful language. Passages invite rereading over the years; many readers discover that each new reading offers increased understanding about the levels of metaphor and meaning. Almost every colourful picture or scene is about relationships, which all, in one way or another, respond to the creative intentions of the heroine. Even the scene-painting shows the land in active relationship with its inhabitants and with itself. And the whole Island stage seems to have been set so that Anne can arrive to embrace and to disrupt it. Anne is the centre of the story, and she is made to seem essential to the very land. The first sentence of the novel invites the reader to see how the land is waiting to collude with the right kind of spirit in order to defy the oppressive control of Rachel Lynde:

> Mrs. Rachel Lynde lived just where the Avonlea main road dipped
> down into a little hollow, fringed with alders and ladies' eardrops
> and traversed by a brook that had its source away back in the
> woods of the old Cuthbert place; it was reputed to be an intricate,
> headlong brook in its earlier course through those woods, with
> dark secrets of pool and cascade; but by the time it reached
> Lynde's Hollow it was a quiet, well-conducted little stream,
> for not even a brook could run past Mrs. Rachel Lynde's door
> without due regard for decency and decorum; it probably was
> conscious that Mrs. Rachel was sitting at her window, keeping a
> sharp eye on everything that passed, from brooks and children
> up, and that if she noticed anything odd or out of place she would

never rest until she had ferreted out the whys and wherefores thereof.[2]

Montgomery makes it seem that the brook is aware of Rachel's sharp eye, and behaves itself as it glides by her. Within moments of starting the story, the reader is following several stories simultaneously: Rachel the busybody tries to control the behaviour of everyone and everything that lives near her, the landscape is sentient and subtly defiant, and the land and people of Avonlea are one in their wish to evade Rachel's all-seeing eye. In 148 words Montgomery establishes the metaphoric pattern of her book, and the willing reader effortlessly absorbs the fact that several stories will be conveyed simultaneously through descriptions involving natural scenes.

Within moments of our meeting Anne Shirley herself in the second chapter of the book, we learn that she is a mistress of images, proficient in reading and creating them on several levels. Later in the novel we find out that she had been abused and neglected as a child and had created an alternate world of beauty and romance to make living tolerable. When she speaks to Matthew on the Bright River Station platform, we hear the love of romance and chivalry in the very first image she chooses: "I had made up my mind that if you didn't come for me to-night I'd go down the track to that big wild cherry-tree at the bend, and climb up into it to stay all night. I wouldn't be a bit afraid, and it would be lovely to sleep in a wild cherry-tree all white with bloom in the moonshine, don't you think? You could imagine you were dwelling in marble halls, couldn't you?"[3] The metaphoric comparison of the cherry-blossom bough and marble halls is a wonderful shorthand code for Anne's quality of seeing. Like the word "castle" the phrase "marble halls" belongs to tales of chivalry and romance; Anne is picturing herself as a beautiful heroine surrounded by adoring knights in the marble halls of a castle. Montgomery's readers would have known, as Anne did, the popular song "I dreamt I dwelt in marble halls." Ingeniously, Montgomery uses trees three more times in the few pages of Anne and Matthew's eight-mile ride from Bright River to Avonlea. Each time, Montgomery shows the reader something else about Anne and about images themselves.

When Anne and Matthew pass beneath "blooming wild cherry-trees and slim white birches," she asks Matthew what they make him think of, and when he replies, "Well now, I dunno," she explains, "Why, a bride of course – a bride all in white with a lovely misty veil."[4] The adult reader can see how touchingly comic Anne is, assuming as she does, that the shy bachelor will share her fascination with brides and beauty. It matters not a whit to quicksilver Anne that in one moment a cherry tree makes her think of marble halls and, in another, a bride in her veil. Within a very short time she shifts from the delight over the bride to unselfconscious sharing about her misery in the orphanage. She says: "I just love trees. And there weren't any at all about the asylum, only a few poor weeny-teeny things out in front with little whitewashed cagey things about them. They just looked like orphans themselves, those trees did. It used to make me want to cry to look at them. 'Oh, you poor little things! If you were out in a great big woods with other trees all around you and little mosses and Junebells growing over your roots and a brook not far away and birds singing in your branches, you could grow, couldn't you? But you can't where you are. I know just exactly how you feel, little trees.'"[5]

Anne is full of sympathy with the caged trees because she is able to compare their plight with her own. Metaphor has made her empathetic, and it has also given her images of hope. Rather than dwelling on the stunted life of the trees and their permanent confinement, she speaks to them about an alternative way of life that would make them happy. She is able to talk about her own need for a loving home and a supportive community when she can speak about the trees' need for natural woodland life. We learn that while Anne can acknowledge how unhappy the orphanage made her, her facility with analogy and metaphor has a determinedly positive bent. She imagines a way out for herself. In these three images with trees, we learn about Anne's quality of dreaming and about her empathy and optimism.

Montgomery may also be suggesting how quickly Anne forms a meaningful relationship with Matthew. With each image revealed, Anne seems to be experiencing an increase in comfort and safety. At the railway station Anne knew she could be all right for a night since she could imagine herself into one of her own stories; when she sees the later blooms as a bride, she is safely indulging a recurrent fantasy; and when she recalls the trees at the orphanage she is describing a brutal reality she thinks she will no longer have to dream of escaping, since she has now been adopted and freed. Anne may be feeling safer and

happily bonding with Matthew, but the reader knows Marilla is waiting at Green Gables expecting to receive a boy, not a girl. The levels of
meaning in Anne's choice of images are fixed against the backdrop of
surprise.

Only a few moments after explaining her life and some of her dreams
to Matthew, Anne encounters what she will later name the White Way
of Delight and is struck dumb by its beauty. In experiencing its shapes
and colours, Anne is bound permanently to Prince Edward Island and
is at the same time inspired to reach beyond anything place alone can
bring her. The set-up of this one passage suggests to me how Montgomery's knowledge of photography, love for literature, passion for colour,
quest for meaning, and gift for metaphor enabled her to touch her readers so profoundly and encourage them to pursue stories and metaphors
of their own. At the sight Montgomery is about to describe, Anne ex-
claims "Oh, Mr. Cuthbert! Oh, Mr. Cuthbert!! Oh, Mr. Cuthbert!!!" Then
the narrator tells us, "They had simply rounded a curve in the road and
found themselves in the 'Avenue.' The 'Avenue,' so called by the New-
bridge people, was a stretch of road four or five hundred yards long,
completely arched over with huge, wide-spreading apple-trees, planted
years ago by an eccentric old farmer. Overhead was one long canopy
of snowy fragrant bloom. Below the boughs the air was full of a purple
twilight and far ahead a glimpse of painted sunset sky shone like a great
rose window at the end of a cathedral aisle."[6]

This description has three of Montgomery's most important metaphoric shapes. After years of studying Montgomery's two thousand
photographs, I realized that the bend, the arch, and the circle act as a
kind of aesthetic shorthand throughout her novel-writing career. Those
three shapes inform her photographs, and they underpin many of her
most colourful nature descriptions. Each shape suggests a metaphor
that tells a story that the novel then reinforces.

Anne and Matthew come around a bend in a road, they pass under
an arch of branches, and they head for a circle of brightly coloured light
likened to an intricately patterned stained glass window designed to
elevate the spirit beyond earth. We are given a picture of what Anne is
learning about life.

The bend in the road was the most important organizing metaphoric
shape of Montgomery's career. The very last chapter of *Anne of Green
Gables* is entitled "The Bend in the Road," and the penultimate sentence

in the novel is "And there was always the bend in the road!"[7] Montgomery carefully crafted that last chapter and this metaphoric bend in the road so that readers could see how far Anne has progressed since the day of arrival on Prince Edward Island. The older Anne transforms the image into a metaphor for her life's journey. In a passage Montgomery added to her original manuscript as she revised it, Anne tells Marilla: "When I left Queen's my future seemed to stretch out before me like a straight road. I thought I could see along it for many a milestone. Now there is a bend in it. I don't know what lies around the bend, but I'm going to believe that the best does. It has a fascination of its own, that bend, Marilla. I wonder how the road beyond it goes – what there is of green glory and soft, checkered light and shadows – what new landscapes – what new beauties – what curves and hills and valleys further on."[8] Anne is still young at the novel's end – just in her teens – and she expects the unseen landscape around that bend in the road to be green and glorious, full of surprise and beauty. She has just suffered keenly from the death of Matthew, and yet she is brimming with hope, just as, at the beginning of the novel, having suffered from neglect, abuse, and then the orphanage, she has chosen to envision woodlands of liberated trees and trilling birds rather than dwell on the cages of the imprisoned trees.

Like the bend in the road, the arch is emblematic. Inspired by the magic arches in Washington Irving's *The Alhambra*,[9] Montgomery's arches – most commonly formed by tree branches – suggest gateways to fairyland and also the quality of experience on life's journey, as in Tennyson's "Ulysses," where "all experience is an arch wherethro' / Gleams that untravell'd world, whose margin fades / For ever and for ever when I move."[10]

Allied to the arch is the circle of light, which draws the viewer into a pictured story. The beckoning circle of light suggests goals and dreams and frequently involves sunset glory; wherever there is heightened colour in Montgomery, there is heightened feeling and meaning.

What is important in the White Way of Delight scene, the first time in this novel when all three shapes are used together, is the way Montgomery is deliberately preparing the reader to respond to the implied metaphors that the heightened colours and shapes come to suggest through the rest of the story. Anne is on a journey, a quest, and so is the reader who joins her sympathetically; Anne's journey becomes consciously metaphoric by the end of the book, and while young readers may not yet be able to articulate what has happened, I think they understand perfectly the importance of Anne's changes.

If images are fundamental to human thought, and if metaphors are essential to our making sense of these pictures, then a writer whose gift is for creating images and stories, and whose work has appealed to audiences for over a century, has much to tell us about the way we accept and share stories. George Lakoff's recent book, *The Political Mind*, suggests that the fate of political parties, and even of whole countries, relies on the extent to which people unconsciously accept certain cultural frames – or stories – and then feel obliged to support the rhetoric that spins from them, even though the original frame and the evolved images no longer have much in common. He explains how, after repeated shocks and threats to safety, the brain can lose its ability to produce chemicals that enable it to process and assess information critically. He warns that whole populations, not just individuals, can suffer from the chemical responses of depression after such shocks as 9/11, tsunamis, the closing of large businesses, or repeated warnings about financial ruin. If we are the stories we tell ourselves, and if we become what we picture, then we do still have hope if we are careful about what we read and what we choose to imprint as memory pictures. I interpret the continued popularity of *Anne of Green Gables* as a sign that our imaginations may still be resilient and our attitudes hopeful.

Montgomery's written descriptions showed me what her black and white photographs also suggested: there is drama in the everyday world; there are metaphors to be perceived and understood through the familiar shapes and colours we find around us. We can choose the elements of the metaphors we want to live by.

Montgomery's visual imagination has only begun to be explored. As cognitive scientists such as Richard Cytowic, Norman Doidge, Oliver Sacks, and others[11] come to understand more about the ways the brain generates and experiences images, I think we will find that Montgomery's novels, journals, letters, photographs, and scrapbooks will be of increasing interest for their insights into the ways an artist perceives, interprets, stores, creates, and recreates images and metaphors, and inspires others to perceive and to generate images and metaphors of their own. Is the embodiment of metaphor part of the cross-cultural translatability of Montgomery's characters? Many of us who are university teachers have lamented that our students are impatient with descriptions and do not take the time with written texts that they will take with images on computer, cell, cinema, or television screens. Perhaps we have not yet understood how we have reconfigured learning pathways and perceptions through the bombardment of various sound and energy waves now surrounding children almost inescapably in Western culture. And perhaps Montgomery's work, and particularly *Anne of Green Gables* and *Emily of New Moon*, may furnish new generations of researchers with ways to measure and enrich what Lakoff and Johnson call "metaphoric rationality," imagination itself.

I suggest that Montgomery will be studied in ways we cannot yet imagine for how she created and understood "memory pictures" and for how her gift for photography and her later fascination with movies are reflected in her own photographic and cinematic creation of scenes. And perhaps most wonderful of all is what we have to learn from Montgomery's passion for colour. What can it mean when someone perceives colour in the way others perceive music? How does synaesthesia give power to Montgomery's images? Again, scientific studies are just beginning to catch up with art in the recognition that sensitivity to colour can be a measure of the brain's ability to perceive and to re-conceive. Maybe someone will be able to tell me some day what my colour-blind father was seeing when he wept with delight at Montgomery's colour-drenched depictions of nature.

As with the images of Anne over time, and as with Montgomery's own changing perceptions of the meaning of womanhood in a culture where women were often paralyzed by convention, so it will be in the next hundred years as scholars work together to uncover new meaning and new ways of understanding. If there is human life on this earth in one hundred years' time, and if restraint and freedom contend with each other in the cultures we now call countries, I can imagine *Anne of Green Gables* will still be read and loved. *Anne* will still be inviting readers to picture and to experience beauty, refreshment, humour, meaning, grief, hope, love, dread, rapture, and defiance. And if researchers are wise, they will want to understand how Montgomery's images continue to cross cultures and time to offer and enable others to experience refreshment, humour, meaning, grief, hope, love, and defiance.

## NOTES

1 Lakoff and Johnson, *Metaphors We Live By*, 193.
2 Montgomery, *Anne of Green Gables*, 1.
3 Ibid., 13.
4 Ibid., 15.
5 Ibid., 17.
6 Ibid., 19.
7 Ibid., 329.
8 Ibid., 324–5.
9 See Epperly, *Through Lover's Lane*, 145–64.
10 Tennyson, "Ulysses," lines 19–21, 11.
11 See especially Cytowic, *The Man Who Tasted Shapes*, and Cytowic and Eagleman, *Wednesday Is Indigo Blue*; also Doidge, *The Brain That Changes Itself*; Feldman, *From Molecule to Metaphor*; Lakoff, *Women and Fire*, and Lakoff and Johnson, *Philosophy in the Flesh*, as well as Lakoff and Turner, *More Than Cool Reason*; Lehrer, *Proust Was a Neuroscientist*; Pinker, *How the Mind Works*; Rich, "A Union of the Senses," and Rich and others, "Neural Correlates"; and Sacks, *Musicophilia*.

## BIBLIOGRAPHY

Cytowic, Richard. 1993. *The Man Who Tasted Shapes*. 2nd ed. Cambridge, Massachusetts: MIT Press, 2003.

Cytowic, Richard, and David M. Eagleman. *Wednesday Is Indigo Blue: Discovering the Brain of Synesthesia*. Cambridge, Massachusetts: MIT Press, 2009.

Doidge, Norman. *The Brain That Changes Itself: Stories of Personal Triumph from the Frontiers of Brain Science*. New York: Penguin, 2007.

Epperly, Elizabeth Rollins. *Through Lover's Lane: L.M. Montgomery's Photography and Visual Imagination*. Toronto: University of Toronto Press, 2007.

Feldman, Jerome A. *From Molecule to Metaphor: A Neural Theory of Language*. Cambridge, Massachusetts: MIT Press, 2006.

Irving, Washington. *The Alhambra*. 1832. New York: Caldwell, nd.

Lakoff, George. *The Political Mind: Why You Can't Understand 21st-Century American Politics with an 18th-Century Brain*. New York: Penguin, 2008.

– *Women, Fire, and Dangerous Things: What Categories Reveal about the Mind*. Chicago: University of Chicago Press, 1987.

Lakoff, George, and Mark Johnson. *Metaphors We Live By*. Chicago: University of Chicago Press, 1980.

– *Philosophy in the Flesh: The Embodied Mind and Its Challenge to Western Thought*. New York: Basic Books, 1999.

Lakoff, George, and Mark Turner. *More Than Cool Reason: A Field Guide to Poetic Metaphor.* University of Chicago Press, 1989.

Lehrer, Jonah. *Proust Was a Neuroscientist.* Boston: Houghton Mifflin, 2008.

Montgomery, L.M. *Anne of Green Gables.* 1908. Toronto: Ryerson Press, 1996.

Pinker, Steven. *How the Mind Works.* New York: W.W. Norton, 1997.

Rich, Anina N. "A Union of the Senses or a Sense of Union?" *Cortex* (2006) 42: 444–56.

Rich, Anina N., Mark A. Williams, Aina Puce, Ari Syngeniotis, Matthew A. Howard, Francis McGlone, and Jason B. Mattingley. "Neural Correlates of Imagined and Synasesthetic Colours." *Neuropsychologia*, vol. 44 (2006): 2918–25.

Sacks, Oliver. *Musicophilia: Tales of Music and the Brain.* New York: Alfred A. Knopf, 2007.

Tennyson, Alfred, Lord. "Ulysses." *The New Oxford Book of Victorian Verse.* Edited by Christopher Ricks. Oxford: Oxford University Press, 1990.

# Uncertainties Surrounding the Death of L.M. Montgomery

MARY HENLEY RUBIO

We will never know with certainty the exact cause of L.M. Montgomery's death. Did she die of an overdose of medication? If so, was it accidental or intentional? Or did she die from natural causes, either those her doctor wrote on her death certificate or something else? There was no autopsy after she was found dead in her bed on 24 April 1942, in her sixty-eighth year, and the circumstances surrounding her death are ambiguous.

As I recount in my biography, *Lucy Maud Montgomery: The Gift of Wings*, Maud's younger son, Dr E. Stuart Macdonald (1915–1982), told me that he believed that his mother had died from an intentional overdose of prescription drugs.[1] Around 1981, he gave me a note – which he had always interpreted as a suicide note – and told me I could either give it to the University of Guelph archives or destroy it. I read it, placed it in an acid-free envelope, and then stored it in a safe location. At the time, I did not question his belief that his mother had taken her own life: in 1942 he was already a medical doctor, and he had been in attendance along with their family doctor, Dr Richard Lane, right after her death.

There seemed no reason to raise further questions, particularly given that the memory clearly caused him enormous pain. In 1981 I had already begun the work of editing Maud's journals and doing interviews for a biography of his mother. Then, in 1982, Stuart died suddenly of a massive brain aneurysm. Elizabeth Waterston and I spent the next twenty-two years editing Montgomery's ten handwritten journals; all that time, the note remained in safe storage at the University of Guelph. As my biography of Montgomery was drawing to a close around 2006, I removed the note from storage and read it again. On this reading, with many years of research into Montgomery's journal-writing process behind me, I was astonished. This "suicide note" was not what I had thought it was, and perhaps not what Stuart had believed it to be.

The note was on a single sheet of paper, handwritten on the back of a 1939 royalty statement, with the handwritten page number "176" at the top. And it was not a suicide note *per se*. Yet I could see why Stuart, as a physician, would have interpreted it as one.

Unfortunately, since he was dead, I could ask no more questions. The few remaining people who had known Montgomery had been parishioners or neighbours, none of them family members on the scene. But I had done numerous interviews with the household maids who were most familiar with Montgomery's lifestyle and writing habits in her Ontario years. An understanding of how Maud wrote, and a degree of insight into aspects of her complex personality and the dynamics of the Macdonald family are central to the context in any interpretation of the so-called suicide note.

Although Stuart was very close to his mother emotionally, he had never been particularly attentive to her writing – it was just something she did, her means of supporting the family. Chester, Stuart's older brother, had always spent a lot of time in their home; Stuart, however, had not. As a young teen Stuart boarded at St Andrew's College in Aurora, Ontario, for secondary school. When he was home in Norval during the summer, he was usually outside with friends, swimming and hiking, and he often slept outside in a tent by the river. After the family moved to Toronto in 1935, and while Stuart was attending the University of Toronto, he spent a great deal of time training as part of the award-winning gymnastics team. When he continued on to study medicine at the university, he still lived at home, but was not there very much – he came for meals, to sleep, and to study in his room. He avoided his brother, Chester, who could be argumentative and difficult. Then, as a young doctor-in-training, Stuart spent most of his time at the hospital. The maids told me, as he did himself, that even when he did not get home, he telephoned his mother every day. He had many conversations with her about the problems with his father and Chester.

He did not involve himself in his mother's professional work beyond very occasionally driving her to evening meetings when Chester, who was her regular chauffeur, could not. In fact, as I discovered, none of Stuart's Toronto classmates had even known that "E. Stuart Macdonald" was the son of "L.M. Montgomery"; as a young man, he was slightly embarrassed by the fact that his mother was so famous. Later in his life, he became proud of her accomplishments; but, as a young man, he wanted to be known for his own achievements as a star gymnast, and then, later, as a skillful, gifted young doctor. He did not want to be tagged as the son of the legendary L.M. Montgomery.

According to his account, when his mother's body was found, the maid called him and Dr Richard Lane, the family doctor. They arrived at approximately the same time. Dr Lane lived across the street from the Macdonalds on Riverside Drive, but his office was downtown. Stuart was also working downtown, at St Michael's Hospital, a round-the-clock obligation for a young resident obstetrician that meant he was rarely home. Stuart recalled Dr Lane saying that he, Lane, would "take care of the body," and Stuart should "take care of" everything else. Stuart told me that he dealt with the note and medicine container(s). His mother's body was removed, and Dr Lane wrote on the official death certificate that the primary cause of death was "coronary thrombosis."

Stuart recalled that he placed the note in his pocket. He was very busy at that time with work responsibilities at St Michael's Hospital. He was soon to leave to serve in the Canadian Navy as a medical doctor, given that it was 1942 and Canada was at war. He now had the additional task of winding up his mother's affairs and arranging his father's move into a nursing home. He was also courting the young nurse Ruth Steele, who became his wife; however, given his mother's poor health, which they hoped would improve, Ruth had not met his mother.

Although Chester was by now a fully fledged lawyer, his mother did not trust him. Instead, she had arranged for a trust company to imple-ment her will. After her death, since Stuart was still in Toronto, the trust company looked to him for many of the decisions, given that it had clearly been Montgomery's choice to have Stuart oversee her liter-ary legacy. She left him the responsibility of dealing with her journals, although any income from them was to be divided between Stuart and Chester (or Chester's heirs, who were at that time the two children from his first marriage, to Luella Reid Macdonald). Her will also cut Chester out of certain portions of his inheritance if he was not living with Luella and his family at the time of his mother's death.[2]

Although Montgomery had been ill for some time, her death came as a shock to Stuart. He recalled coming home some time shortly before it to find her staggering around, as if drunk. Suspecting over-medication, he had taken a blood sample. The test result showed a very high concentration of bromide, one of the sedatives she had been given. She also had been taking prescribed barbiturates, and, like others of that era, she considered brandy to be a medicine, too. In addition, Dr Lane on occasion administered hypodermics to her, most likely in periods of agitation ("attacks of neurasthenia" as they were then called, but today we might ask if Montgomery was also agitated when she was "coming down" from high doses of habit-forming medications like the barbiturate compounds). Most likely the hypodermics contained some form of sedative. Her weight dropped precipitously after 1939, and so she had less body mass to absorb medicines than before. The death certificate states that Dr Lane had visited her that morning, presumably before he went to his office, and one wonders if he had given her a hypodermic.

A little more context: Dr Lane's daughter, Nora, recalled that Mrs Macdonald would often ask her father to drop in, either before or after his office hours, if she or her husband, Ewan, felt unwell. Nora, who later married one of Stuart's medical school classmates, had sometimes taken constitutional walks with "Mrs Macdonald." Nora was very fond of both Ewan and Maud, but she did not know Stuart or Chester very well – Stuart was always out at the hospital, and if Chester was home, he stayed in the house, usually reading. The maids said that Chester roamed freely around the house and often drifted into his parents' bedroom, where his mother did her writing.[3] Unlike Stuart, who had many friends and extra-curricular activities, Chester, the maids said, was a "loner" and spent a high proportion of his time with his mother.

However, during Chester's law course, he started seeing other women. His philandering greatly upset Montgomery and resulted in her revising her will to protect Luella and the children. Following Chester's graduation from law school, she "bought" him into a practice with an established lawyer, and he then moved into a rented home with Luella and their two children. By the time Montgomery died, both Chester's law partnership and his marriage had failed. According to the trust company, Chester was living back at home – a heartbreak to his parents.

I provide a fuller account of Montgomery's will and the end-of-life tensions in my biography,[4] but these details set the basic scene for our contemplation of the meaning of the so-called suicide note. By the time I returned to it, I had come to believe that what had been interpreted by Stuart as a suicide note was the numbered final page to a much longer document, and that this document might have filled in all the missing years at the end of Maud's life since, mid-way through 1939, she had stopped making regular entries in her handwritten journals.

The last entry in Montgomery's handwritten journal was dated 23 March 1942. The so-called suicide note is dated 22 April 1942. She died two days later, on 24 April 1942. The note reads:

> April 22, 1942
> This copy is unfinished and never will be. It is in a terrible
> state because I made it when I had begun to suffer my terrible
> breakdown of 1940. It must end here. If any publishers wish to
> publish extracts from it under the terms of my will they must
> stop here. The tenth volume can never be copied and must not
> be made public during my lifetime. Parts of it are too terrible
> and would hurt people. I have lost my mind by spells and I do
> not dare to think what I may do in those spells. May God forgive
> me and I hope everyone else will forgive me even if they cannot
> understand. My position is too awful to endure and nobody
> realizes it. What an end to a life in which I tried always to do my
> best in spite of many mistakes.[5]

Some points about this note are worth noting here.

The first is that Montgomery saved every scrap of paper and used them for making initial drafts of her writing. She would stack old letters or advertisements, with the good sides up, numbering them in sequence if she were working on a manuscript. She had grown up when paper was a scarce commodity and the need for frugality would have been reinforced during the Great Depression of the 1930s.

In addition, when she was too busy to write in her journals, she jotted down short, dated notes about what had happened on that day or during that week, using scrap paper or envelopes she had slit open. Later, Montgomery would use these to write up expanded entries in her handwritten journals. But if she had a complex story to tell, especially one that might reflect poorly on her, like the story of her romance with Herman Leard, she wrote intermediate drafts, polishing up her story carefully before copying it into her journals. Or, if she did not know how something was going to turn out, like Chester's marriage and success as a lawyer, she would wait until she had more data and could give careful thought to shaping it. After Chester's marriage to Luella, for instance, she waited three years to take up her journal again to set the story down for posterity. If she was badly depressed, she would sometimes wait to write until she felt better: her handwritten journals were an ongoing production until the end of her life, as was the typed version she made of them.

In her final years , Montgomery was in a bind: distressing things were happening that she recognized as an integral part of her life story but which she did not want to commit to a journal intended for eventual publication and that would be read, say, by her grandchildren. And she could not wait indefinitely to see how things would resolve themselves.

As was her custom, she would have been preparing draft notes for her handwritten journals in the period between mid-1939 and 1942, wondering exactly how much to commit to her journals about the real events in her life. In my biography, *Lucy Maud Montgomery: The Gift of Wings*, I suggested that this page "176" might have been intended as the final page in a longer document, one which would have covered the period from her last journal entry in 1939 to April 1942. I thought that she perhaps expected to copy a finished version of it into her final, tenth volume of the handwritten journals, once she decided what to record. Yet, her tenth handwritten journal was not itself "in a terrible state" – it was well written, mostly in a firm hand, until mid-1939, and then it stopped, dropping off with a couple more entries. It appeared that the document that was in a "terrible state" must have been a different manuscript.

Another piece of the puzzle is the statement that "This copy is unfinished and never will be." Maud was emotionally distressed by this time and she could not bear to lay out her humiliations in her permanent journals, which were to be saved for posterity. Any narrative would surely have covered her disappointment with her beloved first son, Chester, and other unhappy events in her life, such as her concern over her diminished professional reputation and her precarious financial situation.[6] Her husband's mental state was an ongoing worry, as well. She may, too, have discovered that Stuart was still communicating with a long-time girlfriend she did not like. But she was more distressed that he would soon be sent overseas as a doctor in the Second World War. She called him her "one good son," and she feared he would be killed.[7]

Maud wanted to control her life story and the way she would be remembered: for this reason, she was loath to record really damaging information about her family, herself, or her own anxieties. She always hoped that events would turn around and she would be able to omit such material. But by 1939 she was aging rapidly and becoming increasingly frail, not to mention more discouraged – and far more dependent on prescribed medications that we now know were dangerous and disorienting. Her handwriting in that period reveals that she had good days and bad ones – perhaps the result of her increasing drug dependency. (She could still write a good hand in personal letters, despite a fall that made handwriting temporarily painful.) The actual entries she recorded in her handwritten journals are few and sketchy. The last full entry for 1939 is in June, and there are no entries for 1940, one only in 1941, and only one final one for 1942:

Friday, June 30, 1939
Tonight, in spite of feeling hurt and bruised and *soiled* I draw a long breath of relief. Mrs. Thompson has gone! [Maud continues to expand on this, venting her anger and frustration with her now ex-maid, Mrs Thompson.]

July 8, 1941
Oh God, such an end to life. Such suffering and wretchedness.

March 23, 1942
Since then my life has been hell, hell, hell. My mind is gone – everything in the world I lived for has gone – the world has gone mad. I shall be driven to end my life. Oh God, forgive me. Nobody dreams what my dreadful position is.

A further point to consider is that in these entries of 1939, 1941, and 1942, taken from her handwritten journals, her despondency is apparent. For some unknown reason, the full account of what happened between mid-1939 and 24 April 1942 is absent from the handwritten record of her life. If there were notes to complete her life book (a possibility that seems very likely, given her dedication to writing a full account of her life), these pages did not get copied into her journals. Maybe, too exhausted or dispirited to write a dismal story, she preferred to wrap up her "life-book" with the short, mysterious entries above.

In the last years of her life, she was also typing up the abridged, edited copy of her handwritten journals, with at least one carbon copy, so that each son could have one. She also thought this abridged version might be published, either during her lifetime or after it, long before the entire handwritten journals could be, with their sharp comments about many people. In the typed copy she removed much unflattering material that she feared might embarrass her two sons, her friends, and her extended family.

In a careful bit of sleuthing, when she was working with the additions to the L.M. Montgomery Archives at the University of Guelph, Vanessa Brown, an archival researcher and Montgomery expert, firmly identified the "longer document" that Montgomery refers to: it was the ninth *typed* journal, which ran to 175 pages. The handwritten "suicide note" labelled page 176 was merely, as it sounds, a note of instruction to Stuart about the publication of her typewritten journals, specifying that she did not want the tenth volume copied or published.

Montgomery had herself begun typing her tenth handwritten volume, and eleven pages survive. Did she type no further, or were these pages lost? Stuart had loaned his mother's journals to Terry Macartney-Filgate, a documentary filmmaker, in the 1970s when the Canadian Broadcasting Corporation (CBC) was making a short movie ("The Road to Green Gables") about Montgomery's life. Macartney-Filgate made duplicates of the *typed* copies, and eventually returned the original and a copy to Stuart.[8] The xeroxes the CBC returned were only of the first nine volumes. Had Stuart held back the tenth volume of her typed copy, as his mother had requested? If Stuart had retained these pages, they could easily have been misplaced in his home before the others were returned: Stuart was very casual with his filing system, and things often lay about for a while.[9] At the time that he gave them to Macartney-Filgate, Montgomery's papers were not considered valuable. For instance, another time Stuart loaned the handwritten volumes to a well-known Toronto publisher, Lovat Dickson, for an indefinite period, to see if they were publishable. Stuart came home one day to find them all stacked on his dining table: they had been delivered by a taxi with the note that the publisher was not interested in publishing them. So it is quite plausible that Montgomery had simply become too discouraged to continue typing beyond these initial eleven pages of volume ten. But additional pages could have been typed and then lost, too.

Since we also know that Chester rummaged through her books, papers, and memorabilia after her death, removing certain things before the Trust Company had finished making their "inventory," he might also have destroyed her final notes for the missing years in the handwritten journals as well as the typed copies of them.[10]

In her obituary, the story was given to the newspapers – perhaps true, perhaps not – that she had just completed a manuscript (the reworked manuscript of *The Blythes Are Quoted*), and that it was turned in to the publisher the day of her death.[11] If she did send a copy of this manuscript to her publisher just before her death, it would indicate that she was writing and of firm mind right up to the end of her life. Alternatively, this statement may have been made in the obituary by Chester or Stuart to deter people from the gossip that Maud had taken her own life, which is what Stuart and Anita Webb, another relative who had been there, believed to be the case. (In my research, I have discovered that material in obituaries is frequently inaccurate for various reasons: faulty memories, lack of time for fact-checking, or because those giving the information want to make certain points about the departed.) If Maud was indeed writing until the end of her life, we could infer that she was determined to replenish her falling income with another novel – not something that one would necessarily expect from a person contemplating suicide later the same day.

At the same time, it is quite plausible that Chester, who was then back at home with lots of time on his hands, and always in need of cash, might have dropped off the manuscript for her (or on his own). Stuart, trained in obstetrics and on frequent call, was exceptionally busy, and often slept over at the hospital on a cot instead of coming home.

An additional wrinkle: *The Blythes Are Quoted* is not really a novel, but a succession of stories and poems that Montgomery cleverly strung together with narrative links in her final years to make another "Anne" novel. Since different versions of this manuscript have survived, it is hard to know which of them might have been placed with the publisher on the day of Montgomery's death. When Benjamin Lefebvre edited this manuscript for his Master's thesis at the University of Guelph, there were slightly different copies in the Guelph Archives, in the McMaster Archives, and in my possession (obtained years earlier when McClelland & Stewart had sent me a copy, asking if I recommended its publication). This manuscript was published in 1974 by McGraw-Hill Ryerson, but in a truncated form called *The Road to Yesterday,* with the links removed, making it a merely a collection of short stories. Stuart had found one copy of the original manuscript among his mother's papers a number of years after her death, and he told me that he circulated it then to various publishers for consideration. (It may have been this version that McGraw-Hill Ryerson used for their truncated 1974 version.[12]) All the muddle over the various manuscripts makes the newspaper account of its history and transmission on the day of Montgomery's death even murkier.[13]

As I finished off my biography under time pressure, I continued to puzzle over this note. What could have happened to the rest of the manuscript that preceded the page "176"? Since it likely would have covered her disappointment and frustration with Chester, I speculated that he might have found the preceding pages and destroyed them. I still suspect that this is what happened. However, as Vanessa Brown observes, it now seems certain that this final handwritten note was only the final direction to Stuart not to publish anything from either her typed (or handwritten) tenth volume if he were to publish the typewritten version.

Another question that remains is: What are we to make of Maud's statement in her final journal entry that she "shall be driven to end my life." That sounds like a very final confirmation of suicidal intent. Stuart recounted to me that, following her death, he had perused her final journal a number of times in an effort to make sense of what had happened, of what had driven her to say this.[14] He said he had found no definitive answer as to why she felt suicidal, and that in wartime many people had tribulations as great or greater than hers.

We know that many people contemplate suicide but do not follow through, either for lack of knowing how or because of a change of heart or mood. If Maud had still been rational, she would have contemplated the effect on her family. She lived in an era when suicide was a shameful thing. (Still reacting this way, Stuart asserted in a letter to the *Globe and Mail* in 1977, just five years before his own death, that his mother had died of natural causes: "Furthermore, she was not depressed in what you call her old age ... She died of a stroke in 1942, and left a legacy which will not be lost."[15]) It was only a few years later that he told me, in private, that he believed his mother had died by suicide.

It is well known that people who take their own lives sometimes plan their deaths carefully so that they do not appear as suicides. Although Montgomery no longer expected Chester to become a success, she did still love this wayward older son. She certainly retained high hopes for Stuart. She would not have wanted to destroy either son, nor to bring humiliation to her entire extended family, especially her innocent little grandchildren.

So one wonders: Why would she have written something so apparently explicit here, when she had stated to Stuart that she intended her complete handwritten journals for eventual publication after sufficient time had elapsed? Could she have been merely expressing her emotions in a dramatic way at a time when she felt too weary to continue writing in her journals, or was too disoriented with medications to be fully rational?

Or could she have written these words to give her life story the tragic ending that had been creeping into her narrative periodically since 1898 in the form of the idea that she and everything she loved were somehow "cursed"? Or could she have feared that her health was so poor that she was unlikely to live much longer anyway, and that she would cloak the ending of her life narrative with mystery and pathos? We can speculate long on what may have been going through her mind, all of which is made more opaque by the fact that Maud was a very complex woman, with wide and frequent mood swings that were intensified by destabilizing medications. And with medications (and doctor-administered "hypodermics") affecting her, we have even less idea what her basic state of mind might have been. We do know, however, that she had been taught to think of suicide not only as a moral failure but also as a sin that would prevent one's entering Heaven in the Christian afterlife.

There are probably many who do not believe it to be morally wrong to lay down a painful life but still would not kill themselves because of the psychological damage to family left behind. Maud speaks very disparagingly in her journals of people who actually do commit suicide, and she was terrified when she thought Ewan might kill himself during his 1934 breakdown (again at a period when he was being heavily medicated with drugs we now know to be very dangerous).

Montgomery had written about suicide twenty years earlier on 10 May 1922:

> Lecky, too, discusses suicide in full. Personally, I have never
> felt the horror in regard to suicide that some feel. My attitude
> towards it is much what I found in Lecky, as quoted of someone.

"Life is forced on us; we did not ask for it; therefore, if it becomes too hard we have a right to lay it down."

. But it is a cowardly thing to do if the doing of it leaves our burden upon others – ay, and a wicked thing. But if it does not I cannot see that it is wicked. It is a wicked and immoral thing to take another person's life, just as it is wicked and immoral to steal another person's money. But if the money is my own, and if I only will suffer from destroying it, it is not wicked to destroy it, though it may be a foolish thing to do.

I don't think I would ever be really tempted to commit suicide as long as I could get enough to eat and wear by any means short of begging. Life, with all its problems has always been an extremely interesting thing to me.[16]

By 1942 Maud felt her burdens were intensified, and, as she sank further into what her doctor called "neurasthenia," she was given more medicine for her "anxiety." She was still quite lucid, as her personal letters to others show; and if her last manuscript went off to the publisher the day of her death, she still was functioning mentally. I recount in the biography that I interviewed one person she talked to her shortly before her death, and he recalled that she spoke of having been ill, but also reported that she claimed her health had more recently improved. He said she was cheerful and helpful over the phone. She gave him useful suggestions for expanding the Canadian Authors Association in the Maritimes. He was shocked to learn of her death shortly thereafter.

To add further complications, I note that I also interviewed another friend from Leaskdale who had visited Montgomery shortly before her death. When this woman said she would visit her again soon, Montgomery told her that she probably would not be there. How should we interpret this statement (if it was accurately recalled, which I believe it was, since it caused this woman to carry enormous guilt for years, thinking that maybe she had missed a cry for help)? Did Maud intend to take her own life? If so, did she hope that an allusion to it might bring some kind of intervention or sympathy? Or was Maud just expressing the feeling that she was weakening physically and might not last much longer? Montgomery's saying that she might not be there at the woman's next visit can be interpreted in various ways.

We must also consider her admonition that "The tenth volume can never be copied." This statement refers to the content of journal number ten, the final one of her handwritten journals, the one we used as copy-text when editing *The Selected Journals of L.M. Montgomery*. This demand could also suggest that she had typed more than eleven pages of the typed version, in which case it would refer to this copy too.

And what are we to make of her statement "I have lost my mind by spells"? What does she mean by "mind"? Does she think she has "lost" her sanity? Or does "mind" to her mean her "creativity," her "will," and her "self-control"? Is she aware of the fact that some of the medications she is taking affect her mind? It is now believed that many of the people committed to mental institutions in the mid-twentieth century were in fact suffering mental disturbance as a result of the overuse of the psychotropic drugs then routinely prescribed for anxiety. Some of these medicines were bromides, which are still used, but only under very controlled circumstances. Barbiturates were also standard medications for anxiety, and they are addictive. Add medicinal brandy to these drugs, as she and Ewan did, and the unintentional result could be lethal.

When Montgomery pleads, "May God forgive me," what is she asking? Forgive her for what? Does this point to suicide, or is she referring to what she perceives as her mental condition – her weakness of will and personal strength at the end of her life? Or is her weakness a lapse of faith in God (a sin in the teachings of her church)? She had always been very professional, determined, and in control, and now she feels her powers are waning – or at least she thinks she no longer has control of her own mind. She also had periods of feeling that she had somehow failed as a mother. It is not difficult to understand why Stuart interpreted this note as asking forgiveness for ending her life. Perhaps it was; perhaps not.

Her complaint that her "position is too awful to endure and nobody realizes it" could refer to many things: (1) her experience of bouts of ongoing depression; (2) her possible suspicion that she is addicted to the drugs she has been taking, and her inability to break free of them; (3) her ignorance of the habit-forming properties of some of these disorienting medications and their side effects on the brain, which left her thinking that her vacillating moods and inability to focus were the result of "losing" her mind; (4) her heartbreak over Chester's professional and personal failures; (5) her precarious financial position at the end of her life; (6) or her fears for Stuart – for instance, that he might marry the wrong woman or be killed in the war; or (7) something else, leading to the conclusion that she had brought all her troubles on herself:

depressed people frequently become prisoners of negative thoughts, particularly about themselves.

And how should we interpret "What an end to a life in which I tried always to do my best"? Does this mean she is going to end her life, or is it merely a statement that she feels her life has progressed along a tragic arc, the theme she has long alluded to in her journals? Is her artistic desire for narrative shape taking control of what she writes here, and is she signalling the end of her life book, summarizing her final analysis? Montgomery's journals had become increasingly important to her. She would also have known that if she recovered, she could always rewrite the story to a different conclusion by carefully slicing out pages in her journals and replacing them – as she had already done before.

In her emaciated, heavily medicated, and depressed state, an accidental overdose would have been quite possible – as would death from natural causes. My own sense of all this is that she was not going to take any chances of dying without there being some kind of artistic closure to the life story in her journals, one that could be revised if things changed. But this supposition does not necessarily indicate that she took her own life. All we can be sure of is that what her son regarded as a suicide note is itself an ambiguous document.

Once I studied this note in light of my own research, I was left with many questions I wish I could have asked Stuart. Her death was a topic he had avoided because he felt (what I regarded as) an irrational personal guilt for not having anticipated and prevented his mother's death, given that he believed, rightly or wrongly, that she had died at her own hand. He indicated that this note had weighed heavily on him all his adult life, and, when he gave it to me, it felt as if he were divesting himself of a toxic item with great relief. He knew he could not, in full conscience, destroy it. But perhaps he thought I might feel it acceptable to do so. Or perhaps he knew me well enough by then to realize that I would never destroy anything of such historical value. At any rate, he was relieved to have it out of his hands, both physically and metaphorically.

Stuart had said to me several times that his mother lived too much in the past, or in the future, but not enough in the present. Of course, the woman he knew as his mother was someone who was already middle-aged at the time of his birth; the mother he actually *remembered* was an older, troubled one. She was no longer the witty, vibrant young woman who, upswept in a promising courtship with his father, had written *Anne of Green Gables* some thirty years earlier. It was touching to watch him meet that vital young woman as he reread and discussed the early journals with me. Unfortunately, his unexpected death in 1982 cut short any further exploration into the personality of the joyous young mother he said he had never known. And it prevented me from asking him all those questions about her death that now emerge, and which Stuart – and Stuart alone – could have answered with total authority.

There remain many questions that I shall always wonder about.

First: did Dr Lane and Dr Stuart Macdonald see any other clear evidence that Montgomery's death was a suicide *before* reading the note and assuming that it was a suicide? Did they actually discuss whether it was a suicide? Is there any chance that the actual *fear* of scandal may have led them to jump to conclusions and concentrate on winding things up quickly?[17]

Second: did Stuart himself find the "suicide note," or did the maid find it and give it to him? If he did indeed find it on her bedside table, as he indicated, was he sure his mother had placed it there that day? Was it only this single sheet, or was it on top of other papers such as her type-written journals, which we know she was rereading?

Third: did he notice that the note was dated and numbered, and that it referred to itself as a "copy" that was "unfinished" and that he was not to publish the tenth volume of her journals? Could one surmise that she might have placed this single sheet on her bedside table to show that her life was written to the end? Finished life story, finished life. Or could we entertain the possibility that she was simply rereading her document as she lay on her bed, feeling unwell as she waited for pills to take effect so that she could rest?

Fourth: it would have been reasonable for both doctors to think that if they announced to the world that the famous L.M. Montgomery had committed suicide, it would become international news.[18] A suicide would have made many people think that mental illness ran in the Macdonald family, damaging any young doctor's career in that era. Because such news would have distressed friends, family, and especially her fans, it would likely have affected her reputation and future book sales. Thus, there was good reason to cover things up as quickly as possible. Dr Lane would have understood this and thought that the quicker the death was attended to, and the faster his famous patient buried, the better. Was that thinking behind the absence of an autopsy? Or did they just think that Montgomery was dead and an autopsy would not bring her back? In 1942, with Hitler threatening the world, there were other things to worry about than the cause of Montgomery's death.

Fifth: there is another possible angle, as well. Dr Lane would have been embarrassed that his famous patient had died under his watch, presumably following his regimen of medicines. What if he had given the frail Montgomery an injection earlier in the day, and she had lain down to rest on her bed, maybe even taking more of his pills to give her a better rest? When he wrote that her primary cause of death was "coronary thrombosis," and that she had "arteriosclerosis and a very high degree of neurasthenia," he seems to be covering all bases, without any further investigation. Is it possible that he had his own reasons for not wanting an autopsy?

Sixth: did Dr Lane himself ever contemplate the possibility that Montgomery's "neurasthenia" might have been intensified by drug dependency? And that some of her agitation and disorientation might have been caused by withdrawal symptoms?[19] Did Dr Lane and Stuart ever discuss drug dependency? Did Stuart ever talk seriously to his mother about it, and the dangers of combining bromides, barbiturates, and brandy? (Hollywood celebrities were still dying of these combinations in the latter half of the twentieth century.) If so, how would she have reacted? Did he (or she) know at that point that dependency or addiction or both can make a mind unstable and lead people to erratic behaviour? Would he (and she) have seen drug dependency as a moral failure on her part?

Seventh, and finally: where was Chester when Montgomery's body was found? When did he appear? We know that Chester would have had reason to poke around in his mother's bedroom regularly to see if she was contemplating more changes to her will which would affect him. What other materials might he have removed before the insurance company changed the locks on the house so that he could not get in?

I continue to wonder if the decision not to have an autopsy resulted in Stuart's feeling unnecessary guilt all his life, given the possibility that his mother may have died from a natural cause, however suspicious the circumstances. What we do know is that the suicide (or suspected suicide) of a loved family member can create lifelong psychological complications for those left behind. It is hard to imagine that even in the throes of a depression, Maud would have placed this burden on her children and grandchildren, especially if she had been functioning well enough to complete her last manuscript and send it to the publisher on the day of her death. Yet, devastating depression can lead people to act impulsively and irrationally; so, however much we speculate, we will never be certain about Montgomery's final thoughts and emotions on the last day of her life.

## NOTES

1 Rubio, *Lucy Maud Montgomery*, 575.
2 Final legal documents and Montgomery's will are in the University of Guelph archives.
3 When he was in law school and living at home again, his wife Luella and children lived temporarily with her widowed father in Norval. The plan was for them to set up housekeeping together again after he graduated.
4 Rubio, *Lucy Maud Montgomery*, 521–80.
5 Ibid., 575. The "suicide note" is now housed in the L.M. Montgomery Collection at the University of Guelph.
6 These issues are covered in more detail in Rubio, *Lucy Maud Montgomery*, 353–7, 362–91, 432–3, 464–7, 505, 529–39, 572.
7 This gave her another reason to set up the Trust Company as her executor.
8 If memory serves me correctly, Stuart also gave him some or all of the handwritten journals to peruse.
9 It was the CBC's duplicate copies of the typed journals which Stuart would mark up later when he attempted to edit the journals himself.
10 He would not have dared destroy any of the handwritten journals because they were clearly left to Stuart in his mother's will. We know that Montgomery reread her handwritten journals, as well as the typed ones, at some point in 1942 because she wrote a handwritten note in each copy in that year. For instance, in the 30 December 1935 entry of the typewritten journals, where she says this is "a mad world ... and no one can ... predict what madmen may do," she wrote in pencil, "Oh, oh, 1942." And she continued to correct typos in both of the carbons and originals of these typed versions of her journals, so she was at work on them until the end of her life.
11 A copy of Montgomery's death notice is in the "pink binder" of my as yet uncatalogued archives at the University of Guelph. It was picked up from the *Globe and Mail* the following day in the *New York Times* with only minor changes.
12 I no longer have McClelland & Stewart's cover letter, nor do I recall the origin of the copy they said they were sending me, nor the date sent. It might have

been from their vaults, or it might have been a copy of the one Stuart had sent to them, which they were just getting around to considering.

13  See Benjamin Lefebvre's speculations about these different manuscripts in his Master's thesis and later writings, including Montgomery, *The Blythes Are Quoted*.

14  If there were more pages than eleven of the typed journals, and he also read them, they could have been lost at this point, getting mixed with newspapers that were being thrown out.

15  *Globe and Mail*, 3 November 1977, located in the as yet uncatalogued Mary Henley Rubio Collection at the University of Guelph.

16  Montgomery, *Selected Journals*, 3:55 (entry of 22 May 1922).

17  Stuart's account to me gave me the impression that the note was what made him think his mother had committed suicide, but since I did not question him further, I can't be sure he intended me to think this.

18  As it was, there was gossip about her death for years; I was often asked after the talks I gave between 1980 and 2008 if it was true that she had committed suicide.

19  Elsie Bushby Davidson, a maid, spoke to me of those "damned pills" – veronal – which Maud and Ewan were taking back in the Leaskdale years, and continued to take.

## BIBLIOGRAPHY

*Globe and Mail*, 3 November 1977.

Montgomery, Lucy Maud. *The Blythes Are Quoted*. Edited by Benjamin Lefebvre. Toronto: Viking Canada, 2009.

– *The Selected Journals of L.M. Montgomery*. Vol. 3, 1921–1929. Edited by Mary Rubio and Elizabeth Waterston. Toronto: Oxford University Press, 1992.

Rubio, Mary Henley. *Lucy Maud Montgomery: The Gift of Wings*. Toronto: Doubleday, 2008.

– Mary Henley Rubio Archival Collection, University of Guelph. Uncatalogued at the time of this publication. (Includes Montgomery's obituary; Dr E. Stuart Macdonald's letter to the *Globe and Mail* about the cause of his mother's death.)

# A Century of Critical Reflection on
## *Anne of Green Gables*

BARBARA CARMAN GARNER

The L.M. Montgomery phenomenon has gathered momentum ever since the publication of *Anne of Green Gables* in 1908 established Montgomery's fame as a writer of popular fiction. A retrospective of the reception of this best loved of Montgomery's novels attests to the uniqueness of this "first classic" of Canadian children's literature. Reviewers of popular literature, historians of Canadian literature, academic scholars, librarians, and writers have all voiced their opinions. The questions asked by the early reviewers, as Mavis Reimer observes, tend to recur in later critical literature.[1]

The first reviewers of *Anne* established a pattern for discussing Montgomery's novel. They showed as much interest in Montgomery herself, and in the landscape of Prince Edward Island, as they did in her enchanting tale. They tried to assess the extent to which the landscape, people, and values depicted in Montgomery's fiction reflected her personal experiences. This holistic approach of looking at author and work together is mirrored by critics writing after the publication of her letters and journals, which enabled critics to appreciate the variety of subtle ways in which Montgomery's life writing and fiction intersect. Many critics interweave details from Montgomery's *Selected Journals*, published in five volumes, and from her correspondence with her pen pals, Ephraim Weber and George B. MacMillan, to contextualize their responses to her fiction.

Recent responses to *Anne* address the following issues and many more. Is Anne a romance, a *bildungsroman*, or a fairy tale? To what extent does the novel reflect Montgomery's own childhood and the historical community of Cavendish that became the Avonlea of the *Anne* books? Just how much realism is there in Montgomery's fiction? How conservative, even nostalgic, is Montgomery? What can one conclude about the moralizing in *Anne*, the portrayal of family, or Montgomery's privileging of female friendship? To what extent is Montgomery influenced by "first-wave feminism"? Why does the novel still appeal to a modern readership? How does *Anne* transform lives? The result is a dizzying array of theories about and assessments of the character and world of *Anne*.

In Anne, Montgomery created a character with a rich inner life, whose dynamism and social context become all the more apparent through the criticism that has proliferated since the publication of Montgomery's correspondence and journals. When we investigate the "auto-" discourses of her life writing, a religious dimension that clearly informs her oeuvre also becomes more evident. The immortal Anne, whom one early reviewer called "half imp, half angel, whose mental and spiritual growth is vividly set forth,"[2] can best be appreciated by interrogating the mental and spiritual dimensions of Montgomery's theory of character. It ultimately becomes clear that in Montgomery's life writing as well as in her novels, her own "mental and spiritual growth is vividly set forth."

Montgomery admits that in writing *Anne* she "cast 'moral' and 'Sunday School' ideals to the winds and made [her] 'Anne' a real human girl."[3] She tried to place the novel with the reputable publishers she knew, but when they all refused, she thought she might someday cut the book to the required seven chapters for "the aforesaid Sunday School paper."[4] In her 1917 account of the process of publishing *Anne*, she admits: "I never dreamed that it would appeal to young and old. I thought girls in their teens might like to read it, [and] that was the only audience I hoped to reach."[5] These later comments on her intended audience are telling; however, her earliest comments to correspondents about her anticipated readership reveal greater ambiguity. After reading *The Spectator* review sent to her by MacMillan, she tells Weber in a letter of 2 September 1909, "I can't really believe that my little yarn, written with an eye single to Sunday School scholars, should really have been taken notice of by *The Spectator*."[6] She configures her audience for *Anne* slightly differently in an earlier letter to Weber: "It is merely a juvenilish story, ostensibly for girls; [but] as I found the MS. rather interesting while reading it over lately I am not without hope that grown-ups may like it a little."[7] Similarly, she tells MacMillan when she first mentions

*Anne* to him in September 1907, "It is a juvenilish story of and for girls but I rather hope some grown-ups will like it too."[8]

Months later, when she mentions to MacMillan the reviews she has received, she admits surprise "that they seem to take the book so seriously – as if it were meant for grown-up readers, and not merely for girls."[9] Montgomery provides MacMillan with a brief overview of reviews her clipping service has sent her, but she catalogues these reviews much more fully for Weber. In her journals she does not record individual reviewers' comments, but in 1930, after rummaging through old scrapbooks, she does compile a list of contradictory comments about her novels from those early reviews. *Anne* heads the list, and these pages make for an interesting read.[10]

Montgomery admits to Weber that she had hoped to learn something from the reviews but was disappointed. She could not envisage the pattern that they, in their somewhat simplistic way, would establish for future Montgomery research. She did, however, appreciate the inter-relatedness of her own auto-discourses, and how they nurtured her spiritual well-being. In *The Alpine Path*, Montgomery reveals particular aspects of Anne's early life that were her own.[11] When she first mentions the book in her journal, she comments: "Many of my own childhood experiences and dreams were worked up into its chapters. Cavendish scenery supplied the background and Lover's Lane figures very prominently. There is plenty of incident in it but after all it must stand or fall by 'Anne.' She is the book."[12] Both Montgomery's Presbyterian upbringing and her personal religious views significantly influenced the way she configured Anne's spiritual growth.

Character is a central focus of early reviews of *Anne of Green Gables*. Early reviewers noted the charm of Anne, as well as Montgomery's integration of character and setting. For example, *The Canadian Magazine* in November 1908 termed the novel "a character study" in "a picturesque section of Prince Edward Island."[13] This appreciation correlates with Montgomery's focus in composition, as she confesses in a 1923 written interview: "In my own writing character is by far the most interesting thing to me – then setting ... my flair is for these things."[14] She confides, "The whole story was modeled around the character of 'Anne' and arranged to suit her."[15]

Although early reviewers heralded Anne as a departure from protagonists in established fiction for young readers, they also compared her to previous child heroines. Both *The Outlook* (22 August 1908) and *The Spectator* (13 March 1909) identify Anne as a "Canadian companion" to Kate Wiggin's *Rebecca of Sunnybrook Farm*. *The Outlook* states, "But the book is by no means an imitation,"[16] and *The Spectator* affirms, "There is no question of imitation or borrowing."[17] Anne's potential relationship with American texts led reviewers to catalogue similarities and differences. The *Saint John Globe* comments, "Like Miss Alcott's girls, [Anne] has become in this story of her life at Green Gables a friend,"[18] a relationship echoed by *The Spectator* reviewer, who finds the novel "in direct lineal descent from the works of Miss Alcott."[19] The *Boston Herald* reviewer is reminded of "the captivating humor of 'Mrs. Wiggs of the Cabbage Patch.'"[20] This placement of Anne in "direct lineal descent" from Alcott is echoed in later critics' attempts to assess Anne's relationship to her American cousins.

While Tanfer Tunc in this volume attests to the potential of cross-border cousins, comparing Anne with American heroines can lead to disconcerting and misleading conclusions, as Virginia Careless as well as Mary Rubio and Elizabeth Waterston warn.[21] Careless, for example, faults many literary scholars who have compared Anne with a variety of American cousins by suggesting derivative similarities that are at best cultural similarities, such as methods of dress and hair style current at the time the respective books were written, and not similarities indicative of influence or borrowing, as these scholars suggest. Careless illustrates her point most succinctly through the many comparisons of *Anne* with *Rebecca of Sunnybrook Farm*. Here she contrasts the assessments of the early reviewers, who saw no indication of imitation or borrowing when they made their comparison, with those of many modern critics, who, by turning their "similar details" into "causal links," suggest that Montgomery borrowed from Wiggin, and thus cast aspersions on the author's creative imagination.

Several reviews, including one in *The Globe*, differentiate *Anne* from the problem novels that had become such a "craze."[22] *The Spectator* reviewer remarks: "To all readers weary of problems, the duel of sex, broken Commandments, and gratuitous suicides, Miss Montgomery provides an alternative entertainment; all the more welcome because what we get in place of these hackneyed features is at once wholesome and attractive."[23] These comments suggest that this reviewer envisages a broad readership for Montgomery's novel.

The review in the *Montreal Daily Herald*, perhaps the first Canadian review of *Anne* (21 July 1908), proclaims *Anne* to be "one of the few Canadian stories that can appeal to the whole English-speaking world," and predicts that Anne will appeal to "every reader old and young."[24] *The Outlook* reviewer states that "it will please grown-up people quite or nearly as much as the school-girls for whom it is primarily designed,"[25] and the *American Library Association Booklist* reviewer (November 1908) follows suit, claiming that *Anne* is "a story that all girls from 12–15 and many grown-ups will enjoy."[26] The question of the novel's intended audience still remains. However, as Beverly Lyon Clark, among others, argues, the rigid segmentation of the adult and juvenile markets was a later twentieth-century development.[27] Reimer rightly identifies "the family story" or "girls' books" genre to which most of the books being compared with *Anne* belong.[28]

The literary merit of Montgomery's fiction has been questioned over the years, but her stature as an intriguing and important female writer sharply increased between the publication of *The Green Gables Letters* in 1960 and the first volume of her journals, edited by Mary Henley Rubio and Elizabeth Waterston in 1985.

In 1989, as an eighty-year retrospective of *Anne*, Mary Harker and I annotated articles, early reviews, and theses discussing *Anne* which had appeared up to that point, and assembled complementary materials in a vertical file designed to accompany the annotated bibliography, which appeared in *Canadian Children's Literature*.[29] Some of the popular magazine articles about Montgomery appeared as twenty- and sixty-year retrospectives. In my introduction, I focused on the importance of Montgomery's auto-discourses, and suggested: "A careful reading of the *Selected Journals*, and not just for the period covering the writing and publishing of *Anne of Green Gables*, is necessary if a well-rounded evaluation of Montgomery's own opinions on life in general, and on *Anne* in particular, is to be gleaned."[30] The journals and letters reveal much about Montgomery that was a matter of conjecture to early reviewers and critics writing prior to 1960.

Scholars commenting on Montgomery's critical reception have noted a new interest in Montgomery attributable not only to the publication of her life writings but also to a change in the literary-critical environment in the 1970s and 1980s. As early as 1966, Waterston commented on Montgomery's critical reception: "Literary critics throughout the western world saw at once the values she had achieved. If subsequent sophisticated criticism agreed to laugh at or by-pass the creator of 'Anne,' critics today are less ready to be patronizing."[31] In 1993 Waterston devoted a chapter of her book *Kindling Spirit: L.M. Montgomery's "Anne of Green Gables,"* to "Critical Reception."[32] Other scholars have discussed the criticism of Montgomery's fiction, and of *Anne* in particular. Of note is Mavis Reimer's summary in *Such a Simple Little Tale* (1992).[33] Reimer documents differences in critical responses that reflect changes in public opinion concerning Montgomery's *Anne*. These changes are most pronounced in the criticism written since 1975, when *Canadian Children's Literature* published a special issue paying tribute to Montgomery; Canadian Children's Press published *L.M. Montgomery: An Assessment*, a reprint of the seven articles from *Canadian Children's Literature*, the following year.[34]

Helen Siourbas's survey of Montgomery criticism in "L.M. Montgomery: Canon or Cultural Capital?" designates Sorfleet's collection as "the first book devoted to literary criticism on Montgomery," and identifies two perspectives emphasized in the essays that constitute it – "her national importance and the limitations of the genre in which she writes."[35] Siourbas cites Gillian Thomas's opinion that "in part the shortcomings of the sequels of *Anne of Green Gables* developed naturally from the genre of the sentimental novel to which they belong,"[36] and adds that in the 1970s, Montgomery "is seen as having a cultural, but not a literary, importance because she writes sentimental children's fiction."[37] She concludes: "Since the author's death in 1942, literary criticism on Montgomery's work has gone from being absent to being apologetic to boldly proclaiming that Montgomery is canon."[38]

The L.M. Montgomery Institute Web site also notes this change: "Active engagement has replaced much of the former tolerance, indifference, or hostility. The complex story of the coming together of these two audiences (the popular and the academic) is part of Montgomery's legacy to Twenty-First Century publishing history and to readers around the world."[39] The founding of the institute in 1993 testifies to the increasing interest in Montgomery studies.

As evidenced in this volume, L.M. Montgomery scholarship has also become more international. The dialogue among critics since the publication of Montgomery's journals and countless critical essays, especially those published as a result of the biennial Montgomery conferences at the L.M. Montgomery Institute, have made readers more aware of trends in Montgomery scholarship. In 1992 Mavis Reimer noted a difference between American and Canadian critical responses to Anne and lamented that, at that time, critics from the different countries did not reference each other's work.[40] Gerson in 2002 also differentiates Canadian and American responses to Montgomery: whereas Canadian essayists "lay adult claim to Montgomery by omitting any reference to youthful readers … American essays on Montgomery published in specialized collections all affirm her categorization as a children's author, many in relation to the emerging field of 'girl culture.'"[41] The last decade of critical response, however, evidences scholars of many nationalities frequently building on one another's work.

In the 2004 spring/summer issue of *Canadian Children's Literature* (*CCL*), entitled *Reassessments of L.M. Montgomery*, Benjamin Lefebvre's editorial "Assessments and Reassessments" sets Montgomery criticism in context and notes the variety of critical articles on Montgomery published in that periodical alone: "Indeed over the last 30 years, *CCL* has published 51 articles and 33 reviews on Montgomery."[42] Lefebvre addresses the question of intended readership of Montgomery's fiction, agreeing with Carole Gerson's observation that "many of these articles do not treat her as an author of juvenile fiction."[43]

Rubio, for example, argues that Montgomery's "early novels were written for a general audience, not children," adding that she was categorized as "a writer of popular fiction."[44] As a writer of domestic fiction, Montgomery ended her romances in marriage, but she "also embedded a counter-discourse which showed that marriage could pose grave dangers"[45] to a woman, and deployed a significant amount of satire, irony, and humour.[46]

Other critics are similarly concerned with defining the genre of Anne, along with its limitations and possibilities. For example, T.D. MacLulich, writing in 1985, theorizes about the original novel's realism to contemporary audiences and the nostalgic view of life it represents to modern eyes.[47] Montgomery herself sheds light on the "limited" realism of her fiction in her answer to the question, "What is the elemental hold of fiction on the human mind?" She defends her choices on the basis of the "deep desire in every one of us for 'something better than we have known,'" and asserts that "'romance' is and always will be, and always should be more popular than 'realism.'"[48] Sugars in this volume continues the dialogue between realism and romance.

Who can begin to assess the impact the various movie adaptations of *Anne* (1919, 1934, and 1985) have had on viewers, or what renewed interest they spawned in the Montgomery enterprise? The same can be asked about *Anne of Green Gables: The Musical*, plays such as the one by Paul Ledoux, ballets, and other media presentations of *Anne*. In her survey of the reception history of *Anne*, Gerson draws attention to the difficulty of distinguishing the academic reception of the novel from the "massive renewal of interest in her from ... the realm of popular television and its myriad spin-offs."[49] Although she recognizes the importance of the publication of the journals for those writing about Montgomery, she believes "a direct causal relationship might be difficult to argue, as in most cases the *Journals* are treated more as background to Montgomery's fiction than as topics of analysis in themselves."[50] However, most scholars agree that explicating the journals provides us with a more dynamic view than a reading of the novels alone permits. In an article entitled "The Architect of Adolescence" (1985), Rubio documents in an informed way the parallels between Montgomery's life and Anne's.[51] Fifty-three years of soul-searching and self-analysis are contained in Montgomery's journals. As Carolyn Hunt observes, "the published portions of the journals reveal a carefully fashioned presentation of the author's outer and inner life."[52] Many Montgomery critics have shown just how carefully fashioned that presentation is.

What makes the life writing of Montgomery's journals so complex is her use of a variety of different auto-discourses. She frequently moves beyond standard journal or diary writing, and employs a discourse similar to that Gabrielle Roy used in her autobiography – what Roy's biographer François Ricard terms "a re-creation or re-enactment of the past from memory and imagination, strongly flavoured with emotion and subjectivity; a past that never fails to quicken and live in the very process of its recall."[53] As Montgomery revised her life story, she not only relived past years, as she herself notes, but also "quickened" them as she rewrote entire entries in her journals. As Rubio noted in 1984, "To read the novels Montgomery wrote ... in conjunction with her diaries is to enter a magical zone where one can witness the fabric of real life being taken apart, and the threads reconstructed into the cloth of fiction."[54]

Both happiness and pain are necessary ingredients of the complex selfhood each person develops to confront daily life. Cecily Devereux, in her article entitled "'See my Journal for the full story': Fictions of Truth in *Anne of Green Gables* and L.M. Montgomery's Journals," helps readers access the complex narrative voice Montgomery adopts in *Anne* and illustrates how that voice is linked to Montgomery's own experience: "The idea that Anne was Montgomery's adult response to her remembered childhood unhappiness is a potent one. In fact, it is difficult not to speculate that Montgomery in 1905 was investing her novel with the same kind of therapeutic function of writing out that she repeatedly maintains was performed for her by her journals."[55] Similarities between Anne and her creator are innumerable, as indicated in Montgomery's 1917 autobiography *The Alpine Path* (first published in book form in 1975), her published *Journals*, *The Annotated Anne* (1997), Cecily Devereux's Broadview edition of *Anne* (2004), and articles such as the one by Rubio cited above. Devereux, after listing those similarities, comments: "It is not entirely clear whether Montgomery is configuring the novel as a document of her life or as a text in which she has inscribed the symptoms of her own condition ... In fact it is possible she is doing both, with a deliberate ambivalence ... As she notes in her journal at the time of *Anne*'s acceptance: 'Many of my own childhood experiences and dreams were worked up into its chapters.'"[56] Irene Gammel, in her introduction to Part 4 of *The Intimate Life of L.M. Montgomery* (2005), in which Devereux's essay also appears, observes that "fiction provided a safe screen of disguises and transpositions for Montgomery to work through intimately personal materials ... From *Anne of Green Gables* to *A Tangled Web*, Montgomery's fiction invites biographical readings that trace the author's projection of autobiographical selves into fictive characters."[57]

If we subscribe to Devereux's theory of a re-configuration of Montgomery's life in Anne's, Montgomery's retrospective passages in the journals not only add to their intertextual complexity, as many other well-known critics of her work have argued, but they also lend a new dimensionality to our understanding of Montgomery's Anne.[58] An interesting discussion of Montgomery's journal-writing as autobiographical process is also found in Margaret E. Turner's "Autobiographical Process in the L.M. Montgomery Journals."[59] Turner suggests not only that Montgomery tells us how to read the journals as "a public record," but also that "she tells us in the journals how to read the fiction."[60]

How many dimensions of Montgomery's inner self, or, as others might phrase it, how many selves, are found in the journals? Janice Fiamengo speculates that the hellish side of Montgomery's inner turmoil is "written out" there: "Repeatedly she psychologized hell to emphasize her possession by darkness and dispossession of hope, stressing the horrifying split between a self blessed by grace and one cast into eternal darkness."[61] Pain became for Montgomery a "strategy of self-articulation."[62] The reflections of Fiamengo, Devereux, and Gammel indicate not only how multi-layered Montgomery's writing is, but also the extent to which Anne becomes an integral part of Montgomery's psyche. Notwithstanding, Montgomery wanted to keep the shadows, to which Fiamengo and others draw attention, out of her fiction. She proclaims, "I would not wish to darken any other life – I want instead to be a messenger of optimism and sunshine."[63] Indeed, Fiamengo, Devereux, and Gammel lead us to believe that Montgomery was trying to write sunshine into her own life through the creation of *Anne*.

Gerson offers a perceptive comment about Montgomery's journals. She paraphrases Rubio and Waterston's observation[64] that Montgomery "shaped her life to fit the narrative of the journals,"[65] and suggests: "I think it quite possible that this professional storyteller shaped her own story retrospectively. In a sense, the journals can be seen as sequels to her life and her published books."[66] Gerson's theory relates to Montgomery's retrospective reconstructions of portions of her life story as she revised sections of her journals. However, I would add that the journals are only "sequels" in that they were published posthumously, and may not represent reality or the final word, as most critics who write about the tension between the inner and outer lives of Montgomery argue. Perhaps Margaret Steffler's suggestion of "reading the journals as an extension and completion of the reading of the novels"[67] is more in keeping with Montgomery's intention.

One specific link between Anne and her creator, often implied but rarely explored in the early reviews and criticism, is the way in which a religious discourse informs *Anne of Green Gables*. That discourse is sometimes voiced by Marilla or Mrs Allan, but most often it acquires its freshness through Anne's own somewhat novel pronouncements. This discourse derives from Montgomery's own experiences of religion both as a child in Cavendish, and, after her secret engagement to Ewan in 1906, as a woman contemplating her role as a future minister's wife. Montgomery's religious discourse shows how the natural world reflects God's spirit, a feature some critics have misconstrued as paganism. This religious undercurrent in the fiction reveals the interconnectedness of Montgomery's auto-discourses; the fiction, as Gammel and others have argued, is an auto-discourse that reflects the persona of its author.

We know from the journals and correspondence that religion is intricately bound up with the moral and social norms to which Montgomery was committed, and plays a very important role in the lives of members of her fictional Prince Edward Island communities. When critics do address this discourse, they privilege Montgomery's negative or unorthodox pronouncements in her correspondence and journals. Careful analysis of these documents reveals the premises on which she built her Christian faith. Montgomery's musings in her correspondence with Ephraim Weber and in her carefully edited personal journals, intended for public perusal only after her death, indicate the importance of faith in her daily life. Stages of her Christian journey are marked by periods of doubt, despair, and skepticism, but underpinning all her religious discourses, be they in her fiction or in her life writing, is her continuing affirmation of a faith in God.

Anne's views on religious practices constitute a sub-theme in the novel. (Jean Mitchell's contribution to this volume engages questions about the cultural context and meaning of some of these practices.) Rubio recognizes that "the inner story [of Anne] also takes part of its form from Montgomery's personal values."[68] Anne's religious discourse echoes Montgomery's. Anne's unwitting remarks about the minister, the Sunday school superintendent, her Sunday school teacher, and prayer express feelings Montgomery expressed in her journals. Anne's "speaking out," I would argue, mirrors Montgomery's "writing out" in her journals and correspondence. So close to the truth of Marilla's inner but unspoken thoughts are Anne's remarks that the reader realizes that Montgomery, as Monica Hilder suggests,[69] is calling for a return to a more sincere expression of religious faith. When Marilla tells Anne, "you should never find it hard to say your prayers," she quips, "Saying one's prayers isn't exactly the same thing as praying."[70] It is clear that the

Allans, the new minister and his wife who represent an ideal for Anne, embody, especially in the person of Mrs Allan, an ideal that Montgomery herself later aspired to achieve as a minister's wife.

The characterization of Mrs Allan as minister's wife, Sunday school teacher, and friend suggests that Montgomery prefigures in her fiction aspects of an idealized self that is still in the future rather than current or in the past. In a similar way, the early criticism of *Anne* prefigured the way critics have analyzed the text, the import they have attributed to Montgomery's fictional narrative voice in the context of her varied auto-discourses, and their recognition of lacunae in the existing body of criticism, for instance, the lack of attention given to Montgomery's religious discourse. Their scholarship has definitively informed readers' appreciation of "where the voice comes from."[71]

## NOTES

1 Reimer, *Such a Simple Little Tale*, 172.
2 *The Spectator*, 13 March 1909, 427.
3 Montgomery, *Selected Journals*, 1:330.
4 Ibid., 1:331.
5 Ibid., *The Alpine Path*, 76.
6 Ibid., *The Green Gables Letters*, 93–4.
7 Ibid., Letter, 2 May 1907, 51.
8 Ibid., *My Dear Mr. M.*, 35.
9 Ibid., 39.
10 Ibid., *Selected Journals* 4:36–43. The references to *Anne* occur on pages 36–7.
11 Ibid., *The Alpine Path*, 73–5.
12 Ibid., *Selected Journals*, 1:330.
13 "The Way of Letters," *The Canadian Magazine*, 87.
14 Heilbron, *Remembering Lucy Maud Montgomery*, 205.
15 Ibid., 200.
16 *The Outlook*, 22 August 1908, 957–8.
17 *The Spectator*, 13 March 1909, 427.
18 *The Saint John Globe*, 8 August 1908, 10.
19 *The Spectator*, 13 March 1909, 427.
20 *The Herald* (Boston), quoted in *The Nation*'s title-page advertisement for new books, 16 July 1908, i.
21 Careless, "L.M. Montgomery and Everybody Else"; and Rubio and Waterston, Preface.
22 *The Globe* (Toronto), "In the World of Books," 15 August 1908, 5.

23  *The Spectator*, 13 March 1909, 426.

24  *The Montreal Daily Herald*, 21 July 1908, 4.

25  *The Outlook*, 22 August 1908, 958.

26  *American Library Association Booklist*, 274.

27  Clark, *Kiddie Lit*.

28  Reimer, *Such a Simple Little Tale*, 174.

29  Garner and Harker, "*Anne of Green Gables*," and vertical file.

30  Ibid.

31  Waterston, "Lucy Maud Montgomery," 199.

32  Ibid., *Kindling Spirit*, 19–24.

33  Reimer, *Such a Simple Little Tale*. See particularly Introduction, 1–10; "Contexts and History of Reception," 176–83; and "Scholarship and Criticism," 183–90.

34  Sorfleet, *L.M. Montgomery: An Assessment*.

35  Siourbas, "L.M. Montgomery," 135.

36  Ibid.

37  Ibid.

38  Ibid., 139.

39  Epperly, "The Changing Perception."

40  Reimer, *Such a Simple Little Tale*.

41  Gerson, "*Anne of Green Gables* Goes," 27.

42  Lefebvre, "Editorial: Assessments and Reassessments," 7.

43  Gerson, "*Anne of Green Gables* Goes," 26.

44  Rubio, *Harvesting Thistles*, 1.

45  Ibid., 5.

46  Ibid., "Satire, Realism, and Imagination," 27–32.

47  MacLulich, "L.M. Montgomery's Portraits," 84.

48  Heilbron, *Remembering Lucy Maud Montgomery*, 205.

49  Gerson, "*Anne of Green Gables* Goes," 21.

50  Ibid., 21.

51  Rubio, "*Anne of Green Gables*," 74–6.

52  Hunt, Preface, xi.

53  Ricard, Foreword, v.

54  Rubio, "L.M. Montgomery: Where Does," 112.

55  Devereux, "'See my Journal,'" 253.

56  Ibid., quoting Montgomery, *Selected Journals* 1:331.

57  Gammel, *The Intimate Life*, 239.

58  See Devereux, "'See my Journal,'" and Gammel, *The Intimate Life* and *Looking for Anne*.

59  Turner, "'I mean to try,'" 93–100.

60  Ibid.

61  Fiamengo, "'the refuge of my sick spirit,'" 178.

62  Ibid., 184.

63  Montgomery, *Selected Journals*, 1:339.

64  Rubio and Waterston, *Writing a Life*, 36.
65  Gerson, "'Dragged,'" 56.
66  Ibid.
67  Steffler, "'This has been,'" 82.
68  Rubio, "L.M. Montgomery: Where Does," 118.
69  Hilder, "'That Unholy Tendency,'" 41.
70  Montgomery, *Anne of Green Gables*, 123.
71  Rubio, "L.M. Montgomery: Where Does the Voice Come From?"


## BIBLIOGRAPHY

*American Library Association Booklist*. Review of *Anne of Green Gables*, by L.M. Montgomery, vol. 4.8 (Nov. 1908). 274. Reprinted in "Book Reviews," in Montgomery, *The Annotated Anne of Green Gables*, 487–8.

Careless, Virginia A.S. "L.M. Montgomery and Everybody Else: A Look at the Books." In Hudson and Cooper, *Windows and Words*, 143–74.

Clark, Beverly Lyon. *Kiddie Lit: The Cultural Construction of Children's Literature in America*. Baltimore: Johns Hopkins University Press, 2003.

Devereux, Cecily. "'See my Journal for the full story': Fictions of Truth in *Anne of Green Gables* and L.M. Montgomery's Journals." In Gammel, *The Intimate Life of L.M. Montgomery*, 241–57.

Epperly, Elizabeth Rollins. "The Changing Perception of L.M. Montgomery's Writing." In *Picturing a Canadian Life: L.M. Montgomery's Personal Scrapbooks and Book Covers*. Confederation Centre of the Arts, 2002. http://lmm.confederationcentre.com/english/covers/collecting-7-1.html (accessed 20 December 2011).

Fiamengo, Janice. "'… the refuge of my sick spirit …': L.M. Montgomery and the Shadows of Depression." In Gammel, *The Intimate Life of L.M. Montgomery*, 170–86.

Gammel, Irene. *Looking for Anne: How Lucy Maud Montgomery Dreamed Up a Literary Classic*. Toronto: Key Porter, 2008.

–, ed. *The Intimate Life of L.M. Montgomery*. Toronto: University of Toronto Press, 2005.

–, ed. *Making Avonlea: L.M. Montgomery and Popular Culture*. Toronto: University of Toronto Press, 2002.

Garner, Barbara Carman, and Mary Harker. "*Anne of Green Gables*: An Annotated Bibliography." *CCL: Canadian Children's Literature*, vol. 55 (1989): 18–41.

– Vertical File on L.M. Montgomery's *Anne of Green Gables*: A Companion to "*Anne of Green Gables*: An Annotated Bibliography." National Library of Canada, Ottawa.

Gerson, Carole. "*Anne of Green Gables* Goes to University: L.M. Montgomery and Academic Culture." In Gammel, *Making Avonlea*, 17–31.

– "'Dragged at Anne's Chariot Wheels': The Triangle of Author, Publisher, and Fictional Character." In *L.M. Montgomery and Canadian Culture*, edited by Irene Gammel and Elizabeth Epperly, 49–63. Toronto: University of Toronto Press, 1999.

*The Globe* (Toronto). "In the World of Books." Review of *Anne of Green Gables*, by L.M. Montgomery. 15 August 1908: 5.

Heilbron, Alexandra. *Remembering Lucy Maud Montgomery*. Toronto: Dundurn Press, 2001.

Hilder, Monica B. "'That Unholy Tendency to Laughter': L.M. Montgomery's Iconoclastic Affirmation of Faith in *Anne of Green Gables*." CCL: *Canadian Children's Literature*, vol. 113–14 (2004): 34–55.

Hudson, Aïda, and Susan-Ann Cooper, eds. *Windows and Words: A Look at Canadian Children's Literature in English Canada*. Ottawa: University of Ottawa Press, 2003.

Hunt, Caroline C. Preface. *Dictionary of Literary Biography: Documentary Series: An Illustrated Chronicle: Four Women Writers for Children 1868–1918*. Vol. 14, 149–204. Edited by Caroline C. Hunt. Detroit: Bruccoli Clark Layman, 1996.

Ledoux, Paul. *Anne: Adapted from the Novel* Anne of Green Gables. Toronto: Playwrights Canada Press, 1999.

Lefebvre, Benjamin. "Editorial: Assessments and Reassessments." *Reassessments of L.M. Montgomery*. CCL: *Canadian Children's Literature*, vol. 113–14 (2004): 6–13.

MacLulich, T.D. "L.M. Montgomery's Portraits of the Artist: Realism, Idealism, and the Domestic Imagination." In Reimer, *Such A Simple Little Tale*, 83–100.

Montgomery, L.M. *The Alpine Path: The Story of My Career*. 1917. Markham, Ontario: Fitzhenry, 1975.

– *Anne of Green Gables*. Edited by Cecily Devereux. Peterborough, Ontaario: Broadview Press, 2004.

– *The Annotated Anne of Green Gables*. Edited by Wendy E. Barry, Margaret Anne Doody, and Mary E. Jones. New York: Oxford University Press, 1997.

– *The Green Gables Letters from L.M. Montgomery to Ephraim Weber, 1905–1909*. 2nd edition. Edited by Wilfrid Eggleston. Ottawa: Borealis, 1981.

– *My Dear Mr. M.: Letters to G.B. MacMillan from L.M. Montgomery*. Edited by Francis W.P. Bolger and Elizabeth R. Epperly. Toronto: McGraw-Hill Ryerson, 1980.

– *The Selected Journals of L.M. Montgomery*. Vol. 1, 1889–1910; Vol. 4, 1929–1935. Edited by Mary Rubio and Elizabeth Waterston. Toronto: Oxford University Press, 1985; 1998.

*The Montreal Daily Herald.* Review of *Anne of Green Gables*, by L.M. Montgomery. 21 July 1908: 4. Reprinted in "Book Reviews," in Montgomery, *The Annotated Anne of Green Gables*, 484.

*The Nation.* Review of *Anne of Green Gables*, by L.M. Montgomery. 37.2246 (16 July 1908): i. Reprinted in "Book Reviews," in Montgomery, *The Annotated Anne of Green Gables*, 483.

*The Outlook.* Review of *Anne of Green Gables*, by L.M. Montgomery. 22 August 1908: 957–8. Reprinted in "Book Reviews," in Montgomery, *The Annotated Anne of Green Gables*, 487.

Reimer, Mavis, ed. *Such a Simple Little Tale: Critical Responses to L.M. Montgomery's "Anne of Green Gables."* Metuchen, New Jersey: Children's Literature Association and Scarecrow Press, 1992.

Ricard, François. Foreword to Roy, *Enchantment and Sorrow*, v–vi.

Roy, Gabrielle. *Enchantment and Sorrow: The Autobiography of Gabrielle Roy.* Translated by Patricia Claxton. Toronto: Lester & Orpen Dennys, 1987.

Rubio, Mary Henley. "Anne of Green Gables: The Architect of Adolescence." In Reimer, *Such a Simple Little Tale*, 65–82.

–, ed. *Harvesting Thistles: The Textual Garden of L.M. Montgomery: Essays on Her Novels and Journals.* Guelph, Ontario: Canadian Children's Press, 1994.

– "L.M. Montgomery: Where Does the Voice Come From?" In *Canadiana: Studies in Canadian Literature. Proceedings of the Canadian Studies Conference, Aarhus, 1984,* edited by Jorn Carlsen and Knud Larsen, 109–19. Aarhus: Canadian Studies Conference, 1984.

– "Satire, Realism, and Imagination in *Anne of Green Gables.*" CCL: *Canadian Children's Literature,* vol. 1.3 (1975): 27–36.

Rubio, Mary Henley, and Elizabeth Waterston. Preface. In Montgomery, *Anne of Green Gables,* by L.M. Montgomery, vii–ix.

– *Writing a Life: L.M. Montgomery.* Toronto: ECW Press, 1995.

*The Saint John Globe.* Review of *Anne of Green Gables,* by L.M. Montgomery. 8 August 1908: 10. Reprinted in "Book Reviews," in Montgomery, *The Annotated Anne of Green Gables*, 486.

Siourbas, Helen. "L.M. Montgomery: Canon or Cultural Capital?" In Hudson and Cooper, *Windows and Words,* 131–41.

Sorfleet, John Robert, ed. *L.M. Montgomery: An Assessment.* Guelph, Ontario: Canadian Children's Press, 1976.

*The Spectator, A Weekly Review of Politics, Literature, Theology, and Art.* Review of *Anne of Green Gables,* by L.M. Montgomery. 13 March 1909: 426–7. Reprinted in "Book Reviews," in Montgomery, *The Annotated Anne of Green Gables*, 489.

Steffler, Margaret. "'This has been a day in hell': Montgomery, Popular Literature, Life Writing." In Gammel, *Making Avonlea,* 72–83.

Turner, Margaret E. "'I mean to try, as far as in me lies, to paint my life and deeds truthfully': Autobiographical Process in L.M. Montgomery's Journals." In *Harvesting Thistles: The Textual Garden of L.M. Montgomery*, edited by Mary Henley Rubio, 93–100. Guelph, Ontario: Canadian Children's Press, 1994.

Waterston, Elizabeth. *Kindling Spirit: L.M. Montgomery's "Anne of Green Gables."* Toronto: ECW Press, 1993.

– "Lucy Maud Montgomery: 1874–1942." In *The Clear Spirit: Twenty Canadian Women and Their Times*, edited by Mary Quale Innis, 198–220. Toronto: University of Toronto Press, 1966.

"The Way of Letters." Review of *Anne of Green Gables*, by L.M. Montgomery. *The Canadian Magazine.* November 1908: 426–7. Reprinted in "Book Reviews," in Montgomery, *The Annotated Anne of Green Gables*, 489.

Wiggin, Kate Douglas. *Rebecca of Sunnybrook Farm.* London: Adam and Charles Black, 1950.

# The Terrain of the Classic:
## Allusions and Intertexts

# L.M. Montgomery and the Significance of "Classics," Ancient and Modern

MARGARET DOODY

When we speak colloquially of "a classic," or certainly of a "children's classic," we are referring to some work of modern literature, usually fiction; commonly, if paradoxically, the phrase has come to be used chiefly of works of the nineteenth and twentieth centuries. In former days the term "a classic" would mean something like *Hamlet* or *Paradise Lost*; now it more usually means a well-known work that has been around for a while – so *David Copperfield* and *Jane Eyre*, once popular reading, are now advertised as "classics." We tend to ignore the once-primary use of the word to refer to classical literature. At one time "a classic" could only refer to a work pertaining to "the classics" – that is, a work written in Latin or Greek.

It is not generally noticed that the work of Lucy Maud Montgomery offers a number of references to "the classics" in that sense. Anne Shirley studies Latin, and so do many – not all – of her friends, those who intend to go on to high school. Jane Andrews has trouble with it, as she complains after her first day at Queen's when she has to construe "twenty lines" of Virgil as homework: "I ought to be home studying my Virgil – that horrid old professor gave us twenty lines to start in on tomorrow."[1] What we would call elementary and junior high school education under teachers like Mr Phillips, Miss Stacy, and, in the *Emily* books, Mr Carpenter consists of a traditional academic curriculum supervised by a provincial government that prescribes courses and set texts. Vocational training might be included, but the road to success is the academic path. The sign of the educated citizen is an ability to read Latin.

From the Renaissance, the learning of Latin had been the key to all educational endeavour, to instruction itself, to engagement in research, and to conversation across national and linguistic boundaries. It fostered the exchange of ideas. It became a mark of class and power, and a mode of advancement of the bright and ambitious. The true citizen of the virtuous republic (usually figured as a male member of an elite group) knew Latin. In a democratic country, then, it seemed reasonable, even noble, that all children should learn some Latin. This seemingly sacred knowledge was extended to bright children in rural schools. Although Montgomery's Jane Stewart, of Lantern Hill, is expert in domestic science, she too has to read Latin.

Successful males traditionally read Latin with ease. A modern reader will be surprised to realize that Gilbert Blythe, doctor-to-be, does not specialize in or even apparently study the sciences in his undergraduate career. At Redmond, we are told, "he took High Honours in Classics and the Cooper Prize."[2] Gilbert has excelled in the traditionally highest masculine area of study. He only takes up the scientific part of his career, so it seems, in the three years he spends at medical school. High school studies include mathematics (algebra and geometry). But nobody studies biology, physics, or chemistry – as their mid- and late-twentieth-century counterparts would do (as Canadian Maritimers like myself did when we went in for "Matrics, or matriculation examinations"). Latin, not science, is still the language of power.

Struggling with Latin, with lines to "construe," is a common task for Montgomery's protagonists; Montgomery's young women patiently resort to grammar books and dictionaries. The language book can seem like a barrier. On her first day, when she stays after school to study for the Entrance Examination, Anne feels sorrow at seeing Diana leave and go out into the beautiful outdoors; the pains of separation and the welling tears are hidden behind the dry book: "A lump came into her throat, and she hastily retired behind the pages of her uplifted Latin grammar to hide the tears in her eyes."[3] Latin is an affair of never-ending grammar, an arid non-language severing the girl from nature and from friendship. Learning Latin is customarily represented by Montgomery as a matter of hard work and dry reference materials. Her fellow student at Redmond, Priscilla, picks up a Greek lexicon: Latin and Greek are dictionary languages. At Redmond, we are told, "the girls of Patty's Place settled down to a steady grind of study ... Anne devoted herself to English, Priscilla pored over classics, and Philippa pounded away at Mathematics."[4] Devoting oneself to a subject is different from "poring" or "pounding" – Anne has obviously chosen the better (or at least the happier) part by specializing in English in her college studies. But earlier, she proved herself worthy by pursuing the high school academic program and enabling herself not only to become a teacher but to pursue the far-off dream of going to college.

At the beginning of *Anne of Avonlea*, Anne is conscientiously trying to make herself work at her Latin: "A tall, slim girl, 'half-past sixteen' ... had sat down on the broad red sandstone doorstep of a Prince Edward Island farmhouse one ripe afternoon in August, firmly resolved to construe so many lines of Virgil."[5]

But as she looks out at the beautiful landscape "fitter for dreams than dead languages," Anne muses on nature and on her own future as a teacher: "the Virgil soon slipped unheeded to the ground."[6] While she is thus musing, her Jersey cow escapes into Mr Harrison's field, and she is interrupted by her irate and unattractive neighbour, who unpleasantly accuses her of wasting her time: "'And I can tell you, you red-headed snippet, that if the cow is yours, as you say, you'd be better employed in watching her out of other people's grain than in sitting round reading yellow-covered novels' ... with a scathing glance at the innocent tan-coloured Virgil by Anne's feet."[7]

Are the truly classic "classics" barriers to real life? Are they dead and deadening – a contrast to life and to novels? Montgomery's references to learning ancient languages and construing lines constantly relegate "the classics" to a world of necessity and of labour.

When Montgomery speaks of modern literature we hear a very different tone. It is all English literature. Her references go back to Shakespeare – and certainly the King James Version of the Bible, with both open and embedded quotations enriching almost every page. But there is little else of the Renaissance. The eighteenth century is well represented in Montgomery. The poet James Thomson, eighteenth-century author of *The Seasons*, is an object of imitation for *Emily of New Moon*. Emily also has read the late eighteenth-century Gothic novels of Ann Radcliffe. Alexander Pope is a presence, his *Essay on Criticism* deliberately and playfully misquoted in the latter part of *Anne of Green Gables*, describing the young peoples' studies: "Hills peeped o'er hills and Alps on Alps arose."[8] Pope describes something appealing to Montgomery: creative strenuousness rather than student efforts. The nineteenth century is very richly present. The reference to *Jane Eyre* in *Emily of New*

*Moon* offers a perhaps belated admission on the author's part that in her early Anne as well as in her orphan Emily she was indebted to Brontë. But the novel is read and known by a male reader, Dean Priest, who marks the poem indicating Rochester's passion for Jane. Emily (who may be named, in part at least, after Emily Brontë) is evidently "that child of shower and gleam"[9] – the way Rochester sees Jane. The erotic enters through the "classic." Yet *Jane Eyre* was still an ambiguous and vexed "classic," in some eyes an improper book; even at the end of the nineteenth century, it could be mentioned as the sort of book girls should not read – and it is Dean who has certainly read it, not Emily.

Such examples illustrate the blurred line between the "classical" (in the demotic sense) and the merely "popular," a line always difficult – perhaps impossible – to draw. Montgomery seems to understand the difficulty of drawing this line – unlike her friend Ephraim Weber, who took it seriously. Comments of Paul Tiessen and Hildi Froese Tiessen on the tone adopted by Weber in his correspondence are to the point: "In conversation with Weber, a man who with some pleasure was ready to imagine himself as highbrow when he joined in the Monday-night meetings of the Athenian club in Outlook, Saskatchewan in the early 1920s … Montgomery felt compelled to negotiate a space for herself between her unequivocal intolerance of new art forms and her growing complicity with an ethos defined by popular cultural forms that Weber, for the most part, explicitly resisted."[10]

I see Montgomery's stance in relation to literary genres and values as less embarrassed and more mischievous – and she is likely to have been as aware of the provinciality of an Athenian club of Outlook, Saskatchewan, as the Tiessens seem to have been. It is true that Montgomery felt challenged by and angry at new twentieth-century forms, styles, and attitudes – I think because they assumed a cosmopolitan authority she could not attain. Also, they are almost all posited on a basis of male experience and superiority. (Virginia Woolf came too late in the day to help women writers born back in the nineteenth century.) I do not, however, think Montgomery feels genuinely depressed or overthrown by the challenges of the "classic" or of "literature." She consistently avails herself of the ambiguity.

Throughout her writing Lucy Maud Montgomery treats any concept of "the classic" with a good deal of playfulness. She appears to relish the ambiguity of literary positioning, begging the distinction between the "popular" and the "classic" or "literary." Novels and poems of the nineteenth century both recur in her novels as simultaneously or alternately "classic" and "popular," as suits her. Tennyson's "Lancelot and Elaine" is for Anne's school a scholastic text set by a civil servant, "the Superintendent of Education having prescribed it in the English course for the Prince Edward Island schools."[11] The faceless "Superintendent" presumably thinks Tennyson's poem a suitable modern "classic." But Montgomery comically treats Tennyson's poem as a phenomenon of pop culture in the girls' adoption of it. They re-naturalize it as *play*, as that which can be re-represented, and as an adolescent image. A "classic" can be simply defined as a written work that has to be studied for examinations. Montgomery de-classifies and de-classicizes the poem about Elaine – or rather, the girls do this themselves, performing a comic rescue mission on Tennyson's work.

Rather cleverly, not to say mischievously, Montgomery places "female" classics in male libraries. In *Emily of New Moon*, not only is *Jane Eyre* in Dean Priest's collection, but we were earlier told that the heroine has read Ann Radcliffe's novels when she found them in Dr Burnley's bookcase.[12] That bookcase became forbidden to her when she was discovered to be reading a book on the human body. The male bookcase of secret knowledge is associated with Radcliffe's studies of evil and mystery, in a passage that heralds the soon-to-arrive Dean Priest. Women's writings can be rendered as if they are "classics" by being given male readers and owners. But classics, so it is hinted, are, if properly understood, repositories of secret power and erotic knowledge.

Recent or current writers are always difficult to place in the "classic" scale. For many readers and critics, a writer like Charles Dickens remained a mere "popular" read, vulgar and entertaining, not to be read in the useful daytime – rather the way in which some of us treat television. Yet modern writers can make claims.

Bret Harte makes claims for himself and for Dickens when in his eulogy "Dickens in Camp" (1870),[13] he praises the novelist for being able to reach the loggers in the western woods. When Gilbert quotes Harte's poem during a walk in the park, we may think of this as a mere tribute to the soothing effects of pine trees. But Harte's poem is a tribute to the divine spell created by a novelist, and the quotation[14] heralds several references to Dickens that crop up in *Anne of the Island*. Anne reads *The Pickwick Papers* for relaxation: "Now that spring examinations were over she was treating herself to Dickens."[15] So Dickens is a familiar and popular writer, his book a light relaxation – a treat, unlike the "classics" (on which exams must be written). Dickens is to be enjoyed, not studied. A light-hearted discussion of *Pickwick Papers* ensues.[16] Yet the introduction of this particular novel marks an ominous beginning for a chapter entitled "Gilbert Speaks," the chapter containing Gilbert's first marriage proposal to Anne. *The Pickwick Papers*, like its model in Rabelais, is a novel hostile to marriage. Most of its plots involve getting out of marriage entrapments; its major plot line is the avoidance of matrimony. L.M. Montgomery is not using reference to the novel at a low level or as an almost accidental realistic allusion to the kind of thing people really read. She employs it in a sophisticated system of reference.

Yet we may ask: Is it true that the only sophisticated reference we can expect from Montgomery – the only subtle use of other texts – involves the use of modern English texts? Does Montgomery really ignore the content of all classical literature? I would contend that at least in one instance some attention is paid to the interior content of classical literature, a spot where Latin literature is more than dictionary work demanding painful decoding. In that opening scene of *Anne of Avonlea*, the tan-coloured Virgil may seem the mere shell of literature, a "classic" in being dutifully acknowledged, yet not part of the life-blood.

Yet, I would contend that the subject matter immediately following contains a comic play upon a famous character and scene in Virgil's *Aeneid*. In the eleventh Book of that twelve-book epic, we find the story of the woman-warrior Camilla, leader of the tribe of the Volscians. This beautiful enemy to the invading Aeneas has already been described in the seventh Book: "She was able to bear the onrush of battle, and to outstrip the winds. She might have flown over the tips of the growing corn nor damaged the delicate young stalks of grain in her running."[17]

Young Camilla is a formidable fighter. Unlike other women, she is not afraid of conflict. A determined virgin, she is greatly beloved of the chaste goddess Diana and is determined to remain a virgin maid: "Sola contenta Diana / aeternum telorum et virginitatis amorem."[18] Camilla spends her time in male pursuits. Camilla is a crack shot as an archer, though chiefly known for her remarkable swiftness in running. She kills many enemies. Yet, alas, beguiled by the view of golden spoils, she loses her guard so that she can be killed by her enemy, the deeply hostile Arruns. (On Arruns, the grieving goddess Diana immediately takes vengeance.) Although her ending is unfortunate, Virgil's Camilla is one of the most beloved of his inventions. Her delicacy, grace, and power have attracted commentators and translators. Pope, though not Virgil's main translator, is keenly aware of the Roman poet. He summons up Camilla in a famous passage of his *Essay on Criticism* – the poem we know that Lucy Maud Montgomery knew, as she had recently quoted it in *Anne of Green Gables*:

> When Ajax strives, some Rocks' vast Weight to throw,
> The Line too labours, and the words move slow,
> Not so, when swift Camilla scours the Plain,
> Flies o'er the unbending Corn, and skims along the Main.[19]

"Corn" in British English, means "grain," chiefly wheat – certainly not maize. Pope redraws Virgil's beautiful hyperbolical picture: Camilla can run over a young wheat field without trampling the stalks.

Now, in the second major scene of *Anne of Avonlea*, the comic scene in the second chapter, Montgomery picks up the tale of the heroine's encounter with the angry Mr Harrison, who is so contemptuous of her and her book. In this sequence she is, I think, inspired by her own use of language in *Anne of Green Gables*, and specifically her use of Pope's *Essay on Criticism* and her description of Anne as the swift runner: "Anne could run like a deer ... run she did with the impish result that she overtook the boys."[20] The original cause of Harrison's wrath was invasion of his oat field by Anne's Jersey cow. (No classical or British wheat field, but a field of prosaic Maritime oats.) Anne, travelling with Diana, comes upon the Jersey cow browsing yet again in Mr Harrison's now rain-dampened oat field. She impetuously jumps out of the vehicle and runs into the field to head the animal off: "Anne is at first swift in the chase: Not a word said she, but she climbed nimbly down over the wheels and whisked across the fence before Diana understood what had happened. 'Anne, come back,' shrieked the latter ... 'I must go and help her, of course.' Anne was charging through the grain like a mad thing."[21] Anne is normally an exceedingly good runner; readers of the first *Anne* book know this. But in this instance she is hampered by a thoughtless excursion into the wet vegetation.

Extraordinarily, on this occasion "Diana could run faster than Anne, who was hampered by her clinging and drenched skirt."[22] Although assisted by the chaste Diana, the ultra-virginal and customarily swift Anne is comically unsuccessful. It takes the girls ten minutes to head the cow off. Far from skimming the tops of the grain stalks and leaving them unbowed, Anne has trampled the grain: "Behind them, they left a trail that would break Mr. Harrison's heart when he should see it."[23]

Flustered and angry, Anne yields to the temptation of selling the offending cow immediately to "Mr. Shearer of Carmody,"[24] who offers her twenty dollars. A comic Camilla, Anne is misled by the gleam of wealth as well as the eradication of a problem and doesn't stop to think what danger might lie in store. She gives an opportunity to her hostile Arruns/Harrison. It seems to me that in this rarest of instances we catch Montgomery making use of a classical story and character. For once, she has allowed Virgil to be represented by something more than the dinginess of lexicons and the trials of school assignments.

And Mr Harrison's ignorant jeer becomes true – for the tan-coloured Virgil has turned into a novel. Montgomery knows that all classics are material to be played with. And she is not only playing with Virgil, but picking up her own descriptions and allusions in *Anne of Green Gables*, too. In doing this she concocts a merry classical mix that comically includes some hidden acknowledgment that her first *Anne* book is also a classic. And that means that her book too can be teased, played with, and re-examined.

## NOTES

1   Montgomery, *Anne of Green Gables*, 270.
2   Ibid., *Anne of the Island*, 307.
3   Ibid., *Anne of Green Gables*, 235.
4   Ibid., *Anne of the Island*, 206.
5   Ibid., *Anne of Avonlea*, 1.
6   Ibid.
7   Ibid., 7.
8   Montgomery, *Anne of Green Gables*, 253. The original line is in Pope's *Essay on Criticism*: "Hills peep o'er hills and Alps on Alps arise!" (1.232).
9   Montgomery, *Emily of New Moon*, 272.
10  Tiessen and Tiessen, "Epistolary Performance," 230.
11  Montgomery, *Anne of Green Gables*, 221.
12  Ibid., *Emily of New Moon*, 224.

13  Harte, "Dickens in Camp," 88–9, 89–90.
14  The quotation from Harte is in chapter 6 of *Anne of the Island*, 60: "And so in mountain solitudes o'ertaken / As by some spell divine, / Their cares drop from them like the needles shaken / From out the gusty pine."
15  Ibid., 138.
16  Ibid., 139–40.
17  "Bellatrix ... / dura pati cursuque peduem praevertere ventos. / Illa vel intactae segetis per summa volaret / gramina nec teneras cursu laesisset aristas." *Aeneid* VII 11.807–10, 59.
18  Virgil, *Aeneid* XI 582–3, 276.
19  Pope, *Essay on Criticism*, 11.370–3, 27.
20  Montgomery, *Anne of Green Gables*, 114.
21  Ibid., *Anne of Avonlea*, 13.
22  Ibid.
23  Ibid., 14.
24  Ibid., 16.

## BIBLIOGRAPHY

Brontë, Charlotte. *Jane Eyre*. New York: Penguin, 2003.
Harte, Bret. *Representative Selections, with Introduction, Bibliography and Notes by Joseph B. Harrison*. New York: American Book Company, 1822.
Montgomery, L.M. *Anne of Avonlea*. Toronto: Ryerson Press, 1946.
– *Anne of Green Gables*. Toronto: Penguin, 2008.
– *Anne of the Island*. Toronto: Ryerson Press, 1949.
– *Emily of New Moon*. Toronto: McClelland & Stewart, 1998.
Pope, Alexander. *An Essay on Criticism: The Rape of the Lock and Epistles to Several Persons (Moral Essays)*. Edited by Raymond Southall. Plymouth: Northcote House, 1988.
Radcliffe, Ann. *The Castles of Athlin and Dunbayne: A Highland Story*. New York: Arno Press in co-operation with McGrath Publishing Company, 1972.
– *The Mysteries of Udolpho*. London: J.M. Dent and Sons, 1959.
Tennyson, Alfred, Lord. *The Poems of Tennyson*. Edited by Christopher Ricks. London: Longmans, 1969.
Thomson, James. *The Four Seasons*. London: J. Walker, Paternoster Row and J. Harris, 1809.
Tiessen, Paul, and Hildi Froese Tiessen. "Epistolary Performance: Writing Mr. Weber." In *The Intimate Life of L.M. Montgomery*, edited by Irene Gammel, 222–38. Toronto: University of Toronto Press, 2005.
Virgil. *Aeneid VII–XIII*. Translated by H.R. Fairclough. Revised by G.P. Goold. Cambridge, Massachusetts: Harvard University Press, 2000.

# "So– so– *commonplace*": Romancing the Local in *Anne of Green Gables* and *Aurora Leigh*

PAUL KEEN

It is impossible to read *Anne of Green Gables* in an unmediated way. Particularly in Canada, one catches sight of the phenomenon, of the novels and character in quotation marks, as it were, long before one reaches the words on the pages. I want to consider the question of what the extraodinary appeal of *Anne of Green Gables* across generations and oceans (and, it must be added, across an amazing array of products, Web sites, and storefront windows) might teach us about the paradoxical venture of giving to airy nothings a local habitation and a name. I begin, by way of a comparison, not with Shakespeare or, for now, with Elizabeth Barrett Browning's *Aurora Leigh*, but with a sonnet entitled "Epic" by the Irish poet Patrick Kavanagh.

> I have lived in important places, times
> When great events were decided, who owned
> That half a rood of rock, a no-man's land
> Surrounded by our pitchfork-armed claims.
> I heard the Duffeys shouting "Damn your soul"
> And old McCabe stripped to the waist, seen
> Step the plot defying blue cast-steel –
> "Here is the march along these iron stones."[1]

Local battles, surely, but, as the poem wryly acknowledges, this was also "the year of the Munich bother." The shadow of major historical events – the poem was written in 1938, the year of the Munich Agreement, which ceded part of Czechoslovakia to Germany – triggers a temporary crisis in this fidelity to the importance of the local. "I inclined /

To lose my faith in Ballyrush and Gortin," the poet admits, but not for long:

> Homer's ghost came whispering to my mind.
> He said: I made the Iliad from such
> A local row. Gods make their own importance.[2]

Gods may well make their own importance, but, the poem implies, a strong enough faith in the value of the local is what breathes life into these stories in the first place. The irony, of course, is that it is Homer, the great epic poet of classical literature, from long ago and far away, who delivers this message about staying true to one's own world, and it arrives in the borrowed form of the sonnet rather than in more home-grown terms. Literary timelessness and neighbourhood politics go hand in hand; they are offered as mutually reinforcing rather than discordant aesthetic registers.

If Lucy Maud Montgomery's novel conveys a similar conviction that "I have lived in important places," it, like Kavanagh's sonnet, grounds this claim in the godlike value of the local. The name itself – *Anne of Green Gables* – has become so familiar that it is easy to ignore how thoroughly it binds Anne to an association with the local – and not just the world of Avonlea – "a little triangular peninsula jutting out into the Gulf of St. Lawrence"[3] – but with the house itself, the local within the local. But, ironically, what is most striking about Anne, and what may be most compelling about her, is her disdain for quotidian reality. It may be fashionable today to align one's self with the practice of everyday life, but Anne wanted none of it. Convinced, as Earle Birney said of Canada, that her new world is haunted by its lack of ghosts, Anne explains that she and Diana have had to invent them because "all the places around here are so– so– *commonplace.*"[4] From her first day in Avonlea, Anne performs her love of the area as resistance, and resistance as rewriting – *Lake of Shining Waters* rather than "Barry's Pond," *White Way of Delight* rather than "the Avenue." She embraces her new world by denying it in favour of a world of romance which she knows full well does not exist. And rather than encouraging us to resent or pity her, Anne's moments of resistance tend to be among the book's most compelling passages. "My life is a perfect graveyard of buried hopes," she reveals, immediately acknowledging that she borrowed the sentence from a book she once read.[5] Being derivative is the best part of the game. Anne operates like a *bricoleur*, to use the word that Jacques Derrida borrowed from Lévi-Strauss,[6] seizing on literary fragments from whatever source best serves her purpose. She lives, more than anywhere else, in a world of discourse. Even the book's title inscribes this ambivalence. If, on the one hand, it aligns Anne with Matthew and Marilla's house, its form also suggests the chivalric world of her romantic imagination. "Anne of Green Gables," like "Lancelot of the Lake," or "Sir Galahad of Camelot." In this volume, Cynthia Sugars aptly describes the ambivalence toward the romance – and the local – as discourse between "Matthew's school of critics" and "Miss Stacy's school of critics."

This tension between the commonplace and the romantic is embedded in the highly literary etymology of the very word "commonplace." If Anne is a *bricoleur*, in Derrida's and Lévi-Strauss's sense, her endless recycling of quotations and allusions suggests that she is herself a living version of a now largely obsolete literary phenomenon: the common-place book, in which people recorded important passages to be recalled or referred to later. As the *Oxford English Dictionary*'s entry suggests, the word "commonplace" was always marked by the same tension that animates its use in *Anne of Green Gables*. If, on the one hand, it suggests "a striking or notable passage, for reference or use, in a book of common places or commonplace-book," it also and more generally means the opposite of this: "a common or ordinary topic," "anything common and trite; an ordinary every-day object, action, or occurrence," "triviality." The classic and the parochial remain fused within the same definition. Anne's simultaneous denunciation of "all the places around here" for being "so– so– *commonplace*" and her extraordinary attachment to the singularity of everything about the place registers this etymological duality on a more purely subjective level. Her reaction echoes the tendency of the word to suggest, almost in spite of itself, an intimacy rather than a gulf between that which is striking or notable, and therefore worthy of being remembered, and that which is trivial, ordinary, or mundane.

This duality is reinforced by the ways that Anne's self-consciously literary style evokes a further tension within historical ideas about the common-place book itself. If, traditionally, the common-place book was the place where one stored what was memorable, keeping the extraordinary handy for reuse in one's own work, by the nineteenth century it had become more widely thought of in the opposite terms: as the degraded refuge of a mediocre writer, the resource that made it easy to make the memorable mundane. In an influential review of Walter Scott's *Waverly* novels in *The London Magazine*, John Scott had offered as high praise the fact that "there is nowhere in his writings the least indication possible of the common-place book."[7] If the ordinary or commonplace can also become aligned with the extraordinary (the contents of a common-place book), this uncanny process, which encodes two apparently incommensurable perspectives within the same concept, also works in the other direction. Used in the wrong ways or by the wrong people, the common-place book can be debased to the trivial realm of hack writers, whose need to copy betrays their poverty of real imagination. The publication of L.M. Montgomery's journals and other life writing over the past decades reveals these books as common-place books that inscribe the author's own ambivalent place in discourses of literary merit and validity of derivation.

In Montgomery's *Anne of Green Gables*, Anne's insistent rewriting of everyday places in comically overwrought literary terms suggests an undisclosed line of continuity between all of these multiple inferences: the complexities that animate her reaction to the "commonplace" world around her are amplified by her own tendency to behave like a living, breathing common-place book in both of the two very different ways that people responded to the concept. In endowing the ordinary world around her with a seemingly endless stream of hopelessly elevated references, she inadvertently renders the romantic mundane, not through a lack of imagination (the problem of the hack writer) but through imaginative excess.

Nor is it just her adopted neighbourhood that must be rewritten. "Will you please call me Cordelia?" she famously responds when asked her name.[8] Asked what she knows about herself, she answers that she prefers to tell what she "imagine[s]," to which Marilla equally memorably responds, "I don't want any of your imaginings. Just stick to bald facts."[9] Except, of course, that Marilla never really wins these battles. Nor does the world of facts. However much she may herself mature over the course of the novel (a point that is foregrounded in descriptions of it as a *bildungsroman*), Anne causes far more change in those around her (and almost always for the better) than they do in her. Like a red-haired version of the uncanny, Anne exposes all those things about Marilla that at some level Marilla understood but could never afford to acknowledge, "those secret, unuttered, critical thoughts" that she "had really thought deep down in her heart for years, but had never given expression to," but which "had suddenly taken visible and accusing shape and form in the person of this outspoken morsel of neglected humanity."[10] Except, of course, that the neglected humanity that is most forcefully registered is not just in Anne but in Marilla's own world of unacknowledged interiority.

The doubled relevance of Marilla's discovery of this neglected humanity anticipates Freud's own description of the uncanny, in his 1919 essay, as that unsettling recognition that what is apparently foreign, new, radically different, is really only what has been there all along, repressed, deliberately forgotten, kept out of sight; the spectre of what "ought to have remained ... secret and hidden but has come to light."[11] But, then, Montgomery had already framed this experience in precisely these terms. "It seems uncanny to think of a child at Green Gables somehow," Rachel Lynde declares at the outset of the novel. "There's never been one there, for Matthew and Marilla were grown up when the new house was built – if they ever were children, which is hard to believe when one looks at them."[12]

As Rachel Lynde seems to intimate, the uncanny, or *unheimlich*, can also be translated as the *unhomely* – the unsettling intuition that those things which make us feel most at home in the world are, at the same time, bound up with the things that seem most foreign to us. But however strongly Rachel Lynde may have associated this paradox with Green Gables, the home or *heimlich* is never merely the building itself – the place where there had never been children and where it seems odd to think of them – but rather, as Freud insisted, the relation of the adult to those forms of imaginative insight that are most forcefully associated with childhood. Anne's presence renders Green Gables uncanny by affording Marilla a glimpse of her secret, unexpressed thoughts and feelings.

If this complex identification with and resistance to the local is true of Anne the character, and of the feelings she inspires in those adults who know her, it is equally true of the novel's endless allusiveness, which embeds its account of provincial life within a broader literary world that stretches back across the Atlantic and south of the border.

The enduring popularity of *Anne of Green Gables* may well have much to do with its celebration of local culture, but its literary commitments are always centrifugal: a way of taking flight, much as Anne does, into a bookish world – a parade of references – that has little to do with Prince Edward Island. Or, that may be too flat-footed a response. If the novel's shrewd depiction of Anne's endlessly romanticizing flights of fancy is itself a wonderfully realistic account of a youthful poetic spirit, its allusiveness may, like Kavanagh's poem, illuminate rather than evade the complexities of local customs.

All of this becomes especially complicated in terms of the one allusion that I want to focus on here, and that is to Elizabeth Barrett Browning's long poem, *Aurora Leigh*. It's not much. A single-line, indented quotation in chapter 33, and it is invoked as a description of Marilla's thought, not Anne's: "One moonbeam from the forehead to the crown."[13] Ironically, the line actually appears in *Aurora Leigh* in a list of the sort of empty compliments that a man must use in order to win a woman's love even though he does not necessarily mean them.[14] It is far less significant than the more insistent references to Robert Browning or Tennyson or Shakespeare or Walter Scott or Felicia Hemans or Charlotte Brontë or any other of a number of famous writers. Jennie MacDonald's paper in this volume notes it as a borrowed insight into sartorial significance in *Anne of Green Gables*, but it is not even cited in Rea Wilmshurst's itemized list of quotations and allusions from the *Anne* novels; nor does it rate a mention in Irene Gammel's *Looking for Anne: How Lucy Maud Montgomery Dreamed Up a Literary Classic*. And it is far from the most interesting or pertinent line that Montgomery could have chosen from that novel-length poem.

In their annotated edition of "Literary Allusion and Quotation in *Anne of Green Gables*," Margaret Anne Doody and Wendy E. Barry comment, in reference to the allusion to *Aurora Leigh*, that "both Aurora Leigh and Barrett Browning were doubtless significant to Montgomery, as to other women writers ... That Anne is a moonbeam illustrates not only her beauty but her virginity, her unripened quality, her spiritual power."[15] As they rightly note, Barrett Browning's "Lady Geraldine's Courtship" is a more prominent, and in many ways a more interesting intertext, complicating as it does Anne's straightforward interest in conventional heterosexual romance by emphasizing her grief "at the very thought of Diana as a bride."[16] But, as I have been arguing, the real significance of Montgomery's allusion to *Aurora Leigh* lies not in the personal parallels between the two protagonists' development but in the broader social questions their stories evoke. Doody and Barry's suggestion that "the Brownings belong to the most positive end of the poetic spectrum of Montgomery's prose" is complicated by *Aurora Leigh*'s often dark subject matter, from its engagement with issues of urban poverty and sexual assault to its uncompromising analysis of the relations between personal and social repression.[17]

As Elizabeth Epperly emphasizes in *The Fragrance of Sweetgrass*, *Aurora Leigh* played a far greater role in the *Emily* series, where its prominence reinforces Montgomery's more fully developed effort to explore the tensions inherent in a woman's struggle, on the one hand, for artistic and professional success and, on the other, for personal fulfillment.[18] As Epperly points out, having Emily record in her diary four lines from the point in *Aurora Leigh* where "Aurora has said farewell to her Romney Leigh and begun her years of struggle as a writer in London" underscores the emotionally fraught nature of Emily's personal and literary struggles.[19] In *Anne of Green Gables*, in marked contrast, there is only one brief and largely forgettable allusion. But that is precisely what makes it interesting.

Critics of *Anne of Green Gables* have rightly paid far more attention to the references to Robert Browning's poetry, which frame the whole of the novel as the epigraph and the core of the final sentence, as well as appearing at various points within the text itself. But my point is not as much about closing the gap between the two – *Anne of Green Gables* and *Aurora Leigh* – by engaging in a study of influence as about asking how their relationship might complicate the idea of influence, and in doing so, might help to illuminate crucial aspects of the novel itself. Like its own version of the uncanny, *Anne of Green Gables* seems to need to hold Barrett Browning's poem at a distance, even as it explicitly acknowledges it, precisely because the poem illuminates so much about the novel itself. What, or how much, if anything at all, for instance, to make of the alliteration and assonance between the two names – Avonlea and Aurora Leigh?

The fact that the parallels between the two stories are so striking makes the differences, which are both subtle and sometimes jarring, all the more interesting. *Aurora Leigh* is, after all, a coming-of-age story about a high-spirited orphan girl with a poetic soul and literary aspirations, who overcomes an unsympathetic, often hostile environment that cloaks its emotionally repressed state in unflinching moral didacticism. Nor, as Elizabeth Waterston has recently argued, were these similarities limited to the characters themselves: "Montgomery herself had been a virtual orphan in the home of stern grandparents, her own pretty young mother having died, and her father having left his twenty-month-old daughter behind him when he went west to the Canadian prairies."[20] As Cora Kaplan noted in her influential edition of *Aurora Leigh* for The Women's Press, it was the first long poem by a woman in English in which the heroine herself is an author and in which that sense of literary vocation is a central aspect of the story. And it shares all of Anne's unruly sense of irrepressible energy. *Aurora Leigh* is above all else a manifesto for Barrett Browning's vision of the poet as nuisance:

> bursting through
> The best of your conventions with his best,
> The speakable imaginable best
> God bids him speak, to prove what lies beyond
> Both speech and imagination.[21]

For Barrett Browning, this spectre of disruption – bursting through conventions – was both an aesthetic commitment and a political creed. She recycled the image in a letter that discussed the poem: "My chief intention just now is the writing of a sort of novel-poem as completely modern as 'Geraldine's Courtship,' running into the midst of our conventions and rushing into drawing-rooms and the like 'where angels fear to tread'; and so, meeting face to face and without mask the Humanity of the age, and speaking the truth as I conceive of it, out plainly."[22] Virginia Woolf recycled the same image, insisting that "Elizabeth Barrett was inspired by a flash of true genius when she rushed into the drawing-room and said that here, where we live and work, is the true place for the poet."[23] One can imagine Anne making the same entrance, and the melodrama of the apology that would follow.

*Aurora Leigh* was famous, as Montgomery would certainly have known. Ruskin hailed it as the greatest poem that the nineteenth century had produced in any literature.[24] Swinburne insisted that: "the advent of 'Aurora Leigh' can never be forgotten by any lover of poetry who was old enough at the time to read it. Of one thing they may all be sure – that they were right in the impression that they had never read, and never would read anything in any way comparable with that unique work of audaciously feminine and ambitiously impulsive genius."[25] But, like Anne's misdeeds in the eyes of so many locals, *Aurora Leigh* was also infamous. Elizabeth Barrett Browning's brother, George, dismissed it as "worse than *Don Juan* ... unfit for the reading of any girl."[26] Barrett Browning wrote with great amusement to a friend that she had been told of a woman sixty years old who believed that her morals had been injured by reading it and that her character was in danger if it were known that she had looked at the book. Reports came to her of women in England who read it in secret and swept it from their drawing-room tables, lest a man should see it.[27]

My point in rehearsing these anecdotes is to suggest the various reasons that Montgomery might have been so attracted to Barrett Browning's poem and been cautious about aligning herself with it. And this is especially true in terms of the vexed issue of Montgomery's status as a conservative feminist, concerned with women's status but deeply committed to the existing social order.[28] Woolf's subsequent claim, that "with her passionate interest in social questions, her conflict as artist and woman, her longing for knowledge and freedom [*Aurora Leigh*] is the true daughter of her age"[29] offers a measure of this ambivalence: the shared preoccupations but also the fundamental differences which define the relation between these texts. It was not for nothing that the American feminist Susan B. Anthony presented her own treasured copy of *Aurora Leigh* to the Library of Congress in 1902, six years before *Anne of Green Gables* was first published.[30] Unlike Montgomery's more cautious relationship to first-wave feminism, *Aurora Leigh* was animated by an uncompromising rejection of the alienating effects of patriarchal thought that finds its most acute expression in its depiction of the overly moral, spiritually impoverished, and deeply alienated state of the spinster aunt that Aurora is sent to live with as an orphan: "She stood straight and calm, / Her somewhat narrow forehead braided tight / As if for taming accidental thoughts."[31] Like the most negative version of Marilla – Marilla as she might have been portrayed in an unsympathetic light – the aunt functions as all that Aurora will ultimately have to reject:

> She had lived, we'll say,
> A harmless life, she called a virtuous life,
> A quiet life, which was not life at all
> (But that, she had not lived enough to know)[32]

Like so many female guardians in nineteenth-century novels, Aurora's aunt is both her opposite and her oppressor. Which is, of course, where the two stories most obviously part ways. Marilla's "unholy tendency to laughter which she was dismayed to find growing upon her"[33] at Anne's more spontaneous judgments suggests both a warmth and humour and a willingness to grow as a result of Anne's example that Aurora's aunt is never endowed with. The result is far less radical in terms of social critique but perhaps more profound in its sympathy for people's genuine, if measured, capacity to get the best of these alienating pressures and constraints.

Rather than pursuing this question of the way *Anne of Green Gables* both acknowledges and evades *Aurora Leigh*'s more polemical feminist commitments, I want to turn to a second question that is implicit in this particular textual allusion – one on which they may have been in far closer agreement – and that is to *Aurora Leigh*'s emphasis on the commonplace. Having dramatized her protagonist's triumph over various forces of oppression, Barrett Browning's poem extends this optimism to her age generally, explicitly attacking her nineteenth-century contemporaries' longing for a lost, heroic past as a healing response to what Carlyle had called the asphyxia of the soul which defined the present.[34] Refusing to abandon her faith in the present-day in favour of some mythologized version of the past, Barrett Browning insisted that "All actual heroes are essential men. / And all men possible heroes."[35] She likened the dangers of historical immersion – of becoming too local – to the example of Mount Athos, which Alexander had wanted to be carved into the enormous figure of a conqueror like some Classical-age Mount Rushmore. Only from a distance could its features become visible. Peasants gathering firewood on the hill would never know they were "gathering brushwood in his ear" until they were five miles away, at which point they would finally be distant enough to be able to make it out.[36] "'Tis even thus / With the times we live in, – evermore too great / To be apprehended near."[37] Which, for Barrett Browning, is why the poet's "double vision,"[38] both immersed within and standing back a little

from her age, is uniquely important; but the integrity that this commitment to a "living art, / Which thus presents and thus records true life"[39]
implies will necessarily be as disruptive as it is honest:

> Nay, if there's room for poets in this world
> A little overgrown (I think there is),
> Their sole work is to represent the age,
> Their age, not Charlemagne's, – this live, throbbing age,
> That brawls, cheats, maddens, calculates, aspires,
> And spends more passion, more heroic heat,
> Betwixt the mirrors of its drawing-rooms,
> Than Roland with his knights at Roncesvalles.[40]

*Anne of Green Gables* has been widely praised for its similar commitment to the "passion" and "heroic heat" of the here and now. Montgomery's declaration that "all things great are wound up with all things
little"[41] manifested itself in her dramatization of a provincial world that
was as emotionally intense as it was insistently local. But her text is
animated by a complex relation to these "little things" that echoes Barrett Browning's emphasis on the poet's "double vision," and which I can
best describe in terms of the opposite impulses of *Anne of Green Gables*
(the novel) and Anne of Green Gables (the character). Where the novel
revels in the minute goings-on of rural life, Anne prides herself on an
often comical disdain for "commonplace" life and on her love of romance, including an infatuation with the medieval chivalric world rejected by Barrett Browning. She harbours a "secret regret that she had
not been born in Camelot," which was "so much more romantic than
the present."[42] Whereas *Anne of Green Gables* (the novel) insists on the
primacy of domestic life as the only adequate basis for its story, Anne of
Green Gables (the character) yearns for escape into the fictional world
of imagined landscapes and distant literary worlds. But the distance between these perspectives is neither static nor arbitrary. On the contrary,
Anne's growing respect for the commonplace functions as a crucial
index of her ethical maturation. Her desire to be remarkable is fulfilled,
not (as she had liked to imagine) by becoming a missionary elsewhere,
but in her decision to forego the Avery Scholarship in order to remain
at home with Marilla; her imagination finds its ultimate nourishment

not in the escapist allure of Camelot or imaginary worlds, but in the bend in the road which lies before her by the end of the novel. Gods make their own importance, she discovers. She remains committed to romance, but romance is increasingly defined in terms of its alignment with, rather than distance from, the pressure of "all things little"[43] in the name of the primacy of duty. This process of maturation might help to illuminate some of the complexities involved in Montgomery's highly qualified allusion to Barrett Browning's more scandalous text of decades earlier.

## NOTES

1 Kavanagh, "Epic," 136.
2 Ibid., 136.
3 Montgomery, *Anne of Green Gables*, 54.
4 Ibid., 203.
5 Ibid., 88.
6 Derrida, "Structure, Sign, and Play."
7 Scott, "Living Authors," 17.
8 Montgomery, *Anne of Green Gables*, 76.
9 Ibid., 88–9.
10 Ibid., 130.
11 Freud, "The Uncanny," 345.
12 Montgomery, *Anne of Green Gables*, 60–1.
13 Ibid., 296.
14 Barrett Browning, *Aurora Leigh*, 4:1013. This and all subsequent references are to book and line number.
15 Doody and Barry, "Literary Allusion and Quotation," 460.
16 Ibid.
17 Ibid.
18 Epperly, *The Fragrance of Sweetgrass*, 191–6.
19 Ibid., 191–2.
20 Waterston, *Magic Island*, 10.
21 Barrett Browning, *Aurora Leigh*, 2:469–73.
22 Ibid., *The Brownings' Correspondence*, 103.
23 Woolf, *The Common Reader*, 137.
24 Ruskin, *The Elements of Drawing*, 227.
25 Swinburne, *Complete Works*, 16:4.
26 George Browning, quoted in Taplin, Introduction, xx.

27  Barrett Browning, quoted in Taplin, ibid.
28  For fuller discussion of Montgomery and feminism, see Åhmansson, Dean, and Devin.
29  Woolf, *The Common Reader*, 139.
30  Reynolds, Preface, viii.
31  Barrett Browning, *Aurora Leigh*, 1:272–4.
32  Ibid., 1:288–91.
33  Montgomery, *Anne of Green Gables*, 173.
34  Carlyle, *Past and Present*, 39.
35  Barrett Browning, *Aurora Leigh*, 5:151–2.
36  Ibid., 5:171.
37  Ibid., 5:181–3.
38  Ibid., 5:184.
39  Ibid., 5:221–2.
40  Ibid., 5:200–7.
41  Montgomery, *Anne of Green Gables*, 179.
42  Ibid., 255.
43  Ibid., 314.

## BIBLIOGRAPHY

Åhmansson, Gabriella. *A Life and Its Mirrors: A Feminist Reading of L.M. Montgomery's Fiction*. Stockholm: Uppsala, 1991.

Barrett Browning, Elizabeth. *Aurora Leigh*. New York: Norton, 1996.

– *The Brownings' Correspondence*. Edited by P. Kelley and S. Lewis. Vol. 10. Winfield, Kansas: Wedgestone Press, 1992.

Carlyle, Thomas. *Past and Present*. Edited by Richard D. Altick. Boston: Houghton Mifflin, 1965.

Dean, Misao. *Practising Femininity: Domestic Realism and the Performance of Gender in Early Canadian Fiction*. Toronto: University of Toronto Press, 1998.

Derrida, Jacques. "Structure, Sign, and Play in the Discourse of the Human Sciences." In *Writing and Difference*, translated and introduced by Alan Bass, 278–94. Chicago: University of Chicago Press, 1978.

Devin, Anna. "Imperialism and Motherhood." *History Workshop Journal*, vol. 5 (1978): 9–65.

Doody, Margaret Anne and Wendy E. Barry. "Literary Allusion and Quotation in *Anne of Green Gables*." In *The Annotated Anne of Green Gables*, edited by Wendy E. Barry, Margaret Anne Doody, Mary E. Doody Jones, 457–62. New York: Oxford University Press, 1997.

Epperly, Elizabeth. *The Fragrance of Sweetgrass: L.M. Montgomery's Heroines and the Pursuit of Romance*. Toronto: University of Toronto P, 1992.

Freud, Sigmund. "The Uncanny." 1919. *Penguin Freud Library: Art and Literature*. Vol. 14. Translated by James Strachey. Edited by Albert Dickson. Harmondsworth: Penguin, 1985.

Gammel, Irene. *Looking for Anne: How Lucy Maud Montgomery Dreamed Up a Literary Classic*. Toronto: Key Porter, 2008.

Kaplan, Cora. Introduction to *Aurora Leigh and Other Poems*, by Elizabeth Barrett Browning. London: The Women's Press, 1978.

Kavanagh, Patrick. "Epic." *Collected Poems*. New York: Devin-Adair, 1964.

Montgomery, L.M. *Anne of Green Gables*. Edited by Cecily Devereux. Peterborough, Ontario: Broadview Press, 2004.

Reynolds, Margaret. Preface to *Aurora Leigh*. New York: Norton, 1996.

Ruskin, John. *The Elements of Drawing*. Miuneola, New York: Dover Publications, 1971.

Scott, John. "Living Authors: (Being a Series of Critical Sketches) No. I. The Author of the Scotch Novels." *The London Magazine*, vol. 1 (January, 1820): 11–22.

Swinburne, Algernon Charles. *Complete Works*. Vol. 16. Edited by Edmund Gosse and Thomas James Wise. London: Heinemann, 1925–27.

Taplin, Gardner B. Introduction to *Aurora Leigh*, by Elizabeth Barrett Browning. Chicago: Academy Chicago Publishers, 1979.

Waterston, Elizabeth. *Magic Island: The Fictions of L.M. Montgomery*. Oxford: Oxford University Press, 2008.

Wilmshurst, Rea. "L.M. Montgomery's Use of Quotations and Allusions in the 'Anne' Books." *CCL: Canadian Children's Literature*, vol. 56 (1989): 15–45.

Woolf, Virginia. *The Common Reader*. Second Series. New York: Harcourt, 1948.

# "Matthew's school of critics":
# Learning to Read *Anne of Green Gables*

CYNTHIA SUGARS

*Don't stick up your ears now, imagining that the great*
*Canadian novel has been written at last. Nothing of the sort.*
*It is a merely juvenilish story, ostensibly for girls; [but] ...*
*I am not without hope that grown-ups may like it a little.*[1]
L.M. Montgomery, Letter to Ephraim Weber, 2 May 1907

As the above excerpt from L.M. Montgomery's letter to Ephraim Weber suggests, Montgomery had foreseen the debates about *Anne of Green Gables*'s status as a literary classic well before its publication. Her words anticipate the terms that Desmond Pacey invoked in his swift dismissal of the book in *Creative Writing in Canada* in 1952: "*Anne of Green Gables* is a children's classic, and it would be silly to apply adult critical standards to it."[2] Pacey's elitist values led him to paint the book as "the kind of escape literature which a materialistic and vulgar generation craved."[3] Since then, there has been a good deal of discussion, contention, even consternation, in literary critical circles about whether *Anne of Green Gables* is to be classified as a work of popular children's fiction or as a work of "genuine" literature – a false dichotomy that is based in an unimaginative (as Anne might say) sense of both. Carole Gerson's detailed study of the reception of Montgomery's work outlines the "growing scholarly capital"[4] that Montgomery has experienced in academic contexts, from the modernists' dismissal of her work in the early and mid-twentieth century to her rise in status in the late 1980s and early 1990s following the publication of her journals and the founding of the L.M. Montgomery Institute at the University of Prince Edward Island in Charlottetown. Nevertheless, an evaluative bias against Montgomery's work remains evident even today in the teaching canon of Canadian literature, namely in her relative absence from university-level courses devoted to Canadian Literature, as opposed to courses in Children's Literature.

Montgomery adamantly wanted to write a book that was not bound by the rules of conventional juvenile fiction, which demanded what she termed an "insidious" moral message. As she insisted in her journals, she had in mind a piece that would be "art for art's sake."[5] When writing *Anne of Green Gables*, she stated, "I cast 'moral' and 'Sunday School' ideals to the winds and made my 'Anne' a real human girl."[6] While Montgomery rejected the didacticism of children's writing in her insistence on representing Anne as a realistic character (and hence, as a girl with many faults), it is also true that Montgomery, writing at the turn of the century, was positioned between two predominant literary genres, romance and realism (the latter associated, in the decades to follow, with literary modernism). Writing to Ephraim Weber in 1929, Montgomery very clearly rejects the form of realism practised by Morley Callaghan, whose approach she describes as an attempt "to photograph a latrine or pig-sty meticulously." The sky and landscape, she insists, are just "as 'real' as the latrine and can be all seen at the same time. Callaghan sees *nothing* but the latrine and insists blatantly that you see nothing else also. If you insist on seeing sky and river and pines you are a 'sentiment-alist' and the truth is not in you."[7]

The idealization of Anne throughout the novel, the episodic plot structure, and the romance-driven storyline could easily place the novel in the category of literary romance. On the one hand, romantic narratives have long been dismissed by literary critics as being sentimental, predictable, overwrought, escapist, and "false." A "real human girl" would presumably not fit into this world. On the other hand, the absence of a direct moral message might seem to comply with the demands of literary romance, which was often criticized for its irreligious and corrupting influence on readers' imaginations (as was literary modernism). And yet, one might say that the apparent realist mode of *Anne of Green Gables* is held up to scrutiny by the overt romantic readings offered by Anne within the novel. Indeed, *Anne of Green Gables* ironizes its protagonist's romanticizing tendencies, yet at the same time, Anne's romantic vision is her most enduring and appealing quality. Where Anne fits within "art for art's sake" and "a real human girl" is another tangle altogether, since supposedly juvenile fiction might only be slotted into the latter, while romance might be accommodated to neither. This web of realism, romance, high art, and moral message – as all become folded into the definition of a literary classic and encrypted within the text of *Anne of Green Gables* – forms the subject of this essay.

Toward the end of *Anne of Green Gables*, Anne explains to Marilla why she and her friends have given up their "story club": "It was silly to be writing about love and murder and elopements and mysteries," she tells Marilla.[8] Instead, the students are to follow Miss Stacy's advice and write about "what might happen in Avonlea in our own lives."[9] Yet, as the reader of the novel clearly knows by this point, Anne's statements cannot always be taken at face value. Her excesses might soar in a flight of fancy or plummet into an equally extreme retreat into the prosaic. In both instances, the imaginative leap is key. Imagination, as Anne so often insists, is what lends things permanence and depth, just as it also contributes to the enduring quality of a literary "classic." If it is disparaged by the critical "write-about-what-you-know" school of Miss Stacy for being romantic and false, it is nevertheless what "Matthew's school of critics" seeks: poetic resonance and a suspension of disbelief. Indeed, the plethora of "classic" literary intertexts by Shakespeare, Browning, Longfellow, Wordsworth, Byron, Tennyson, Brontë, Hemans, Scott, and so many others that are sprinkled throughout *Anne of Green Gables* fall into the category of romantic literature ... which might suggest that a literary classic is one that combines both elements: scope for (romantic) imagination *and* an element of homegrown or intuitive mimetic truth.

This essay argues that *Anne of Green Gables* contains its own designation as a literary classic encrypted within it, and furthermore, that it instructs us in how to read *Anne* itself *as* a classic, with its heroine functioning as a kind of metonym for the text itself (the text which she, in effect, writes by infusing the local landscape of Avonlea with poetry). One thing that Anne must teach Marilla is how to become a sympathetic reader more like Matthew. "I don't believe in imagining things different from what they are," Marilla retorts when Anne suggests that they pretend that Marilla is her aunt.[10] Yet the social realist, "Miss Stacy" school of literature, which denies that crucial imaginative leap, is wholly distinct from Anne's approach to literary appreciation, and from readers' appreciation of *Anne of Green Gables*. In effect, *Anne of Green Gables*'s self-reflexive commentary on its own literary status places us both in "Matthew's school of critics" (committed to poetic resonance and suspension of disbelief) and at the same time in Miss Stacy's school of critics (devoted to local realism and modest moral instruction), the very position that is enabled by those works we celebrate as literary classics.

An important moment of literary critical pedagogy is embedded early in the novel, when we are first introduced to Anne. When Matthew goes to pick up his newly arrived "orphan" at the train station in Bright River, the narrator offers a lesson in critical exegesis, a lesson in what we could call reading for surfaces versus reading for subtext: "An ordinary observer would have seen this: A child of about eleven, garbed in a very short, very tight, very ugly dress of yellowish gray wincey ... beneath the hat, extending down her back, were two braids of very thick, decidedly red hair. Her face was small, white and thin."[11] Miss Stacy would recognize the "real world" of Avonlea in this description. But the narrator, who is surely a "kindred spirit" to Anne, as becomes evident later in the novel, continues: "So far, the ordinary observer; an extraordinary observer might have seen that the chin was very pointed and pronounced; that the big eyes were full of spirit and vivacity; that the mouth was sweet-lipped and expressive ... in short, our discerning extraordinary observer might have concluded that no commonplace soul inhabited the body of this stray woman-child."[12] An "extraordinary observer," in other words, would have read something deeper into the straightforward scene of an orphan girl waiting at a train station. This reader would undertake that imaginative leap between text (the child) and reader (the observer) that is so crucial to interpreting (and writing) a literary classic.

This elaboration of two types of readers might be compared to Slavoj Zizek's outline of two forms of reading in *Looking Awry*. In his analysis, there are two ways of reading the relation between realist interpretation and "distortion": "If we look at a thing straight on, matter-of-factly, we see it 'as it really is,' while the gaze puzzled by our desires and anxieties ('looking awry') gives us a distorted, blurred image."[13] On the other hand, "if we look at a thing straight on, i.e., matter-of-factly, disinterestedly, objectively, we see nothing but a formless spot; the object assumes clear and distinctive features only if we look at it 'at an angle,' i.e., with an 'interested' view."[14] In the latter instance, the object becomes more "real" by virtue of its having been "distorted." This is precisely what hap-

pens when Anne reads her environment. She lends it symbolic, emotional, and psychic depth, thereby granting it a "meaning" that it does
not have in its commonplace reality. In the train station scene, then,
Montgomery gives instructions for reading against the conventions of
Avonlea's exegetical realist tradition, instructions on reading not only
Anne herself but also the novel *Anne of Green Gables*. If a literary classic is defined, in part, by its being no "commonplace" sort of book – in
other words, a book that cannot merely be read for surfaces – so, too,
*Anne of Green Gables*. (Anne herself makes this evaluative distinction
on numerous occasions, as, for example, when she identifies the catechism readings, and the Lord's Prayer, as almost poetry, but not quite.)

This lesson is evident in Anne's reading of the painting of "Christ
Blessing Little Children" in chapter 8. Being the "extraordinary observer" that she is, Anne "reads" the painting as a fictional fantasy and
an autobiographical realist text, both of which require acts of imagination: by inserting herself into the fictional scene (imagining herself as
the shy girl in the corner in the blue dress), she imbues the artwork with
both personal and universal resonance. Indeed, a literary classic's uni-
versality is only powerful in so much as it speaks, in some form, to the
personal experience of the reader. Reader identification, with its basis in
imaginative fantasy, is, in effect, what both the Matthew and Miss Stacy
schools of critics have in common. Writing (or reading) about what you
know and suspension of disbelief are not mutually exclusive; the "real"
(what you know) is also the "fictional" (what is imagined). Montgomery
self-consciously plays with and confuses these categories throughout
*Anne of Green Gables*, in part by having us read Anne as a kind of book,
in part by having the book posit readings of itself.

There are, of course, multiple levels of "reading" in the novel: Anne's
reading of Avonlea; Anne's reading of works of literature; other characters' readings of Anne's stories; other characters' readings of Anne
herself; our reading of Anne; our reading of Anne reading Avonlea; our
reading of *Anne of Green Gables*; the narrator's reading of the story she
is relaying. It is clear that Montgomery's encryption of various kinds
of reading (and reader-response) informs the ways we as readers are
implicitly positioned to assess the book. In other words, we are ex-
horted to respond to the character Anne, and the book *Anne of Green
Gables*, as "extraordinary" readers and to resist the temptation to read
for surfaces.

Within the novel, Anne insists on investing the landscape of Avonlea with the permanence of imaginative gloss, which in turn becomes part of the "real world" landscape of the novel we read. In short, she transforms Avonlea (as Montgomery does Cavendish) into a classic landscape. Readers inevitably remember the moments when Anne renames the landmarks of Avonlea, particularly during the initial wagon ride with Matthew, who becomes entranced by her ability to romance the landscape that he has long taken for granted, in effect making it more "real" by fictionalizing it. According to Margaret Doody, one of the editors of *The Annotated Anne of Green Gables*, Avonlea is full of hidden riches that people do not see.[15] If Avonlea, as Doody suggests, can be interpreted as an anagram for Avalon, King Arthur's secret isle, it is only Anne who recognizes it for the classic setting that it is. As Doody puts it, "Avonlea has partly lost sight of its own identity and inheritance, and thus some of its vision."[16] Indeed, Anne invents the Haunted Wood, as she tells Marilla, to counter its seeming "commonplace" surface reality,[17] a statement that identifies Anne as one of those "extraordinary" readers who can plumb the depths and romantic potential of her provincial surroundings. Marilla's scolding of Anne for her imaginative propensities is rooted in Anne's tendency to reify her fictions. The fictions gain power when they cross over into the real-world of Anne herself, for what happens is that Anne's fantasy of the Haunted Wood appears more real to her than the wood itself, making her incapable of crossing it at night. What bothers Marilla is not that Anne makes up stories, but that Anne's stories force people to become aware of the "storied" nature of their existence – that Miss Stacy can be trumped by Matthew.

Yet as we know, this tendency of Anne's is also what attracts Marilla to her in the first place, as when she so gloriously dramatizes her impending eviction from Green Gables, thereby fictionalizing her own reality: "Oh, this is the most tragical thing that ever happened to me."[18] These different capacities for "reading" have their counterpart, of course, in the stream that passes by Rachel Lynde's house, which has "dark secrets" that Mrs Lynde, as the conventional, "ordinary" reader, cannot discern. The stream is re-interpreted under Mrs Lynde's disciplinary but ultimately unperceptive gaze as orderly and "well-conducted." As we discover in her failure to uncover Matthew and Marilla's secret, Mrs Lynde is not a particularly astute reader. Try as she might, she cannot glean the reasons for Matthew's departure, notwithstanding the series of "clues" – Matthew's white collar, the crab-apple preserve – which she tries in a Holmesian fashion to decipher. Neither the stream, nor Anne – nor *Anne of Green Gables* – can be read for surfaces alone.

If Anne is intent on turning the landscape of Avonlea into the stuff of classic literature, she herself comes to function as a kind of metonym for the novel (as we saw in the train station scene when she is "read" by two different kinds of interpreters). Anne is faulted by various characters for her flights of fancy. Yet what sets her apart from her fellows, what makes her an "original," is the fact that she is a "classic": that is, she contains hidden depths and is beyond the commonplace. If Anne is in many ways akin to Flaubert's Madame Bovary, in that both are under the sway of romantic literature, the difference is in the way we read her. Anne is like a good book: she is unpredictable, multi-layered, imaginative, eloquent, diverting, original. For the characters in the novel, she alleviates the tedium of the everyday. Like a literary classic, Anne herself has a lasting quality that distinguishes her from run-of-the-mill other girls. As Old Miss Barry says of "that Anne-girl": "I get tired of other girls – there is such a provoking and eternal sameness about them. Anne has as many shades as a rainbow."[19] Anne's enduring quality and layers of depth render her a classic in the best literary sense. Moreover, as she matures and becomes educated, she does not lose these qualities but in a sense perfects them, a transformation that is emblematized in Anne's physical appearance, as she metamorphoses from the diminutive "Carrots" to the classic beauty with the "Titian hair,"[20] a transformation chronicled by Jennie MacDonald in this volume.

These concerns achieve an instructive self-reflexivity in Anne's story club. Miss Stacy assigns her class a composition exercise to write about a walk in the woods,[21] a version of writing about what they know. Interestingly, this task does not worry Diana, who appears to find Miss Stacy's literary bias relatively easy to replicate. She is far more perturbed by a different assignment, the demand that they write "a story out of our own heads."[22] The more difficult and challenging task of composing a work of imaginative literature is the rationale behind Anne's formation of the story club, which is created as a kind of school in literary composition and analysis: its goal is to "cultivate their imaginations"[23] – the very effect that Anne, and literary "classics," have on the readers who encounter them. Even though the narrator disparages Diana's naive response to Anne's romantic story-club tales by lumping her among "Matthew's school of critics,"[24] the fact is that Anne's evocative creative talents, like those of her classic literary predecessors, enable her to have a double impact on readers: her stories invite them to suspend their disbelief and, as Anne puts it, they have a real-life "wholesome effect,"[25] under which could be included the "cultivation of the imagination."

This is where things get interesting, for Anne's justification of the story club misses the mark expressly because she adopts Miss Stacy's approach to literary functioning, thus humorously misapplying, by literalizing, critical assumptions about the morally redemptive influence of "classic" literature (and, interestingly, of juvenile fiction). Believing in the transformative power of imaginative literature, Anne insists that the redeeming feature of her stories is that there is a moral in each tale: "All the good people are rewarded and all the bad ones are suitably punished ... The moral is the great thing."[26] However, the novel's perspective on this kind of reductive literary pedagogy is telling, since we are alerted more than once that a classic does not "instruct" in the same mimetic way as the lesser literary pieces in the Sunday school tracts and primers that Anne is given to read as part of her education. Indeed, throughout *Anne of Green Gables* it is the cultivation of the imagination, not moral instruction, that is spiritually uplifting. This explains why Old Miss Barry is so smitten with Anne: not because she is a well-conducted child, but because she can "imagine" her way out of any predicament.

This conversation about the story club becomes self-reflexively invoked two chapters later after the Lily Maid episode. At this point, Anne looks back on her career and notes a moral in the very stories we've been reading about her, thereby interpreting for us the "classic" adventures of Anne of Green Gables: "The affair of the amethyst brooch cured me of meddling with things that didn't belong to me. The Haunted Wood mistake cured me of letting my imagination run away with me. The liniment cake mistake cured me of carelessness in cooking. Dyeing my hair cured me of vanity."[27] What is significant is that these are expressly not the "lessons" that inform our reading of (and delight in) these episodes, which makes Anne's reductive interpretation of them all the more amusing. We like these events for their very irreducibility to sentimentalized containment. As with the stream at the beginning of the novel, it is not the "well-conducted" and decorous aspects that we value (expressed in Anne's moral imperative in reading her past), but rather the reverse: the irrepressible and hidden depths that point to something beyond the surface analysis of social-realist message. As Anne would be the first to acknowledge, we don't read a classic as we do the catechism: for lessons in daily living. Likewise, we don't read Anne's "mistakes" for the ordinary lessons they contain about social etiquette and decorum, but rather for their very intractability to such interpretation.

The "moral lesson" of the Lily Maid experience, as Anne presents it, is that there is no room for romance in everyday Avonlea, as there had been in previous eras. Anne makes two assumptions: that romance is reserved for the (old) world of the classics; and that romance disguises (and distracts from) a latent realist moral message (which Anne has read into the classic romantic scenes from her past). But of course, the entire novel has been undercutting both prescriptions. There is room for romance in Avonlea, as Anne has been central in applying it there. Miss Stacy's call to write about "what might happen in Avonlea" is expressly what Anne is doing by looking back on it here: etching her romantic exploits into realist narrative form. Likewise, there is room in Anne's imaginings for a moral lesson through her very indulgence in romantic plots – though the moral is not to avoid the sway of romanticism, as her reductive (and ironized) interpretations would seem to imply, but to embrace its depths and, one might say, cultivate the imagination.

"Romance is not appreciated now,"[28] Anne laments, but, as the popularity of the novel attests, it is – which is what Matthew asserts at the conclusion to that chapter: "Don't give up all your romance, Anne."[29] With these words, Matthew voices the thoughts of the reader: like him, the reader is at this point already lamenting the impending "closing of the book" on *Anne of Green Gables*, and more tellingly, is already feeling nostalgic for it. This narrational self-reflexivity reaches its epitome at the end of the novel (chapter 37) when Marilla and Anne review the events of the past, laughing at the "greatest hits" (the liniment in the cake, the hair dye) as if they are rereading the book that has preceded: "What a girl you were for making mistakes in them days, Anne. You were always getting into scrapes. I did use to think you were possessed. Do you mind the time you dyed your hair?"[30] Both inside and outside the novel, Anne's story has achieved an aura of permanence before it is even finished.

A classic text, as these observations suggest, is one that wears well, in part because of what is traditionally perceived to be the transformative power of art. Like such a work, Anne's effect on those around her is spiritually and morally uplifting, but not didactic. As Old Miss Barry proclaims towards the novel's end: "If I'd a child like Anne in the house all the time I'd be a better and happier woman."[31] Like Browning's heroine in "Pippa Passes" (with which the novel concludes), Anne has a redemptive influence on others. But most important, she is oblivious to these powers, which makes her that much more authentic. As so many critics have noted, not only are Marilla and Matthew able to "rescue" Anne, but she is able to redeem them, as well as such unlikely crustaceans as Rachel Lynde. In this sense, the novel's reading of Anne as a classic or "uncommon" soul enacts how we, in turn, are to read the novel: as an "uncommon" work that inspires a combination of imaginative cultivation and reader identification. We have come full circle to Montgomery's own claims for the book as being a work of "art for art's sake" that concerns a "real human girl."

These literary pedagogical features can be extended to what for me is the most significant and interesting act of reading in the novel: the way the book enacts its own reading of itself on a narrational, metatextual level. We know how Anne renames and "stories" the Avonlea landscape, but more interesting are the ways Anne's readings of the landscape become referenced within the novel itself. This happens very subtly over the course of the book in the shift in narratorial point of view. What I'm referring to is the way Anne's imagined names for things – the Lake of Shining Waters, the Haunted Wood, Lover's Lane, the Dryad's Bubble, the Snow Queen – become part of the geography of the narrated text. It happens as early as chapter 4, when the narrator, who has before this adopted an omniscient presence, refers to the "Lake of Shining Waters" as Anne is looking out the gable window toward the Barry house. In the course of the novel, the narrator starts to refer to the "real-world" of Avonlea by the names that Anne has appended to it, so that Anne's imagined and romanticized titles become narratively overlaid atop the "ordinary" Avonlea landmarks. Consider, for example, the description of the coming of spring in the opening of chapter 20: "Spring had come once more to Green Gables ... The maples in Lover's Lane were red-budded and little curly ferns pushed up around the Dryad's Bubble. ... One June evening ... when the frogs were singing silverly sweet in the marshes about the head of the Lake of Shining Waters ... Anne was ... looking out past the boughs of the Snow Queen."[32] Anne's reading thus assumes a kind of permanence within the geography of the text (a simulacral effect that is echoed in Avonlea Village and "Canadian World" in Japan in which the fictional place-names are given "real-life" counterparts). In fact, the narrator says as much when she observes a few lines later: "It was as if all the dreams, sleeping and waking, of its vivid occupant had taken a visible although immaterial form."[33] So, when Marilla chastises Anne a few pages later for "believ[ing] all that wicked nonsense of your own imagination,"[34] this is, in a sense, precisely what happens in the book, where the narration itself begins to invoke (and "believe in") its own imagined creation.

These self-referential moments enact a kind of performative speech act, whereby Anne's (and the author's) act of naming renders as "real" the very imagined world we are reading about as we are reading it. In this way, the novel round-aboutly conforms to Miss Stacy's dictum to "write about what might happen in Avonlea," for in the narrator's renaming of the world of Avonlea, Anne's imaginings achieve a reified ("real") existence. True to the status of many classic literary texts, the fictionalized sites become memorable and therefore "real" to the reader, though here this extra-literary effect takes place within the literary work – which was precisely Anne's purpose in "romancing" the landscape in the first place: to make it more memorable, more real.

This phenomenon has an uncanny counterpart in Montgomery's own contradictions about the "real-life" models for her novel. Insistent that the novel was not based on real-life characters and places, Montgomery nonetheless charted the "real" origins for many of the "imagined" sites in the novel. One such exegetical moment occurs in her journal entry of 27 January 1911. As Irene Gammel points out: "It seems that the author who had reacted so defensively to the Cavendish folk who suggested that she had copied from 'real life' now seemed to agree with them. She carefully identified the Cavendish models for Green Gables, Lover's Lane, the Haunted Wood, Lynde's Hollow, the Lake of Shining Waters, and so on in a lengthy entry that would later allow Parks Canada to establish many of these landmarks as part of the Green Gables tourist site."[35] Even the character of Anne acquired this kind of extra-literary presence in the "Real." In her journal entry of 9 October 1907, Montgomery claimed: "Anne is as real to me as if I had given her birth."[36] And on 27 January 1911, she rhapsodized: "[Anne] is and always has been ... so real to me that I feel I am doing violence to something when I deny her an existence anywhere save in Dreamland ... She is so real that, although I've never met her, I feel quite sure I shall do so some day – perhaps in a stroll through Lover's Lane in the twilight."[37] An overlayering of realism and romance, fact and fiction, is clearly evident in these accounts. As Cecily Devereux argues, Montgomery used her journals as verification of both real-life and fictionalized events. Devereux notes how instances of "self-quotation" (quotations from Montgomery's journals) occur in *Anne of Green Gables*[38] and how "Montgomery's assembling of her life story in her journals has produced a compelling 'real-life' system within which Montgomery, her imagined heroine, her novel, and the geo-physical space of her childhood all signify in relation to one another."[39]

Unsurprisingly, in the spirit of the author's self-referentiality, the most notable renaming in the fictional world of Avonlea is the epithet "Anne of Green Gables." Ironically, the title is coined by Anne to diminish her status as a romantic heroine. Gazing into the mirror in her gabled bedroom, Anne realizes that she can never be the figure of high romance, the Lady Cordelia Fitzgerald, but "only Anne of Green Gables."[40] In one swoop, she takes us from the realm of classic myth to Miss Stacy's world of the already known. And yet the full import of the name is embryonic at this point, since Anne Shirley (the ordinary girl) has not yet fully metamorphosed into Anne of Green Gables (the extraordinary girl) and embarked on her larger-than-life adventures that will, effectively, bring the world of Lady Cordelia to the world of Avonlea. Furthermore, the name is itself an example of Anne's infamous poeticizing of her encounters (Anne becomes "Anne of Green Gables," just as Barry's Pond becomes the "Lake of Shining Waters"), while it is yet another fantasied renaming of sorts, since we never do learn whether Anne's "real" name was originally spelled with an "e." The name is thus a condensation of the two literary-critical registers that the novel navigates: fiction and everyday reality, romance and realism, extraordinary and ordinary.

In effect, Montgomery only half applies Miss Stacy's advice to her own book, for the novel embraces both categories (romance and realism), just as the character of Anne herself encompasses both. *Anne of Green Gables* is a tale of local Prince Edward Island life, to be sure, but it is also a tale that allows "scope for imagination" (a tale of adventure, exploits, romance, melodrama, poetry, and all those things that are central both to the story club and to the "classic" works of literature that are invoked throughout the novel). The effect of *Anne of Green Gables* on its readers, comparable to Anne's effect on those around her, compels us to respond to it as something beyond the "ordinary" and commonplace. If this places us among "Matthew's school of critics," that time-honoured group of literary aficionados ... well, we are in good company. Matthew is, after all, the first interpreter within the novel who reads Anne right.

## NOTES

1   Montgomery, *Green Gables Letters*, 51.
2   Pacey, *Creative Writing in Canada*, 98.
3   Ibid., 98.
4   Gerson, "Anne of Green Gables Goes to University," 27.
5   Montgomery, *Selected Journals*, 1:263.
6   Ibid., 331.
7   Montgomery, *After Green Gables*, 170.
8   Montgomery, *Anne of Green Gables*, 286.
9   Ibid.
10   Ibid., 104.
11   Ibid., 63.
12   Ibid., 63–4.
13   Zizek, *Looking Awry*, 11.
14   Ibid., 11–12.
15   Doody, *The Annotated Anne of Green Gables*, 22.
16   Ibid., 30.
17   Montgomery, *Anne of Green Gables*, 203.
18   Ibid., 76.
19   Ibid., 312.
20   Ibid., 302.
21   Ibid., 241.
22   Ibid., 242.
23   Ibid., 244.
24   Ibid.
25   Ibid., 245.
26   Ibid.
27   Ibid., 261.
28   Ibid.
29   Ibid., 262.
30   Ibid., 324.
31   Ibid., 269.
32   Ibid., 199, 200–1.

33 Ibid., 201.
34 Ibid., 203.
35 Gammel, *Looking for Anne*, 247.
36 Montgomery, *Selected Journals*, 1:332.
37 Ibid., 2:39–40.
38 Devereux, "'See my Journal,'" 254.
39 Ibid., 254–5.
40 Montgomery, *Anne of Green Gables*, 109.

## BIBLIOGRAPHY

Devereux, Cecily. "'See my Journal for the full story': Fictions of Truth in *Anne of Green Gables* and L.M. Montgomery's Journals." In *The Intimate Life of L.M. Montgomery*, edited by Irene Gammel, 241–57. Toronto: University of Toronto Press, 2005.

Doody, Margaret Anne. Introduction to *The Annotated Anne of Green Gables*, by L.M. Montgomery, edited by Wendy E. Barry, Margaret Anne Doody, and Mary E. Doody Jones, 9–34. New York: Oxford University Press, 1997.

Gammel, Irene. *Looking for Anne: How Lucy Maud Montgomery Dreamed Up a Literary Classic*. Toronto: Key Porter, 2008.

Gerson, Carole. "Anne of Green Gables Goes to University: L.M. Montgomery and Academic Culture." In *Making Avonlea: L.M. Montgomery and Popular Culture*, edited by Irene Gammel, 17–34. Toronto: University of Toronto Press, 2002.

Montgomery, L.M. *After Green Gables: L.M. Montgomery's Letters to Ephraim Weber, 1916–1941*. Edited by Hildi Froese Tiessen and Paul Gerard Tiessen. Toronto: University of Toronto Press, 2006.

– *Anne of Green Gables*. Edited by Cecily Devereux. Peterborough, Ontario: Broadview Press, 2004.

– *The Green Gables Letters from L.M. Montgomery to Ephraim Weber, 1905–1909*. Edited by Wilfrid Eggleston. Ottawa: Borealis, 1981.

– *The Selected Journals of L.M. Montgomery*. Vol. 1, 1889–1910; Vol. 2, 1910–1921. Edited by Mary Rubio and Elizabeth Waterston. Toronto: Oxford University Press, 1985; 1987.

Pacey, Desmond. *Creative Writing in Canada: A Short History of English-Canadian Literature*. Toronto: Ryerson, 1952.

Zizek, Slavoj. *Looking Awry: An Introduction to Jacques Lacan through Popular Culture*. Cambridge, Massachusetts: MIT Press, 1991.

# Anne of Green Gables as Centre and Circumference

WENDY SHILTON

*There is no first, or last, in Forever –*
*It is Centre, there all the time –*
Emily Dickinson to her sister-in-law, Sue[1]

*My Business is Circumference*
Emily Dickinson to her literary mentor, Thomas Higginson[2]

A last word, let alone the last word, will never emerge when it comes to *Anne of Green Gables*. Every reader reading *Anne* – no matter what position she or he occupies in temporal, cultural, or geographical space – has something more, and something unique, to say. It is this ongoing, dynamic process of adaptation and evolution in textual and experiential meaning-making over decades of expanding readership that has anchored Anne's acquired status as a "classic." Acquired, I say, because in its earliest days Lucy Maud Montgomery's most famous novel was not considered the stuff of classics by literary specialists. With time, however, important developments in literary and cultural theory over the last century have authorized it to become a classic, underscoring its enduring value in diverse ways for an increasingly diverse reading public.

When I read *Anne of Green Gables*, to add yet another perspective to the mix, I hear two categorically different literary voices murmuring in the background. One belongs to Northrop Frye, the eminent twentieth-century Canadian literary critic; the other is that of Emily Dickinson, the "Vesuvian" poet of mid-nineteenth-century New England. Holding Frye and Dickinson in mind, I want to suggest another thread for the conversation that seeks to better understand *Anne's* continuing affirmation as a classic, a conversation that emanates from the novel's powerful commitment to recognizing and supporting the experience of core human needs across time and space. I will begin with Frye.

In his provocative "Conclusion" to *A Literary History of Canada*, first published in 1945, Frye argued that to assess the status of Canada's place in the literary marketplace at the time, one would need to eschew evaluation as the end of criticism, seeking rather to understand how the verbal imagination in Canadian literature operated more broadly as cultural history. He explains: "The evaluative view is based on the conception of criticism concerned mainly to define and canonize the genuine classics of literature. And Canada has produced no author who is a classic in the sense of possessing a vision greater in kind than that of his best readers ... There is no Canadian writer of whom we can say what we can say of the world's major writers, that their readers can grow up inside their work without ever being aware of a circumference."[3]

Frye relied in the essay on a theoretical axis of centre and circumference to justify his view at the time. "Centre," for him, connoted the literary: that is, meaning produced "centripetally" through story, myth, and metaphor. "Circumference," in contrast, connoted meanings produced through social, cultural, and historical discourse. But the alleged lack of major writers in Canada up to that point, according to Frye, had one advantage, allowing us "to see what literature is trying to do when we are studying a literature that has not quite done it."[4] In other words, to allow an appreciation of the achievement of Canadian literature, a critical approach would have to be reoriented away from an inward, rigorously defined, transcendent literary centre to an outward, more inclusive, general conception of writing as social text in the circumference. Frye stated: "If no Canadian author pulls us away from the Canadian context toward the centre of literary experience itself, then at every point we remain aware of his [sic] social and historical setting. The conception of what is literary has to be greatly broadened for such a literature."[5]

"Greatly broadened," of course, is exactly how we would describe what happened to conceptions of the "literary" within very few decades after Frye's "Conclusion." For the emergent, intersecting lenses of postmodernism, Marxism, feminism, postcolonialism, neurolinguistics, multimodal literacies, and the like would blur, collapse, and dissolve the implied boundaries constructing the axis of centre and circumference, literary text and social text. Fortunately for *Anne of Green Gables* and Montgomery studies, nearly every theoretical spasm and curl would benefit reader appreciation, placing *Anne* firmly in the category of

classic not only in Canadian literature but also far beyond, in world literature. In consequence, is Frye's conceptual axis of centre and circumference now obsolete? To the contrary, as with most of his brilliant legacy. Provided we question and explore his distinctions between nature
and culture, inward and outward, timeless and temporal embedded in
his use of the metaphors of centre and circumference, the theoretical
construct is helpful.

In *The Great Code*, Frye writes: "the real interest of myth is to draw
a circumference around a human community and look inward toward
that community, not to inquire into the operations of nature ... mythology is not a direct response to the natural environment; it is part of the
imaginative insulation that separates us from that environment."[6] But I
find that the drawing power of *Anne of Green Gables* lies in its invitation to readers to move in a quite different direction: that is, rather than
insulating and separating the human imagination and the environment,
the novel asks us to strive to reconnect and integrate them, to see that
imaginative processes actually depend on environmental processes and
that, when understood as irrevocably interdependent forces, both re-
store wholeness to human being-in-the-world. *Anne of Green Gables* is
a classic precisely because it does possess "a vision greater in kind than
that of [its] best readers," and its readers not only can but do "grow up
inside [this] work without ever being aware of a circumference."

Reading Emily Dickinson, I find, helps to illuminate the classic in
*Anne* in the sense I mean here. Like Montgomery's fictive Anne, Dickinson knew, celebrated, and struggled with the challenge of learning to
contain powerfully contradictory emotional forces within. On the one
hand, she found "ecstasy in life, the mere sense of living is joy enough,"[7]
but on the other, she felt herself as both a woman and a writer to be
"the only Kangaroo among the Beauty,"[8] an *isolato*, alienated from a
world that was incapable of nourishing her intellectual, emotional, and
creative needs. The main concerns in her poetry are with core human
needs: physical and emotional nourishment, acceptance and belonging,
dependable self-other relationships, and a flowing, rhythmic interplay
of caring social relations and developing autonomy, self-determina-
tion, and assertiveness. In Dickinson's poetic imagination, we see wild
fluctuations between extremities of emotional experience, scintillating
at one moment with wit and a breathless passion for life, and at another, a hair's breadth from excruciating despair and psychic rupture.

A sampling of many of the opening lines alone from her poems reflects a harrowing fragmentation of subjectivity that yearns for the restorative power of wholeness, healing, integration: for example, "Me from Myself – to Banish,"[9] "I felt a Funeral, in my Brain,"[10] and "My Life had stood – a Loaded Gun."[11]

Dickinson was not at all literally dispossessed of family or roots, but her poems and letters reveal constant preoccupation with the experience of feeling radically estranged. Her poems often translate this emotion into a chronic search for home, fulfillment, a place or space of belonging, of which Poem 579 is a good example:

> I had been hungry, all the Years –
> My Noon had Come – to dine –
> I trembling drew the Table near –
> And touched the curious Wine –
>
> 'Twas this on Tables I had seen –
> When turning, hungry, Home
> I looked in Windows, for the Wealth
> I could not hope – for Mine –
>
> I did not know the ample Bread –
> 'Twas so unlike the Crumb
> The Birds and I, had often shared
> In Nature's – Dining Room –
>
> The Plenty hurt me – 'twas so new –
> Myself felt ill – and odd –
> As berry – of a Mountain Bush –
> Transplanted – to the road –
>
> Nor was I hungry – so I found
> That Hunger – was a way
> Of Persons outside Windows –
> The Entering – takes away –[12]

This poem constructs a liminal moment in which a speaker, on the threshold of altered consciousness that her "Noon – had Come," meditates on the embodied difference between "Plenty" and "Hunger," "Ample Bread" and "Crumb," "Table" and "Nature's Dining Room." She is crossing a subjective boundary through a thinking-feeling process of differentiation, no longer identifying herself among the outsiders, the excluded, or "Persons outside Windows" looking in, but rather as an insider drawing near "Wealth." Ultimately, she recognizes, the difference is that between despair and hope, lack and the promise of fulfillment, dispossession and possession, sensing that "Hunger" is a state that "the Entering" into shelter and embodied communion "takes away." Note, however, that the speaker's arrival does not offer immediate comfort or peace; instead, the unfamiliarity of her present condition leaves her feeling "hurt," "ill," "odd – / As berry – of a Mountain Bush / Transplanted – to the road –." Note, too, that nature is not severed from culture here. The transplant of the berry alters the sense of home not by replacing the mountain bush with the road but by relating the two more closely and clearly, with the mere boundary of a transparent window to connect and delineate outside from inside. The speaker's memory of deprivation and the interim suffering of her "transplanted" state provide the continuity and interdependence of past and present, nature and culture, as she learns for the first time to seek out, cross over, enter into, and inhabit more comfortably an environment that nourishes and supports her growing acceptance of, and self-identification with, sustenance and sufficiency.

A sense of place, for Dickinson, is contingent on a strong sense of embodied presence. Place and presence, moreover, as revealed in Poem 1099, are determined by what the poet frequently refers to as "circumference":

> At Half past Three, a single Bird
> Unto a silent Sky
> Propounded but a single term
> Of cautious melody.
>
> At Half past Four, Experiment
> Had subjugated test
> And lo, Her silver Principle
> Supplanted all the rest –

> At Half past Seven, element
> Nor Implement – be seen
> And Place, was where the Presence was
> Circumference between –[13]

This poem describes an event, with a beginning, middle, and end, in the space of which a change, a difference, has occurred. Within four hours, a "single Bird" has tentatively signalled its existence, emerging onto the horizon ("silent Sky") of the speaker's awareness through song, has reached, through an implied crescendo, maximal musical glory (who can tell the singer from the song when "silver Principle" takes over?), and then receded into silence. However, far from being left with nothing, or absence, the speaker-hearer realizes that "Place" has emerged from , and merged with, the point where "Presence was," and the meaning of both is produced only when the two are related through the arc or "Circumference between." The meaningfulness of this event, then, is the poet's opportunity – and responsibility – to determine. For Dickinson, it is the meaning-maker, the poet, who defines circumference. Circumference is the embodied experience of a boundary embracing – what she calls in Poem 258, "the internal difference, / Where the meanings, are –."[14] Poetry is the symbolic translation of that embodied sense; it is "The poet," she writes in Poem 448, who "Distills amazing sense / From ordinary Meaning – " and gains "a Fortune – / Exterior – to Time –."[15]

Montgomery's Anne, like Dickinson, has a passion for language and a responsive imagination; she knows that language has the power to transform experience through art into beauty. And beauty heals, makes whole. Language that works for Anne, as it were, connects emotion and meaning, the physical and the cognitive or metaphysical. "When I hit on a name that suits exactly," Anne explains to Matthew, "it gives me a thrill."[16] (Note that Anne's evaluative criterion for suitable names echoes a statement Dickinson once made about poetry: "When I feel physically as if the top of my head were taken off, I know that is poetry."[17]) Anne's meaning-making is a fine-tuned process of sensing, "listening" to her body state, pausing to discover feeling before identifying it through its most fitting  form in language. Anne's allegedly meaningless chatter is often a form of sensing, groping for certainty along the edges of meaning; at the same time, she is able to dwell speechless in uncertainty for a time while meaning becomes focused. When she sees, for example, the apple trees in bloom along the roadway near the outset of the novel, we are told that "its beauty seemed to strike the child dumb";[18] she strains to find the right word to express her emotion – an ache she describes as at once "queer," "funny," and "pleasant." For her, the words "pretty" and "beautiful" don't "go far enough." Precision in language, especially the language of embodied emotion, is crucial to her for meaningful, fulfilling expression. Rejecting the empty local conventionality of "the Avenue" as a suitable name for the tree-lined road, she says, "There is no meaning in a name like that,"[19] and then recasts it in more satisfying terms as "the White Way of Delight."

Anne's ground for meaning, then, is the certainty of her own embodied experience as a central reference point. But her "problem," as an orphan, is her lack of rootedness, relatedness, or immediate attachment to a meaningful environment to affirm and support her judgment. Anne tells Matthew at the beginning, "I've never had a real home"; as Margaret Doody writes, she is "a wandering spirit, looking for a location."[20] Interestingly, Anne also actively associates the promise of home, attachment, and belonging with the feelings she experiences in witnessing beauty: "It gives me that pleasant ache again just to think of coming to a really truly home."[21] Like Dickinson, Anne has an exceptional consciousness and range of emotion. Her capacity to feel rapturously optimistic about life has a counterforce in her degree of suffering and sorrow, which almost always emanates from crushing doubts and disappointments concerning issues of belonging and home. Shortly after she tells Matthew that she feels "glad to be alive – it's such an interesting world," she is devastated to learn that she is not wanted: "Suddenly she seemed to grasp the full meaning," crying out in despair, "You don't want me! ... Oh, what shall I do? I'm going to burst into tears!" – whereupon we are told she "proceeded to cry stormily."[22]

Deprived of parents and family, Anne has known herself only as a means to others' ends: as a child-care worker; as an institutionalized ward of the state. Endearing and delightful though many of her incongruities and idiosyncracies of character are to readers, we also cannot escape the poignancy underlying them as "symptoms" of severely disrupted early attachment and maladaptation to an unwelcoming and untrustworthy environment of contingency. The wisdom of her body is her greatest resource, but her formative experience has been that of a rejected body, and therefore she has difficulty identifying with it. Until she can accept and feel at home within this body, she harbours a profound ambivalence toward it – hence her strong reactions and misguided actions. Anne must come to accept herself intrinsically, as a means not to others' ends but to her own purposes and designs. But self-acceptance is not given; it must be created through ongoing experiences of exchange, give and take, in a context of accepting and trusting relationships from which an accepting "I" emerges. Anne, to return to Dickinson's words, must experience an embodied shift from being one of the "Persons outside Windows" to one of those "Entering in."

Part of the power of *Anne of Green Gables* is that it depicts a context not only for Anne's development but for all who enter into relationship with her. For the reality she enters is fluid, not fixed, and Anne, as so many readers have observed, is as much a positive agent of change as she herself is changed within this transformative context. Her unexpected arrival and preternatural behaviour disrupt Marilla's lifelong emotional and expressive rigidity, stirring a rewiring, so to speak, in her formerly unyielding felt life. By the end of the novel, we are told that "she had learned to love this slim, gray-eyed girl with an affection all the deeper and stronger from its very undemonstrativeness."[23] Anne's presence fosters a shift in the passive Matthew, too, from trance-like timidity and near-mute communication to much more explicit assertion, through gesture and speech, of his desires. Though both Marilla and Matthew figure in differing ways as literary types of despair in the beginning, with Anne's ongoing influence and the requirement that they enter into responsive exchange with her in their environment, they co-evolve with her, becoming more deeply related to themselves and to each other.

Avonlea may seem an Eden, but Anne brings a force of realism that shatters pastoral illusion. For me, the key verbal exchange that effects a core emotional breakthrough for all, one which secures the new turn of relations in this novel, occurs shortly after Anne's arrival. When Matthew and Marilla do not know what to say or do with Anne's piercing accusation, "You don't want me," Marilla is said to step "lamely into the breach" by replying, "Well, well, there's no need to cry about it."[24] Anne's response constitutes the crux of the novel: "Yes, there IS need!"[25] Too untamed by standards of social compliance to deny or mask raw, visceral truth, Anne's statement is a proclamation, kerygmatic in its transformative power. Anne, who knows and has the power to name emotion, has the strength to admit what others cannot: that core embodied needs are the forces that drive and sustain life and growth. Meeting them is essential; fulfilling them in caring reciprocity is health. Possessing this wisdom and resistant to all attempts to suppress it, Anne breathes new life into the lives of all, awakening them to acknowledge and respond to their own experience of need. "What good would she be to us?" asks Marilla as she debates with Matthew whether to keep Anne; "We might be some good to her," is Matthew's "sudden and unexpected reply."[26] Much later, toward the end of the novel, Matthew reflects, "She's been a blessing to us ... the Almighty saw we needed her, I reckon."[27]

*Anne of Green Gables* possesses both centre and circumference within the context of ongoing meaning-making and living process. Its "classic" story or *mythos* of an unwanted child who finds love, home, and happiness resonates within but also far beyond the trope of orphanhood of Western culture. For though it may evoke the archetypal *topos* of home as Eden or Paradise regained, its representation of core human needs – needs that cross boundaries of time and space, however shaped and re-shaped they are by cultural specificity and political differences – points toward an ever-relevant vision of individual and community renewal through more co-operative, more empathic, more caring relationships. *Anne's* circumference, then, is bounded and defined entirely by the individual and collective needs of each reader reading it, the "internal difference" experienced by each reader able to identify with the *mythos* at the novel's centre.

> The Poets light but Lamps –
> Themselves – go out –
> The Wicks they stimulate –
> If vital Light
>
> Inhere as do the Suns –
> Each Age a Lens
> Disseminating their
> Circumference –
>
> Emily Dickinson[28]

## NOTES

1  Dickinson, *The Letters*, 268.
2  Ibid., 288.
3  Frye, "Conclusion," 340–1.
4  Ibid.
5  Ibid.
6  Ibid., *The Great Code*, 37.
7  Dickinson, *The Letters*, 342a, quoted by Thomas Higginson.
8  Ibid., 288.
9  Dickinson, *The Poems*, 709.
10  Ibid., 340.
11  Ibid., 764.
12  Ibid., 579.
13  Ibid., 1099.
14  Ibid., 258.
15  Ibid., 448.
16  Montgomery, *Anne of Green Gables*, 15.
17  Dickinson, *The Letters*, 324a.
18  Montgomery, *Anne of Green Gables*, 13.
19  Ibid., 14.
20  Doody, Introduction, vii.
21  Montgomery, *Anne of Green Gables*, 14.
22  Ibid., 17.
23  Ibid., 173.
24  Ibid., 17.
25  Ibid., 18.
26  Ibid., 21.
27  Ibid., 200.
28  Dickinson, *The Poems*, 883.

## BIBLIOGRAPHY

Dickinson, Emily. *The Letters of Emily Dickinson*. Edited by Thomas H. Johnson. Vols. 1–3. Cambridge, Massachusetts: Harvard University Press, 1958, 1986.
– *The Poems of Emily Dickinson, Variorum Ed.* Edited by Ralph W. Franklin. Vols. 1–3. Cambridge, Massachusetts: Harvard University Press, 1998.
Doody, Margaret Anne. Introduction to *Anne of Green Gables*, by L.M. Montgomery. Cambridge, UK: Worth Press, 2010.
Frye, Northrop. "Conclusion." *Literary History of Canada, 1st Ed.* General Editor Carl F. Klinck. Toronto: University of Toronto Press, 1965, 1945.

– *The Great Code: The Bible and Literature.* Toronto: Academic Press, 1982, 1981.

Montgomery, Lucy Maud. *Anne of Green Gables.* Cambridge, UK: Worth Press, 2010.

# Provoking the Classic:
# Class, Colonialism, and Christianity

# "Nice Folks": L.M. Montgomery's Classic and Subversive Inscriptions and Transgressions of Class

CAROLINE E. JONES

The literature that we come to know as "classic" often treads a fine line between reinscribing a society's conventions, particularly of gender and class, and challenging those same values. As has oft been noted, L.M. Montgomery's work offers strong support to contemporary feminist readers, with strong female characters exercising their voices and agency in opposition to many social mores; indeed, many of her texts featuring outspoken girls have come to be regarded as possessing the hallmarks of "classic" literature. However, Montgomery was more ambivalent about subverting her culture's ideologies of class, and transgressions of class lines occur less frequently. In fact, many of Montgomery's passive ideologies (those of which she was likely unaware) tend to reinscribe class distinctions. After all, in the historical and social context in which she was writing, class and social standing had much to do with blood and breeding: the "naturally" established order. While with certain characters Montgomery appears to advocate a progressive, egalitarian ethic, her texts far more often underscore conventional ideologies of class, ideologies that centre on innate breeding (qualities inherited through "blood" and family), rather than individual character. Montgomery's conflicted depictions of class in *Anne of Green Gables* provide rich material for analysis. They particularly emphasize how Montgomery reinscribes popular perceptions of the "natural" social order, and invite us to explore how those reinscriptions solidify the novel's status as "classic."

While I will employ several class theories in this reading of Montgomery's work, including Karl Marx's theories of economic class, Pierre Bourdieu's ideas of cultural and symbolic capital, and Mikhail Bakhtin's discussions of language, I ultimately frame this discussion in terms of blood and birthright. Montgomery's narrative relies fundamentally on the clichéd notion that "blood will tell," a somewhat fatalistic but entirely appropriate idea for her place and time. In most of her characters we find merit ultimately determined by blood – "good" characters, who have an innate, indescribable sort of elevation of soul and personality, are usually from "good" families. Regardless of the eccentricities of certain family members, these "good" characters and "good" families, refined and with a marked degree of social poise and standing, rise above the common, ordinary members of their communities and, often, enhance and develop their societies' sensibilities.

Theories of and ideas about class – encompassing markers of economics, culture, language, and national or ethnic identity – intersect intriguingly in Montgomery's work, informing my ideas of blood and birthright. From Marx to Bourdieu to Bakhtin and beyond, theorists of class offer lenses that refract Montgomery's class ideologies for twenty-first-century sensibilities, thus problematizing perceptions of the classic *Anne of Green Gables* as a predominantly progressive text that fully transcends its own place and time.

Karl Marx identifies "three great classes of modern society resting upon the capitalist mode of production[:] wage laborers, capitalists, and landlords."[1] Marx himself did not fully anticipate a class structure in which the professions (doctors, lawyers, higher educators, and others whose work requires specific and extended education) figured as prominently as they do, although he stipulated that if "sources of revenue" constitute people into classes, "physicians and officials would also form two classes."[2] Richard Abel suggests that because professionals have no clear alliance with either workers or capitalists, Marx felt they had no significant part to play in the class conflict that he hoped would shift dominant economic and social structures from capitalism to socialism.[3] Unsurprisingly, Montgomery's Prince Edward Island both conforms to and veers from Marx's model of class divisions: on her "magic island,"[4] families generally own land and work it themselves, or if they are unable to do that, lease it to other farmers. Montgomery makes occasional references to such traditional capitalists as small-scale merchants and store owners, but gives more weight to professionals: ministers, schoolteachers, and doctors figure prominently in *Anne*, and all play significant roles in plot and character development.

Matthew G. Hatvany, in a call for a historiographic approach that deconstructs the binary of landlord and tenant as the primary social structure on Prince Edward Island, acknowledges a "loosely defined 'middle class' of merchants, land agents, entrepreneurs and prospering farmers (both freehold and tenant)" even in the province's earliest years.[5] *Anne of Green Gables* was written thirty years after the 1875 demise of the proprietary estate system that had been a dominant social and economic force since 1767,[6] and it is set in a time when a "well-entrenched middle-class" had already established itself.[7] Thus, most of Montgomery's economic systems reflect Hatvany's categorizations of the middle class, and incorporate and expand upon Marx's categorizations, creating their own sub-classes: we see independent farmers, merchants, teachers, and even a few professionals in varying degrees of flexibility and rigidity. In Montgomery's hands, these classifications shift, connect, and transgress their boundaries vexingly – which is just what we expect of her.

Matthew and Marilla's decision to adopt an orphan to help with, and presumably inherit, their family farm, has interesting implications that bear examination in terms of class.[8] Marilla's rationale for their decision, offered to Rachel Lynde in chapter 1, provides context for the arrival of a newcomer as well as some of her own class ideologies. First, she explains that they need reliable help on the farm, as Matthew is sixty and has heart trouble; she complains that most of the hired help available consists of "French boys" and that "as soon as you do get one broke into your ways and taught something he's up and off to the lobster canneries or the States."[9] Marilla adds that they have decided to adopt "a smart likely boy of about ten or eleven … the best age – old enough to be of some use in doing chores right off and young enough to be trained up proper. We mean to give him a good home and schooling."[10] Marilla's approach to the situation is entirely pragmatic: they are aging siblings who have no family to whom they may leave their farm; thus they will simultaneously serve themselves and do their social duty by adopting a child from an orphanage, giving him a home, and turning him into a useful and productive citizen.

When she and Matthew decide to keep Anne, despite her unsuitability to become the future farmer they had envisioned, Marilla remains resigned to doing her duty: "Matthew Cuthbert, it's about time somebody adopted that child and taught her something. She's next door to a perfect heathen ... Well, well, we can't get through this world without our share of trouble. I've had a pretty easy life of it so far, but my time has come at last and I suppose I'll just have to make the best of it."[11] Matthew's approach has been more instinctual; when he expresses a desire to keep Anne despite her sex, Marilla asks, "What good would she be to us?" to which Matthew replies, "We might be some good to her."[12] He senses that Anne, with her passionate longing for a home, and her immediate love for Green Gables itself, could become as much – or more – a part of the farm as any boy might.

Marilla's ideological approach to the adoption is staunchly national-istic. She tells Rachel that Matthew had suggested adopting a boy from Dr Thomas Barnardo's London program, but that "I said 'no' flat to that ... I'll feel easier in my mind and sleep sounder at nights if we get a born Canadian."[13] Her earlier observations on the tendencies of Acadian boys to leave farm employment for the canneries or the United States also implies an assumption of innate shiftlessness in those youths. Marilla is here limited by Montgomery's deep interpellation into the passive ideology that Acadians have no desire to change their social, economic, or cultural status. This ideology circumvents the possibility that those workers may be simply looking for the best opportunity to support themselves – and in fact may simply want the same sort of economic and social independence that the Cuthberts enjoy. Montgomery has es-tablished a passive double standard: the impulse for self-improvement that she lauds in English-Canadians is characterized as unreliability in French-Canadians, largely because that very self-improvement trans-gresses her perception of the established societal role of Acadians in Island life and culture.

Similarly, within the fictional community of Avonlea, we see a well-established social order, generally based on economic status: Montgom-ery offers a range of characters, from educated professionals to well-intentioned and good-hearted but essentially uneducated people. In the absence of the expected orphan boy, Matthew hires a "French" boy – or, correctly, an *Acadian* boy – Jerry Buote, to help with the farm work. Members of the middle class – farmers and householders – are gen-erally satisfied with their lives, and feel no need to expand their intel-lectual, professional, or spiritual horizons. Similarly, it never occurs to Montgomery's Jerry to look beyond the role into which society has cast him from his birth.

In considering transgressions of class in *Anne*, it is necessary to ask, who carries the capital? Bourdieu's ideas of "symbolic" capital (achieved through "reputation or honour") and "cultural" capital (achieved through "intellectual or educational qualifications"[14]) are clearly borne out in Montgomery's ideas of class. While most citizens of Montgomery's villages notably lack the cultural capital of higher education, they do carry strong symbolic capital: in most of her communities, family pedigrees denote distinct social standing: within the middle class – that is, independent farmers – Cuthberts, Lyndes, and Blythes stand as pillars of Avonlea society, while Sloanes and Pyes offer more dubious social credentials and carry markedly less symbolic capital. An elite few – Rev. and Mrs Allan and Miss Stacy – also carry cultural capital. Montgomery's Anne is remarkable in that she innately understands the value of cultural capital and actively pursues it throughout the novel.

In Montgomery's work, wage labourers conform most clearly to Marx's proletariat, a class of people identified by Bourdieu as being deprived of the cultural and symbolic capital Montgomery valued most highly. Marx glorifies the worker as being central to any economy, while Montgomery tends to dismiss labour as an end in itself, unless that labour sustains one's own land and particularly if that labouring for economic independence is supplemented with desire for additional cultural capital. She privileges the values of intellect and learning, educating most of her central characters beyond the village one-room schoolhouse, and ultimately turning Anne Shirley into a professional educator – as distinct from a village schoolteacher. By the end of *Anne of Green Gables*, Anne Shirley and Gilbert Blythe alone express aspirations for education beyond teachers' college. This impulse toward learning sets these two apart from their peers, who remain content with their lives as farmers or small-town schoolteachers.

Perhaps the most uniformly marginalized segment of the population in Montgomery's work is the Acadian community. While Acadian characters appear in most of Montgomery's novels, they are flat constructs, identified pejoratively as "the French." Fulfilling the basic function of "hired help," they are never written as round, well-developed individuals who contribute to the story lines, and they entirely lack cultural and symbolic capital. Marilla's remark about "stupid, half-grown little French boys" early in *Anne of Green Gables*[15] is representative of the way she depicts all such characters in the novel. Montgomery similarly characterizes Mary Joe, the young woman Mrs Barry hires to look after her daughters, not simply as ignorant of how to treat Minnie May's croup, but also as stupid: "young Mary Joe, a buxom, broad-faced French girl from the Creek ... was helpless and bewildered, quite incapable of thinking what to do, or doing it if she thought of it."[16] Anne more charitably attributes Mary Joe's failings to a lack of imagination.[17]

After Anne has mistakenly flavoured a cake with anodyne liniment in place of vanilla, Marilla tells her to feed it to the pigs, adding: "It isn't fit for any human to eat, not even Jerry Buote."[18] If Jerry had demonstrated any sort of character failing, the remark might be de-racialized, but as it stands, Marilla classifies Jerry as negligibly human, just above the status of the Green Gables pigs. Montgomery mentions Jerry Buote three times in the course of the novel: when he is introduced as having asked for work,[19] when he has described newcomer Anne as a "crazy girl" who talks to herself,[20] and here, in the incident of the cake. In none of these encounters does Jerry do or say anything that merits such dismissive treatment.

Montgomery's inclusion of Acadian characters "reflects Anglophone attitudes of condescension to the French."[21] Gavin White's 1995 piece "L.M. Montgomery and the French" reminds us that Montgomery "shared with countless other English-Canadians the view that Canada had been held back by the French vote, which represented an underclass incapable of responding to higher ideals."[22] White ultimately concludes that, while our modern sensibilities with their broader ideologies about race and nationality might regret such blind spots in a beloved icon, we have to recognize that Montgomery was, in these matters at least, a well-interpellated product of her society.[23] While my impulse is to look for a subversive commentary against these dominant attitudes, I do not find any evidence for that position, and must conclude that Montgomery simply allows her characters to voice the "obviousnesses" that the novel's earliest readers would accept without question. (In this volume, Collins-Gearing examines the taken-for-granted assumptions that reveal colonizing attitudes.)

As Bakhtin recognizes, language, while key to characterization and narrative development, also functions as a strong signifier of social status. Montgomery's uses of diction and dialect often reveal her passive assumptions about class. Bakhtin suggests: "At any given moment of its evolution, language is stratified not only into linguistic dialects in the strict sense of the word (according to formal linguistic markers, especially phonetic), but also – and for us this is the essential point – into languages that are socio-ideological: languages of social groups."[24] Marilla's use of language as a gauge to determine Anne's quality[25] offers what may be Montgomery's earliest suggestion of how she (and the audience for whom she wrote) evaluated class. In *Anne of Green Gables* she creates several layers of class, using dialect as indicator. At the bottom are Acadians, from whom we see no dialogue in the first two *Anne* novels. In *Anne of the Island* we find examples of Montgomery's "transcriptions" of Acadian speech rendered as broken and mispronounced; that is, with missing articles or misplaced subjects, and the stereotypical "th" rendered as "d" and the short "i" as a long "e," intimating an inability to master spoken English. The primary Acadian who actually speaks in the *Anne* series is Pacifique Buote (another hired man of Avonlea, who shares a surname with Jerry of *Anne of Green Gables*). In a brief exchange with Anne (which occurs in the heat of her distress over Gilbert Blythe's ill health), Montgomery's Pacifique explains: "I got de word las' night dat my fader, he was seeck. It was so stormy dat I couldn't go den, so I start vair early dis mornin'. I'm goin' troo de woods for shortcut."[26] Additionally, Pacifique's elision of "very" to "vair" and his dropping of terminal consonants in "last," "morning," and "going" offer a stereotypical portrayal of sloppiness in his spoken English.

Next in the linguistic hierarchy are the lowest-class English-Canadians, usually labourers, who have little formal education and often serve as comic relief; some of them offer occasional and unexpected affinity with the more refined protagonist, as well as pearls of folk wisdom. These characters tend to drop or add terminal consonants (especially "t"), elide syllables and words, misuse or mispronounce words, and use "ain't."[27] With these similar linguistic tendencies, Montgomery aligns such characters with her depictions of "the French" as being similarly indifferent to education, intellectual self-improvement, or the acquisition of cultural capital.

Next in the strata, and the most common, is the upstanding, middle-class citizen with a basic one-room schoolhouse village education who tends towards the occasional colloquialism and speech that is direct, idiomatic, and only slightly ungrammatical: most of the characters in *Anne of Green Gables* fall into this category. Rachel Lynde's voice, as introduced in the first chapter, creates a prototype for the people of

Avonlea, and, probably quite deliberately, offers a strong foil for the sin-gularly evocative and rich voice of Anne Shirley. The initial conversa-tion between Rachel and Marilla also demonstrates Marilla's primary colloquialism, using "real" for "really," as she does when greeting Rachel: "This is a real fine evening, isn't it?"[28] Rachel's signature "that's what" appears when she learns of the Cuthberts' plan to adopt an orphan from Nova Scotia: "Well, Marilla, I'll just tell you plain that I think you're doing a mighty foolish thing – a risky thing, that's what."[29] In that single phrase she also uses "plain" for "plainly" as well as the colloquial in-tensifier "mighty." In addition, Matthew's familiar "well now" and his occasional "dunno"s and "mebbe"s[30] are reminders that these characters are the salt of the earth – educated adequately for their lives as farm-ers, with little emphasis on literary aesthetics. Their language is warm, folksy, and engaging, off-putting in neither its formality nor its misuses, indicative of people with ample symbolic capital.

Pristine speakers, for whom grammar and slang are misused only in-tentionally and for effect, comprise the final linguistic category. Anne, in clear contrast to the citizens of Avonlea, uses perfect diction with little or no slang, and has an extensive and grandiose vocabulary, full of literary allusions and vivid imagery. Montgomery later introduces the women who become Anne's intellectual and spiritual mentors, Miss Stacy and Mrs Allan, who also use conventional, if less striking, English. The delayed entrance of these kindred spirits into Avonlea ensures that Anne herself remains at the centre of the story: she is the first character who cherishes both beauty and words, who aligns them and puts them in service to each other, who uses language to express the joys of her heart and soul as well as the complexities of her mind. Her reverence for and uses of language single out Anne as a person of unique status in the heretofore ordinary village of Avonlea. The later arrivals of Miss Stacy, the progressive educator, and Mr and Mrs Allan, the progressive religious and spiritual leaders, quietly validate for the community both Anne's aspirational language and her aspirational ideas.

These distinctions of class through dialect (or lack thereof), syntax, diction, and grammatical rigour function as perhaps the clearest indica-tors of class. Because readers are themselves interpellated into Bakhtin's "social groups," they recognize and welcome as familiar and appropriate the linguistic tropes Montgomery employs. These designations of class through language reinforce our expectations, offering a subtle validation of existing class structures as normal and right. Stories that reflect our sense of social propriety, that "sound like us," that do not challenge our collective sense of the status quo, are more likely to fulfill our expectations of "classic" texts: resonant, clear, and unchanging.

Anne Shirley has become a classic character largely through transgression: her strong and unrestrained voice, her fallibility, and her human foibles. Anne speaks to readers through her imperfections, her mistakes, her frailties. She is also, not coincidentally, one of Montgomery's few entirely integrated upwardly mobile characters. Anne is successful in her assimilation into the upper stratum of Avonlea society for a variety of reasons, including her subversions of conventional Avonlea norms: she is pert, excessively and impulsively verbal, and uninhibited in speaking her mind. She is, of course, smart, loving, and lovable, but her social success is also, and significantly, due in part to the fact that her people were "nice folks." Anne is the quintessential proof of the argument that "blood will tell." From the brief history Anne offers Marilla in chapter 5 of *Anne of Green Gables*, we learn that Anne's parents were educated (both taught in a high school) and poor but respectable: they had a "weeny-teeny little yellow house" and a "woman who came in to scrub."[31] The child Anne imagines that house set in a riot of flowers and with "muslin curtains in all the windows [because m]uslin curtains give a house such an air";[32] her vision is fulfilled in *Anne of the Island* when young-woman Anne goes back to the house and discovers it "almost exactly as I've pictured it ... there *is* a lilac tree by the gate, and – yes, there are the muslin curtains in the windows."[33] The working-class woman who now lives in the house remembers the family and praises Bertha Shirley: "She was a nice little thing. My darter went to school to her and was nigh crazy about her."[34] Montgomery makes sure that the romantic narrative Anne has constructed for her own story, and which she shares with Marilla, is borne out by fact later in the series. The neat yellow house provides an appropriate setting for the Shirleys' lives together, and a suitable background for Anne's brief time with her parents.

Upon her the death of her parents, baby Anne is taken by Mrs Thomas, the aforementioned scrub woman, with whom she lives for eight years, serving as nursemaid to younger Thomas babies as soon as she is able. Upon Mr Thomas's death she is taken by the Hammonds and lives with them for two years "in a little clearing among the stumps."[35] A note in the Norton Critical Edition tells us that these stumps are "trees cut to waist level and left to rot by shiftless farmers clearing a field,"[36] a detail that further reinforces the limited cultural and social influences under which Anne has lived most of her life. Anne tells Marilla that she's gone to school only "a little,"[37] but offers a plethora of poetic pieces she has learned by heart. When asked if Mrs Thomas and Mrs Hammond were good to her, Anne responds, hesitantly, "O-o-o-h ... Oh, they *meant* to be – I know they meant to be just as good and kind as possible."[38]

In what has become, for me, the core piece of evidence indicting Montgomery as passively classist in this novel, Marilla reflects that, though Anne talks "too much," "there's nothing rude or slangy in what she does say. She's ladylike. It's likely her people were nice folks."[39] This terminology is loaded with unexamined value judgments: Marilla, and the reader with her, assumes that only "nice folks" would be capable of Anne's high-minded and articulate flights of fancy; that only "nice folks" could produce a child as sensitive as Anne clearly is; and that only the product of "nice folks" would be inclined to see the good in people who have clearly mistreated her. Anne's is a Cinderella story, and in coming to Green Gables she, like Cinderella, is restored to her social birthright: a nice girl among nice folks. Similarly, she comes into her rightful intellectual inheritance first in attending Queen's and teaching at her own school in *Anne of Green Gables*[40] and *Anne of Avonlea* (1909), then in attending college at Redmond in *Anne of the Island* (1915). Anne eventually lives out her parents' work when she becomes a high-school teacher herself in *Anne of Windy Poplars* (1936). In *Anne of Green Gables*, as Anne's story begins, Montgomery suggests that without her "good blood," Anne would never have managed – nor would she have hoped – to attain the cultural and symbolic capital that is ultimately depicted as her birthright. Nor, of course, could she have expected to transcend the pejorative labels of "home girl" or "charity child."

Anne's decision to defer college, despite winning the Avery Scholarship to Redmond at the end of *Anne of Green Gables*,[41] has been hotly debated, particularly by feminist scholars, since the late twentieth century. I will not pursue that debate, but I must note that the decision solidifies Anne as "the right sort of person" in the eyes of her community. Her sacrifice of the scholarship and her willingness to teach in Avonlea while pursuing her continued education independently demonstrate to community members that she is sufficiently grateful to Marilla for the home and opportunities that the Cuthberts have given her. The novel, in fact, would ring false had Anne decided to let Marilla sell the farm so she could go to Redmond – *Anne of Green Gables* is, after all, fundamentally the story of a search for home. To see that much-longed-for and deeply loved home sacrificed would undermine and discredit everything the reader has come to understand and love about Anne herself. Anne does what Montgomery wants readers to realize is the "right thing" in putting aside her own goals; but Anne is, after all, protecting the very thing at the heart of her journey: her home.

Interestingly, we can read Montgomery herself into both Anne's and Marilla's positions: upon her grandfather Macneill's death in 1898, Montgomery left her own career as a schoolteacher, and later a job at the *Halifax Echo* newspaper, to live with and care for her grandmother. Conversely, as Montgomery wrote *Anne of Green Gables*, she was aware that, as a single (though recently engaged) woman, she could find herself in a precarious position should her grandmother die before Maud herself could be married. The house in which she had grown up would go to an uncle upon her grandmother's death, leaving her with limited options for supporting herself.[42] In a long journal entry reflecting on her decision to accept Ewan Macdonald's marriage proposal, Montgomery writes that she was not actively seeking marriage, but that in light of her "anomalous position" regarding her home,[43] marriage seemed a reasonable alternative: "I dreaded unspeakably the loneliness of the future when I should be alone, absolutely alone in the world, and compelled to make a new home alone in some strange place among strangers."[44] Anne's decision to stay with Marilla assures the reader that her beloved home, unlike Montgomery's, will never be lost to her.

Raymond Williams maintains that: "[hegemony] does not just passively exist as a form of dominance. It has continually to be renewed, recreated, defended, and modified. It is also continually resisted, limited, altered, challenged by pressures not at all its own."[45] Bridget Fowler observes that: "Bourdieu's reception theory denies neither that writers and artists are autonomous nor that they are capable of 'singular achievements', but it does deny that culture is now an instrument of social change," and she further contends that Bourdieu "has underemphasized the potential for art and literature both to be critical and to imagine new alternatives."[46] In light of Bourdieu's theory on the role of artists and writers in both creating social change and maintaining hegemony, we may, again, ask ourselves if social mobility affects a text's ability to achieve "classic" status. I recognize in *Anne of Green Gables* an inverse relationship between class-progressivism and classic status: Anne's Cinderella story resonates with contemporary readers just as it did with readers a hundred years ago – the idea of a virtuous young woman restored to her rightful place is compelling – but the underlying passive ideology of "nice folks" who are innately privileged by virtue of blood and birth remains uninterrogated, hidden. Montgomery encourages readers to accept her vision of Avonlea as a place in which everyone knows, accepts – indeed, embraces – her or his "place" as defined by social conventions and bound by economic status. Anne Shirley transgresses the limitations placed upon her by circumstances of her life because her blood – her "nice folks" – entitles her to do so. Her educated and well-bred parents entitle her to the privileges of the middle class, while her confident and eager voice, as well as her ultimate integration into Avonlea society, have cemented her, and the novel that introduced her to the world, in the status of a classic.

## NOTES

1  Marx, *On Society*, 15.
2  Ibid., 16.
3  Abel, *American Lawyers*, 30–1.
4  Elizabeth Waterston coined this term for Montgomery's fictional depictions of Prince Edward Island in her study of Montgomery's fiction, *Magic Island*.
5  Hatvany, "Tenant, Landlord and Historian," 132.
6  Ibid., 109.
7  Ibid., 116.
8  I am indebted to Jean Mitchell and Jane Ledwell for raising this question in their comments on an earlier draft of this article.
9  Montgomery, *Anne of Green Gables*, 11.
10  Ibid., 12.
11  Ibid., 48.
12  Ibid., 30.
13  Ibid., 12.
14  Fowler, *Pierre Bourdieu*, 31.
15  Montgomery, *Anne of Green Gables*, 11.
16  Ibid., 118.
17  Ibid., 118–19.

18  Ibid., 144.
19  Ibid., 36.
20  Ibid., 69.
21  Rubio and Waterston, in Montgomery, *Anne of Green Gables*, 11n9.
22  White, "L.M. Montgomery," 67.
23  Ibid., 68.
24  Morris, "From M.M. Bakhtin," 75.
25  Montgomery, *Anne of Green Gables*, 40.
26  Ibid., *Anne of the Island*, 237.
27  Mary Vance's petulant "I s'pose you like her better'n me" in *Rainbow Valley* is typical of the author's use of dialect for lower-class, and thus uneducated, people. See Montgomery, *Rainbow Valley*, 39.
28  Montgomery, *Anne of Green Gables*, 10.
29  Ibid., 12.
30  Ibid., 172. Editors Rubio and Waterston acknowledge that Matthew's pronunciations are more colloquial than Marilla's (172n6).
31  Ibid., 38.
32  Ibid.
33  Ibid., *Anne of the Island*, 144.
34  Ibid.
35  Ibid., *Anne of Green Gables*, 38–9.
36  Rubio and Waterston, in Montgomery, *Anne of Green Gables*, 38n2.
37  Montgomery, *Anne of Green Gables*, 39.
38  Ibid., 40.
39  Ibid.
40  Ibid., 219–30.
41  Ibid., 229–30, 240–1.
42  Ibid., *Selected Journals* 1:221, 1:408.
43  Ibid., 221.
44  Ibid., 322.
45  Williams, *Marxism and Literature*, 112.
46  Fowler, *Pierre Bourdieu*, 11.

## BIBLIOGRAPHY

Abel, Richard L. *American Lawyers*. New York: Oxford University Press, 1989.
Bourdieu, Pierre. *Outline of a Theory of Practice*. 1972. Translated by Richard Nice. Cambridge: Cambridge University Press, 1977.
Fowler, Bridget. *Pierre Bourdieu and Cultural Theory: Critical Investigations*. London: Sage Publications, 1997.

Hatvany, Matthew G. "Tenant, Landlord and Historian: A Thematic Review of the 'Polarization' Process in the Writing of 19th-century Prince Edward Island History." *Acadiensis*, vol. 27 (1997): 109–32.

Marx, Karl. *On Society and Social Change*. Edited with an introduction by Neil J. Smelser. Chicago: University of Chicago Press, 1973.

Montgomery, L.M. *Anne of Green Gables*. Edited by Mary Henley Rubio and Elizabeth Waterston. New York: Norton Critical Edition, 2007.

– *Anne of the Island*. New York: Bantam, 1987.

– *Rainbow Valley*. New York: Bantam, 1985.

– *The Selected Journals of L.M. Montgomery*. Vol. 1, 1889–1910. Edited by Mary Rubio and Elizabeth Waterston. Toronto: Oxford University Press, 1985.

Morris, Pam, ed. "From M.M. Bakhtin, The Dialogic Imagination." In *The Bakhtin Reader: Selected Writings of Bakhtin, Medvedev, and Voloshinov*, translated by M. Holquist and C. Emerson, 74–80. London: Edward Arnold, 1994.

Rubio, Mary Henley, and Elizabeth Waterston, eds. *Anne of Green Gables* by L.M. Montgomery. New York: Norton Critical Edition, 2007.

Waterston, Elizabeth. *Magic Island: The Fictions of L.M. Montgomery*. Oxford: Oxford University Press, 2008.

White, Gavin. "L.M. Montgomery and the French." CCL: *Canadian Children's Literature*, vol. 78 (1995): 65–8.

Williams, Raymond. *Marxism and Literature*. Oxford: Oxford University Press, 1977.

# Civilizing *Anne*: Missionaries of the South Seas, Cavendish Evangelicalism, and the Crafting of *Anne of Green Gables*

## JEAN MITCHELL

*"Then there was a missionary book dealing with the Pacific Islands, in which I revelled because it was full of pictures of cannibal chiefs and the most extraordinary hair arrangements."*[1]

*"Matthew Cuthbert, it's about time somebody adopted that child and taught her something. She is next door to a perfect heathen. Will you believe that she never said a prayer in her life until tonight?"*[2]

Embedded in the classic text of L.M. Montgomery's *Anne of Green Gables* is a civilizing project distinctly linked to Canada's first overseas Presbyterian mission. The churchgoers of Prince Edward Island and Nova Scotian Presbyterian congregations, including Maud Montgomery's forebears and family, were instrumental in launching this foreign mission in another far-off corner of the globe, an archipelago in the south Pacific that would later be added to the British Empire. As Mary Rubio has noted, Montgomery's life on the north shore of Prince Edward Island was profoundly shaped by Scottish Presbyterianism, and the Presbyterian Church figured prominently throughout her life, literary work, and marriage.[3] Montgomery also had relatives from the Princetown/Malpeque areas of Prince Edward Island, Annie Montgomery (1847–1917) and Charlotte Geddie Montgomery (1855–1905), who served as Presbyterian missionaries in Persia (Iran) for many years where they were active educators and evangelists.[4] Reading *Anne of Green Gables* against the backdrop of Presbyterian evangelicalism and the early establishment of the South Seas mission shows the surprising ways in which out-of-the-way places are connected and the ways in which traces of those entanglements are present in the popular culture and scholarship that continue to condition our thinking about "others."

The South Sea islands of Melanesia were made infamous by descriptions of their darkness, heathenism, and cannibalism circulated by missionaries and European travellers in the nineteenth century. Early attempts at Christian conversion there ended in the death of the legendary missionary John Williams in 1839 in New Hebrides, the chain of volcanic islands so named by Captain Cook in 1773. Grim reports of hostility to the word of God and news of the martyred missionary attracted the avid attention of Nova Scotian John Geddie, a young, newly ordained minister serving the Presbyterian congregations in the Cavendish and New London areas of Prince Edward Island. After almost a decade in Prince Edward Island looking after the rural congregations and proclaiming the need for a Presbyterian overseas mission, by 1846 John Geddie and his wife Charlotte with their two children had ventured twenty thousand miles to the small island of Aneityum, the most southerly island in the New Hebrides archipelago (known as Vanuatu since its independence in 1980). Amid ongoing reports of danger, they initiated and sustained the first colonial Presbyterian foreign mission from Canada.

Rev. Geddie enjoined the people of Cavendish and the New London area to take part in a civilizing project that extended the parameters of their world; it was an evangelical project constructed on "radical alterity,"[5] which called for the salvation of the "heathen" and "savage" others through Presbyterianism. The work of John and Charlotte Geddie was central to the foundation of the mission society in Canada, the opening of the Pacific mission field, major events of conversion, and the commemoration of martyrs. Their evangelical zeal drew other missionaries to New Hebrides, including Prince Edward Islanders who died there.[6] It is my observation that the evangelical legacy and civilizing project that emerged in the Cavendish area had a profound impact on L.M. Montgomery and her first novel.

The Geddies' story adds to our cultural mapping of Cavendish and suggests a certain kind of cosmopolitanism (however narrow) that was fuelled by restlessness, imagination, and the power of words. Introducing Bible-based education, literacy, and a Protestant notion of domesticity was essential to the projects that linked distant islands such as Prince Edward Island and Aneityum, creating global connections and shaping local histories. Montgomery's novel *Anne of Green Gables* emerged from a context that was in some ways already global: Cavendish was connected to places far beyond its boundaries and to evangelical and imperial agendas that encompassed the globe.

Having worked in the South Pacific, I was aware of the legendary Rev. Geddie. However, I had been unaware of his connection to Cavendish until 2006, when I found details in the archives related to his ordination in Cavendish. While researching this paper, I travelled to Aneityum to find out more about the Geddies' mission. I was again surprised to find that the people whom I met there were very familiar with Cavendish, Prince Edward Island. Members of the Presbyterian Church in Aneityum spoke about Cavendish with some reverence as the place where John Geddie was ordained on 13 March 1838. There were traces of the Geddies' presence on the Island: the ruins of the enormous church that they had the islanders build, a printing press rusting near the shore, and a thriving Presbyterianism somewhat under siege from a new wave of Christian evangelicals. Cavendish was indeed famous on the Island of Aneityum: not for L.M. Montgomery and her novels but rather for the Geddies and their mission. And yet this Christian mission, Montgomery, and her most famous novel are linked in important ways.

Scholars since Edward Said, by drawing attention to the profound and lasting effects of colonial discourses, have suggested how imperial practices have influenced literature and print culture.[7] Religion, particularly missionary practices, is also being examined as "a domain through which cultural difference was articulated, ordered and managed under colonial rule."[8] Nicholas Thomas has observed that the various colonial discourses that are still present in popular culture and scholarship continue to shape our ways of thinking and "owe a good deal to the religious and secular antecedents."[9] Reconsideration remains urgent, for, as Thomas rhetorically asks, "Do we not persist in seeing other societies primarily in terms of what they lack?"[10]

Postcolonial critics have called for further investigation of metropolitan-colonial relationships in order to grasp how ideas of cultural difference were construed and circulated.[11] Such perspectives displace reliance on the static images and stereotypes of the colonized and missionized "other" by providing more nuanced accounts of agency and resistance on both sides of the colonial divide. An exploration of how evangelical projects emerged in places such as Cavendish adds new dimensions to our understanding of the missionizing impulses of the nineteenth century and contributes new insights into what Thomas calls "colonialism's cultures." The efforts of the Geddies and their congregations in the Cavendish and New London areas of Prince Edward Island to establish an overseas mission, and their years of mission work in New Hebrides suggest how this "civilizing" project linked the colonized and colonizing communities. The tropes of darkness and light, and the themes of heathenism, primitivism, salvation, conversion, transformation, and domestication were powerful and ubiquitous in the nineteenth century. They circulated in missionary correspondence, sermons, and related texts, informing the everyday experience of people in vastly different places such as New Hebrides and Prince Edward Island. They also surfaced in popular culture such as in the novel *Anne of Green Gables* (see Collins-Gearing, in this volume).

Close examination of what Thomas has called the "radical alterity of the evangelical project"[12] emanating from the Geddies' mission and its origins in the Maritimes illuminates the sense of otherness that circulates in Montgomery's fiction. Alterity does not simply signify difference-as-otherness but rather draws attention to the way it is produced. The "heathenism" of South Seas Islanders became essential to defining what it meant to be Christian and civilized. In *Anne of Green Gables*, the protagonist may be understood to represent the imperial and colonizing child (again, see Collins-Gearing's comments),[13] but at the same time Anne also represents the disturbing "other" in Avonlea. She is an outsider, without place, without parents and, even more important, without religion. In the novel, Rachel Lynde, who ruminates on the dangers of "imported" orphans such as Anne, is also in charge of the Foreign Mission Auxiliary in Avonlea. Her work in the Foreign Mission is a theme that runs throughout the *Anne* series. In *Anne of the Island*, Rachel Lynde complains about the inferior quality of church ministers: "The one we have now is the worst of the lot ... And he says he doesn't believe that all the heathen will be eternally lost. The idea! If they won't all the money we've been giving to the Foreign Mission will be clean wasted."[14] There are resonances between notions of otherness at home and abroad, and therefore it is important to think about how alterity is constituted and transmitted in everyday life through popular culture.

Marilla's discovery that Anne does not know her prayers earns her the designation of "next door to a perfect heathen" and spurs Marilla's efforts to civilize and domesticate her. There is, then, a double valence embedded in the idea of "civilizing Anne" that is threaded throughout the novel.

Feminist scholars have urged readings of the margins for traces of female agency, collusion, and resistance, in order better to understand how gender was constituted in missionary and colonial projects.[15] The introduction of domesticity by missionary wives was a central part of the civilizing project and its social order, which was articulated through race and gender. And yet, women's work in the overseas mission and their work to support missions at home was often effaced. This is evident in the case of the Geddies' mission, where Charlotte Geddie's pivotal work often went unrecognized. Paying attention to the cultivation of domesticity in places such as Aneityum tells us something about women's work at home and abroad. Historian Bronwen Douglas has argued that even conventional texts can yield stories of both "heathen" and Christian women's agencies if read critically and creatively against the grain.[16] Reading *Anne of Green Gables* as a civilizing text reveals Montgomery's own complex and ambivalent relationship toward religion, evident in her endorsement of Presbyterianism and her contrasting resistance to its authoritarianism, rigidity, and narrow interpretations of spirituality.

That the Geddies connected the Cavendish area to the mission on the Island of Aneityum is evident in the following historicized account of Geddies' mission. On a large tablet behind the altar in the Presbyterian Church in Aneityum it is written: "When he [John Geddie] arrived in [New Hebrides] in 1848 there were no Christians, when he left in 1872 there were no heathens." This extraordinary message is also found in the John Geddie Memorial Church in the Cavendish and New London areas of Prince Edward Island, where it is framed and hangs on the church wall. Geddie became known as "the messenger of love,"[17] but the story of the mission and its intersection with other colonial agendas and the people of New Hebrides is much more complex than the straightforward accounts of the Geddies' singular successes. When the mission was established, the people of New Hebrides were depicted as primitive, their savagery necessitating intervention by Europeans to pacify, convert, and civilize them. Thomas has argued that the "hyperbole of the extreme savagery of the natives was mirrored in the absolute char-acter of temporal distancing"[18] between Europeans and "natives." From the social evolutionary perspective popular in the nineteenth century, societies progressed in a linear movement from savage and barbarian to civilized states. In this context Anne could only be "next door to a per-fect heathen," for the South Sea Islanders were the *perfect* "heathens."

Born in Banff, Scotland, in 1815 and brought up in Pictou, Nova Sco-tia, John Geddie had long been fascinated by London Mission Society reports from around the world describing the triumph of the gospel in far-off lands. From his early days, Geddie yoked his own spiritual and psychological well-being to the salvation of the "uncivilized" in distant and dangerous places. Geddie, as his biographer notes, was prone to "seasons of deep depression,"[19] during which he believed himself be-yond the possibility of salvation, a state of being that has been linked to the Calvinist doctrine of predestination. (Interestingly, this melancholia parallels and prefigures that of L.M. Montgomery's husband, Rev. Ewan Macdonald, whom Montgomery married in 1911.) Small of stature, plagued by ill health, given to depression, John Geddie was an unlikely candidate for the rigours of missionary work among South Sea Island-ers who, as noted above, were characterized as violent and intractable to the word of God.

During his first year in the north shore area of Prince Edward Island, Geddie together with his congregations founded Bible and missionary societies, and in 1840 they sent funds to the London Missionary Society for the first time.[20] Geddie's desire to mount a foreign mission from the Canadian Maritimes was strikingly bold at that time, for churches in the British colonies were seeking financial aid for their own work at home. For many, sending missionaries abroad seemed an impossibility. How, with their limited resources, could the small churches such as those of the Cavendish and New London areas and other Maritime congrega-tions field missions in far-off lands? In the winter of 1843, Geddie started publishing a series of letters in *The Presbyterian Banner* "in which he set forth the claims of the heathen upon the Church."[21] He passionately argued his case for a mission from Prince Edward Island: "To undertake a mission to the heathen is our solemn duty and our high privilege. The glory of God, the command of Christ and the reproaches of those who have gone to perdition unwarned, call us to it. With 600,000,000 of immortal souls as my clients, I beg you to arouse yourselves and to take a worthy part in this noble enterprise which seems destined, in the arrangement of God, to be instrumental in achieving the redemption of the world."[22]

While Geddie was attempting to persuade the Presbyterians of Nova Scotia and Prince Edward Island to field a foreign mission, the Baptist churches of the Maritime provinces managed to send out a missionary to Burma as part of the American Baptist Mission there. We can imagine, given what we know about the denominational rivalry that is so well chronicled in Montgomery's novels and journals, that Geddie would have been even more determined to launch colonial Canada's first overseas mission. Rev. George Patterson, in his 1882 *Missionary Life among Cannibals*, describes the behind-the-scenes manoeuvres through which the congregations of Cavendish and those in other parts of Prince Edward Island and Nova Scotia played a pivotal role in creating the foreign mission to the South Seas. Because there was a great deal of opposition to the mission throughout the Maritime colonies, Prince Edward Islanders' unflagging support, including the monetary contributions they pledged very early on, were crucial in Geddie's campaign to sway the Maritime Synod to endorse the mission. Montgomery's relative Alexander Macneill was one of Geddie's key supporters and attended the crucial Synod meeting that took the decision to support the establishment of the mission.[23]

On 30 November 1846 Rev. John and Charlotte Geddie and their two children sailed from Halifax. Rev. Geddie's parting words succinctly capture the representation of South Sea Islanders that informed the mission project and underlined his surrender to the suffering that invariably lay ahead: "We are going forth to those lands where Satan has established his dark domain. I know that suffering awaits me. But to bear the Redeemer's yoke is an honor to one who has felt the Redeemer's love. Now let us to that dark domain."[24]

The worth of missionaries was often measured by the suffering they endured and by the degree of primitivism and savagery they were believed to encounter. These representations also constantly affirmed the difference between "heathens" and Christians, thereby justifying missionary intervention in the lives of others. Thomas has noted that the narratives of particular mission fields dramatized one or two key prac-

tices to signify savagery and heathenism; in the South Seas cannibalism and the low status of women, especially their treatment as beasts
of burden, indexed the savagery of these islands.[25] (This assessment of
women raises questions about what constituted "low status" for women
in the nineteenth-century imagination of the British Empire.)

As Mary Rubio has noted, emphasis on education gave the Scots a
great advantage as colonizers.[26] While Anne has little formal education
before coming to Green Gables, she is, as Marilla concedes, a "teachable
little thing."[27] Later in the novel, as Anne excels at her studies, Marilla
reminds her, "When Matthew and I took you to bring up we resolved
that we would do the best we could for you and give you a good education."[28] Education was an advantage that Geddie exploited in Cavendish, where he first successfully convinced people about the need
for an overseas missions, and later on Aneityum, where education and
literacy were believed to be essential instruments of the civilizing project. The absence of literacy and the reliance on orality were associated
with primitivism, but, even more important, literacy was required for
reading the Bible. The Geddies' privileged education and literacy and
their printing press were pivotal to the success of the mission's work in
converting the Islanders to Christanity. Upon reaching Aneityum, it is
reported, Geddie quickly produced an alphabet and within six weeks
was able to preach in the local language.[29]

From the beginning, Rev. Geddie had scripture translated and circulated, and by 1863 he had translated the entire New Testament into
Aneityumese.[30] In a remarkably short time the Geddies and their assist-
ants created a network of schools with books in the local language and
churches with Bible readings throughout the entire Island. Today in
Vanuatu the terms for school and church are conflated in the Bislama
term *skul*.

The mission in Aneityum did much more than introduce a new religion through education. The mission imposed a whole new worldview
and an infrastructure of institutions that transformed work, leisure,
celebration, worship, and concepts of self and other. According to Jocelyn Linnekin, the Geddies' mission brought two cultures together in
highly asymmetrical ways and the Island of Aneityum was "next door"
to a "Presbyterian theocracy."[31] She argues that the mission was "fero-
ciously hostile to all cultures but [its] own, and to other Christian de-

nominations (not to mention pagans) ... It would be difficult to find a mission with less cultural sensitivity, yet within twelve years Presbyterianism had conquered ... Aneityum."[32] Despite the success of the Geddies' mission, islanders were dying from "contact" diseases such as measles and tuberculosis. Depopulation emerged as a critical issue for Pacific Islanders, who had little resistance to the diseases brought by "outsiders," reflecting a tragic trend among many indigenous peoples around the world.

In the "civilizing" project, educating and making literate stood alongside a parallel goal of domesticating girls. The introduction of "protestant bourgeois domesticity,"[33] the strategy that accompanied conversion, was central to the work of missionaries. Anne McClintock has explained the significance of domesticity: "So often vaunted as involving a naturally occurring, universal space – ensconced within the innermost interiors of society, yet lying theoretically beyond the domain of political analysis – the cult of domesticity involved processes of social metamorphosis and political subjection of which gender is the abiding but not the only dimension."[34] The "cult of domesticity" was key to the civilizing process and the production of docile, disciplined, and useful converts. Great emphasis was placed on reaching women and girls and teaching them how to sew and undertake a variety of domestic tasks. These activities were directly linked to conversion because those who attended church necessarily had to be covered in fabric skirts and blouses rather than local dress, which, to the missionaries, allowed an alarming degree of nakedness.[35] Sewing and sewing circles were a key medium linking the missionary wives such as Charlotte Geddie and the newly converted young girls and women. Clothing and sewing clothes were read as key symbols of Christianity and modernity, and "the sewing circles enclosed women and girls within collective domestic settings to teach useful skills and to discipline unruly female bodies."[36]

In *Anne of Green Gables*, Marilla, in addition to teaching Anne about religion, also emphasizes making her "useful," which entails introducing her to proper disciplined domesticity. Women in the nineteenth century had to make clothing to provide for their families, and it is in this context that Marilla is concerned about Anne's ability to sew.[37] While Anne does not learn to sew clothes, she reluctantly does learn patchwork, and throughout the novel, clothes are a source of contention between

Marilla and Anne, as Jennie MacDonald's essay in this volume illustrates. Clothes index particular struggles about the status of females and the nature of domesticity.

Acquiring religion and attending Sunday school are linked both to proper clothes and to appropriate reading materials in *Anne of Green Gables*. When Marilla asks Matthew, "Will you believe that she never said a prayer in her life till tonight?" she follows with a determined intention: "I'll send to the manse tomorrow and borrow the *Peep of Day* series, that's what I'll do. And she shall go to Sunday school just as soon as I can get some suitable clothes made for her."[38] The *Peep of Day* series that Marilla sees as indispensable to Anne's religious education was written by Favell Lee Mortimer, an English woman married to an evangelical preacher, in the mid-nineteenth century at the height of British imperial power. The series, translated into thirty-eight languages, circulated throughout the British Empire, selling a million copies. Aimed at children, the series charted the dire repercussions of their wayward behaviour in great and morbid detail, while deriding "heathens."[39]

Likewise, domesticity and textuality were linked at home and in the mission. In her many letters home to the Maritimes, Charlotte Geddie described the more intimate realm of the mission project, such as her work with young girls: "I meet with my boarding school girls four afternoons in the week, to teach them sewing. While they are sewing I endeavor to instruct and amuse them, by telling them of the manners, customs &, of my own and other Christian lands; they are always delighted and listen with the greatest attention."[40] We can only imagine the scene, the stories, and how the young listeners in Aneityum construed Cavendish. Charlotte Geddie's descriptions of the peaceful and productive sewing circles provided a dramatic contrast to the women's downtrodden "heathen" status earlier described by the missionaries. Charlotte Geddie's text is one of many descriptions penned for family and friends at home which were reproduced for larger audiences interested in missionary activities. People "at home" were called upon to continue to support the mission and also learned about the South Seas through presentations at churches by missionaries on furlough, as well as church magazines, popular magazines, children's books, and missionary memoirs that presented detailed descriptions of pagan rituals, martyrdom, and accounts of the elevation of the "heathen."[41]

In one of the quotations used as epigraphs to this chapter, Montgomery in *The Alpine Path* notes that she "revelled" in a missionary book displaying the cannibal chiefs, which was one of the few books she was allowed to read on Sundays. Thomas argues that the power of such missionary publications "arises partly because they are constituted not merely as a private archive but a set of publishable texts which conveyed ideas about a place and a social process – namely the story of conversion – to a mass audience."[42] It was such reports that first attracted John Geddie to mission work, and it is also worth noting that Montgomery contributed to Sunday school publications and even considered serializing the text of *Anne of Green Gables* for Sunday school publications after the manuscript was rejected by several publishers.[43]

Jane Haggis and Margaret Allen have offered further insight into these missionary texts: "Given the pervasiveness of this literature, cheap, plentiful and with wide distributional networks through church and most particularly, Sunday schools, it is at least arguable that the 'emotional communities' of the missionary texts and their attendant paraphernalia made a vital contribution to embedding the hierarchies of race as a deep pervasive and taken-for-granted aspect of the imperial and post-imperial imaginary."[44] Missionary and related texts were a particular and ubiquitous genre of writing that provided those at home with powerful representations of the "heathens" who were being pacified and converted. They also fuelled the production of difference and the sense of otherness that informed popular culture such as Montgomery's novels. The question remains as to whether Montgomery aligned the moral purposes of her book with the contents of these publications.

The recognition that Anne does not know how to pray – or, more specifically, does not know how to be a good Presbyterian – is pivotal to Marilla's decision to keep her at Green Gables and to her determined efforts to "save" Anne by making her "useful." Like other such projects, the civilizing project encoded in the novel has curious and unanticipated effects, offering, as Anne would say, "scope for imagination" for troubling conceptualizations of both "heathen" and Christian. The wonder and the magic of Anne is that she softens Marilla's rather joyless and narrow view of religion, offering a view of religion far different from that of the Geddies, which demanded compliance and effected erasures. What becomes clear in Montgomery's novel is that Anne may not have had religion, but she has a vibrant spiritual worldview that is intensely animated and provides a subtle and yet far-ranging critique of the repressive, proselytizing religion integral to the civilizing process. Anne's affinity to nature places her much closer to an indigenous than to a Presbyterian cosmology (once more, see Collins-Gearing and Garner in this volume). Montgomery's classic heroine is unrelenting in subverting unimaginative ideas about prayer, as evident in the following passage: "Why must people kneel down to pray? If I really wanted to pray I'll tell you what I'd do. I'd go out into a great big field all alone or into the deep, deep woods and I'd look up into the sky – up-up-up-up into that lovely blue sky that looks as if there was no end to its blueness. And then I'd just feel a prayer."[45]

Throughout Montgomery's novel and her life-writing there are insights and intimations about missionary life that I read in the context of the Geddies' legendary legacy and missionary culture more generally. Anne's rather dire assessment of the limited marital options of missionaries appears very early on in the novel. Anne tells Matthew on the drive back from the train station to Green Gables: "I'm so homely nobody will ever want to marry me – unless it is a foreign missionary. I suppose a foreign missionary mightn't be very particular."[46] This passage suggests that Montgomery had considerable knowledge of missionaries and the kind of life they offered to wives. There are a number of other references to missions and missionaries in *Anne of Green Gables*. For example, when Anne thinks about her future, she tells Marilla that she is considering becoming a missionary: "That would be very romantic," she says, "but one would have to very good to be a missionary, and that would be a stumbling-block."[47]

Suffering and martyrdom, also key features of the Christian missionary's life, surface as influential ideas early on in Montgomery's life. In 1889, at the age of fifteen, Montgomery presented her first recitation, entitled "The Child Martyr," at the literary concert in the Cavendish hall.[48] Conversion and intense suffering were also the themes of one of her favourite childhood books, *The Memoir of Anzonetta Peters*, which charts the conversion, suffering, and untimely death of a child.[49]

While Anne changes those around her, she, too, changes over the course of the novel. Observing that she had become "much quieter," Marilla remarks to Anne, "You don't chatter half as much as you used to … What has come over you?" to which Anne replies: "I don't know – I don't want to talk as much ... It's nicer to think dear, pretty thoughts and keep them in one's heart, like treasures. I don't like to have them laughed at or wondered over."[50] Anne's intense oral performances and fanciful imaginings become a casualty of the interiority and individualism cultivated by school, religion, and domesticity. The cultivation of the modern and pacified individual displaces the young Anne who cast spells on those around her.

The evangelical Presbyterian project was an essential part of the history and cultural context of Cavendish and provides insight into Montgomery's childhood, her community, and her creativity. It also, as I have argued, shaped the framing of her classic novel. There were, of course, multiple factors that culminated in the crafting of this classic. Scholars have pointed to the importance of Montgomery's religious upbringing and values, and to the importance of popular culture in shaping *Anne of Green Gables*. However, these influences are not mutually exclusive, as religious beliefs, evangelical practices, and popular culture constitute ideas of self and other in complex ways. It is not a question of sacred or secular influences but rather of the dense entanglements that they represent. Shirley Foster and Judy Simons have noted that *Anne of Green Gables* "certainly has lessons to teach,"[51] but they are neither the narrowly religious nor the more narrowly secularized lessons on offer in other such literature.

The intertextuality of Montgomery's novel reveals the influence of the powerful stories that emanated from the Geddies' texts of conversion and transformation of the "heathen." Montgomery's classic novel may be seen as simultaneously upholding and undermining the evangelical project: Montgomery's novel also demonstrates a resistance to standard readings of evangelical Presbyterianism. She allows Anne's agency to flourish and offers alternative perspectives on spirituality, suggesting that conversion and transformation are complex and bring about unanticipated consequences. Anne first bewitches Matthew and then Marilla, saving them as much as they save her. She also transforms Avonlea. The Aneityumese, too, transformed Presbyterianism – indigenizing it, making it their own, and imbuing it with possibilities that their first missionaries, John and Charlotte Geddie, may not have imagined.[52]

While in Aneityum, I discovered that at each full moon a group of women from the island climb the hills to congregate at a beautiful place to pray together for the entire night. Montgomery's fictional heroine Anne, who longed to pray in the open air, would most certainly have recognized this imaginative impulse of the "other islanders" to pray on a mountain at full moon.

## NOTES

1   Montgomery, *The Alpine Path*, 49.
2   Ibid., *Anne of Green Gables*, 76.
3   Rubio, "L.M. Montgomery: Scottish-Presbyterian Agency," 90. For another perspective see White, "The Religious Thought of L.M. Montgomery."
4   Whytock, "Annie and Charlotte Montgomery."
5   Thomas, "Colonial Conversions," 396.
6   George Gordon, a missionary from Prince Edward Island, and his wife, Ellen Powell, were killed in 1861 on Erromango, an island just north of the Aneityum mission. James Gordon, who wrote *The Last Martyr* about his brother, left Prince Edward Island for missionary work in Erromango, where he too died violently.
7   Said, *Orientalism*.
8   Ballantyne, *Religion, Difference, and the Limits*, 429.
9   Thomas, "Colonial Conversions," 389.
10  Ibid.
11  See Bhabha, "The Other Question"; Cooper and Stoler, "Tensions of Empire"; Douglas, "Christian Citizens"; Thomas, "Colonial Conversions"; and Thomas, "The Inversion of Tradition."
12  Thomas, "Colonial Conversions," 396.
13  See also Bradford, "The Homely Imaginary"; Devereux, "Introduction"; and Rubio, "L.M. Montgomery: Scottish-Presbyterian Agency."
14  Montgomery, *Anne of the Island*, 40.
15  See Douglas, "Christian Citizens"; Grewal, *Home and Harem*; Jolly, "'To Save the Girls'"; and Stoler, *Carnal Knowledge*.
16  Douglas, "Christian Citizens," 2.
17  Patterson, *Missionary Life among the Cannibals*. See also Paton, *Missionary to the New Hebrides*.
18  Thomas, "Colonial Conversions," 370.
19  Patterson, *Missionary Life among the Cannibals*, 25.
20  Ibid., 30.
21  Ibid., 34.
22  Harrison, "John Geddie."
23  Patterson, *Missionary Life among the Cannibals*, 34.
24  Harrison, "John Geddie."

25　Thomas, "Colonial Conversions," 373.

26　Rubio, *L.M. Montgomery: Scottish-Presbyterian Agency*, 91.

27　Montgomery, *Anne of Green Gables*, 60.

28　Ibid., 350.

29　Miller, *Misi Gete*.

30　Ibid.

31　Linnekin, "New Political Orders," 199.

32　Ibid.

33　Douglas, "Christian Citizens."

34　McClintock, *Imperial Leather*, 35.

35　Jolly, "'To Save the Girls,'" 127.

36　Douglas, "Christian Citizens," 4.

37　Doody, "Homemade Artifacts and Home Life," 439–40.

38　Montgomery, *Anne of Green Gables*, 76.

39　Pruzan, *The Clumsiest People in Europe*.

40　C. Geddie, *The Letters*, 25.

41　Johnston, *Missionary Writing and Empire*, 3.

42　Thomas, "Colonial Conversions," 371.

43　Montgomery, *Selected Journals*, 1:331.

44　Haggis and Allen, "Imperial Emotions," 693–4.

45　Montgomery, *Anne of Green Gables*, 73. In her first journal Montgomery wrote of a very similar approach to prayer: "To go away … to the heart of some great solemn wood and sit down among the ferns with the companionship of the trees and the wood-winds echoing through the dim moss-hung aisles like the strings of some vast cathedral anthem. And I would stay there for hours alone with nature and my own soul." Montgomery, *Selected Journals*, 1:162.

46　Ibid., *Anne of Green Gables*, 20.

47　Ibid., 277.

48　Ibid., *Selected Journals*, 1:4–5.

49　Ibid., *The Alpine Path*, 50.

50　Ibid., *Anne of Green Gables*, 367.

51　Foster and Simons, *What Katy Read*, 157.

52　Presbyterianism played a pivotal role in the struggle for independence in the 1970s.


## BIBLIOGRAPHY

Ballantyne, Tony. "Religion, Difference, and the Limits of British Imperial History." *Victorian Studies* (spring 2005): 427–55.

Bhabha, Homi. "The Other Question: Difference, Discrimination and the Discourse of Colonialism." In *Literature, Politics and Theory*, edited by Francis

Barker, Peter Hulme, Margaret Iversen, and Diana Loxely, 147–72. London: Methuen, 1986.

Bradford, Clare. "The Homely Imaginary: Fantasies of Nationhood in Australian and Canadian Texts." In *Home Words: Discourses of Canadian's Literature in Canada*, edited by Mavis Reimer, 177–94. Waterloo, Ontario: Wilfrid Laurier University Press, 2008.

Cooper, Fredrick, and Anne Laura Stoler. *Tensions of Empire: Colonial Cultures in a Bourgeois World*. Berkeley: University of California Press, 1997.

Devereux, Cecily. Introduction to *Anne of Green Gables*, by L.M. Montgomery, 12–38. Peterborough, Ontario: Broadview Press, 2004.

Doody, Margaret. "Homemade Artifacts and Home Life." In *The Annotated Anne of Green Gables*, Edited by Wendy E. Barry, Margaret Anne Doody, and Mary E. Doody Jones, 438–42. New York: Oxford University Press, 1997.

Douglas, Bronwen. "Christian Citizens: Women and Negotiations of Modernity in Vanuatu." *The Contemporary Pacific*, vol. 14 (2002): 1–38.

Foster, Shirley, and Judy Simons. *What Katy Read: Feminist Re-Readings of "Classic" Stories for Girls*. Iowa: Universtiy of Iowa Press, 1995.

Geddie, Charlotte, and Charlotte Geddie Harrington. *Letters of Charlotte Geddie and Charlotte Geddie Harrington*. Truro, Nova Scotia: News Publishing Company, 1908.

Gordon, James D. *The Last Martyrs of Erromango: Being a Memoir of the Rev. George N. Gordon, and Ellen Catherine Powell, His Wife*. Nabu Press, 2010.

Grewal, Inderpal. *Home and Harem: Nation, Gender, Empire and the Cultures of Travel*. Durham: Duke University Press, 1996.

Haggis, Jane, and Margaret Allen. "Imperial Emotions: Affective Communities of Mission in British Protestant Women's Missionary Publications c. 1880–1920." *Journal of Social History* (2008): 691–716.

Harrison, Eugene Myers. "John Geddie, 1815–1872: Messenger of the Love of Christ in Eastern Melanesia." http://www.wholesomewords.org/missions/igeddie.html (accessed 20 December 2011).

Johnston, Anna. *Missionary Writing and Empire, 1800–1860*. Cambridge, UK: Cambridge University Press, 2003.

Jolly, Margaret. "'To Save the Girls for Brighter and Better Lives': Presbyterian Missions and Women in the South of Vanuatu 1848–1870." *The Journal of Pacific History*, vol. 26 (1991): 27–48.

Linnekin, Jocelyn. "New Political Orders." In *The Cambridge History of the Pacific Islanders*, edited by Donald DeNoon, 185–216. Cambridge, UK: Cambridge University Press, 1997.

McClintock, Anne. *Imperial Leather: Race, Gender and Sexuality in the Colonial Contest*. New York: Routledge, 1995.

Miller, R.S., ed. *Misi Gete: Pioneer Missionary to the New Hebrides*. Launceston: Presbyterian Church of Tasmania, 1975.

Montgomery, L.M. *The Alpine Path: The Story of My Career*. Don Mills, Ontario: Fitzhenry & Whiteside, 1975.

– *Anne of the Island*. New York: Bantam Books, 1979.

– *Anne of Green Gables*. New York: Aladdin Classics, 2001.

– *The Selected Journals of L.M. Montgomery*. Vol. 1, 1889–1910; Vol. 2, 1920–1921; Vol. 3, 1921–1929. Edited by Mary Rubio and Elizabeth Waterston. Toronto: Oxford University Press, 1985; 1987; 1992.

Mortimer, F.I. *The Peep of Day (Family Devotional Guide to Bible)*. Whitefish, Montana: Kessinger Publishing, 2004.

Paton, John G. *Missionary to the New Hebrides: An Autobiography*. Adamant Media Corporation, 2001.

Patterson, George. *Missionary Life Among Cannibals: Being the Life of the Rev. John Geddie*. Toronto: James Campbell and Son, 1882.

Pruzan, Todd. *The Clumsiest People in Europe: or, Mrs. Mortimer's Bad Tempered Guide to the Victorian World*. New York: Bloomsbury, 2006.

Rubio, Mary. "L.M. Montgomery: Scottish-Presbyterian Agency in Canadian Culture." In *L.M. Montgomery and Canadian Culture*, edited by Irene Gammel and Elizabeth R. Epperly, 89–105. Waterloo, Ontario: Wilfrid Laurier University Press, 2001.

Said, Edward W. *Orientalism*. New York: Vintage, 1979.

Stoler, Anne. *Carnal Knowledge and Imperial Power: Race and the Intimate Colonial Rule*. Berkeley: University of California Press, 2002.

Thomas, Nicholas. "Colonial Conversions: Difference, Hierarchy, and History in Early Twentieth-century Evangelical Propaganda." *Comparative Studies in Society and History*, vol. 34 (1992): 336–89.

– "The Inversion of Tradition." *American Ethnologist*, vol. 19 (1992): 213–32.

White, Gavin. "The Religious Thought of L.M. Montgomery." In *Harvesting Thistles: The Textual Garden of L.M. Montgomery*, edited by Mary Rubio, 84–8. Guelph, Ontario: Canadian Children's Press, 1994.

Whytock, Jack C. "Annie and Charlotte Montgomery: Teachers and Evangelists in Persia." Unpublished manuscript. 1–18. http://www.csph.ca/papers/CSPH/2011 - Jack Whytock - draft.pdf (accessed on 10 July 2012).

# Narrating the "Classic" on Stolen Ground:
## *Anne of Green Gables*

BROOKE COLLINS-GEARING

With its one hundred years of continuous publication, its translations into numerous languages, its worldwide readers, and the scholarly engagement that continues to surround it, *Anne of Green Gables*
epitomizes the status of classic. Such popularity, in both Western and
non-Western cultures, raises questions about the appeal of a text in
which embedded constructions of home, nationality, childhood, and
land continue to exclude readers from diasporic identities, such as First
Nations peoples. *Anne of Green Gables* and the literary critical tradition
that surrounds it have embodied ideas and processes of identity formation constructed from European and Euro-American colonizers. This
paper will discuss how the idea of the children's classic has been built
on possessing stolen land to construct an identity of national belonging,
place, and history that excludes colonized subjectivities. My purpose is
to dismantle the ways in which *Anne of Green Gables* is bound by and
reinscribes colonizing discourses – not only in historical context but
for today's readers – and, in doing so, to attempt to make these discourses visible.[1]

Margaret Zeegers has said: "Marginalisation can be understood as
being a result of particular constructions of subjectivities through dis-
cursive practices which make invisible certain subjects and subject positions and what is more, they normalise that invisibility. Normalisation
can be understood as a process within power relations that constructs
that which is being marginalised and that which is being privileged as
being beyond question, as part of being a natural state of affairs."[2] The
voices that we hear speaking about *Anne of Green Gables* contribute
to the construction of what is marginalized and what is privileged. To
make visible the ways in which the text and the discourses surround-

ing it ignore its positioning on Mi'kmaq land, its "taken-for-granted" exclusionary devices need to be revealed. To do this, I will use an Indigenous decolonizing analysis of the text, which dismantles early twentieth-century colonial power, revealing the entrenched dominance of colonization today.

In line with the decolonizing methodology of bell hooks, I hope that the text, while maintaining its original appeal and status, can also be seen to offer alternative reading approaches and to include traditionally unacknowledged potential readers by critiquing the status quo: "It is also about transforming the image, creating alternatives, asking ourselves questions about what types of images subvert, pose critical alternatives, and transform our world views and move us away from dualistic thinking about good and bad. Making a space for the transgressive image, the outlaw rebel vision, is essential to any effort to create a context from transformation. And even then little progress is made if we transform images without shifting paradigms, changing perspectives, ways of looking."[3] It is neither my intention, nor my right, to attempt to speak on behalf of First Nations peoples, in particular Mi'kmaq nations; I hope, rather, to address decolonizing strategies that force into visibility normalization processes that centre and privilege Western perspectives.

I am drawn to these questions by my own experience and identity. I grew up in Kamilaroi country in northern New South Wales, Australia. My parents never hid from us that we had Aboriginal heritage, but we also didn't easily identify as Indigenous. It was only when I left the small racially tense and historically segregated town I grew up in (to go to university in a much larger regional city) that I began to understand the effects of colonization, dispossession, and assimilation on many Indigenous peoples and communities. As an undergraduate and postgraduate, I was trained and supported by the Indigenous community on campus. And although my PhD was officially in English, I crossed physical and disciplinary boundaries to move between Aboriginal Studies and literature.

I first read *Anne of Green Gables* when I was a young child. But it wasn't until my sister tried to tell me, back in the early 1990s, that she believed we were very distant relations to Scottish Macneills from Nova Scotia (my mother's maiden name is McNeill) that I reread the book. By this stage, my feelings toward it were mixed. When the editors of this volume asked me to contextualize my relationship with *Anne of Green Gables*, my subjectivity, and my association with the text, I was worried – almost as worried as the day I stood at the podium in 2008, on Mi'kmaq land, to address a massive room full of Montgomery fans, friends, and followers about how this classic text with its century-long history was built on stolen land. The following quotation by Montgomery articulates a relationship with the land that I include here to help me articulate my relationship with the text:

> Peace! You never know what peace is until you walk on the shores
> or in the fields or along the winding red roads of Abegweit on a
> summer twilight when the dew is falling and the old, old stars are
> peeping out and the sea keeps its nightly tryst with the little land
> it loves. You find your soul then ... you realize that youth is not
> a vanished thing but something that dwells forever in the heart.
> And you look around on the dimming landscape of haunted hill
> and long sand-white beach and murmuring ocean, on homestead
> lights and old fields tilled by dead and gone generations who
> loved them – and even if you are not Abegweit-born, you will say,
> "Why ... I have *come home!*"[4]

In Montgomery's use of the word "Abegweit," an anglicization of one of the Mi'kmaq names for what is now called Prince Edward Island, voices of the dispossessed can faintly be heard. While Montgomery's love of the land is undeniable, I could not help but struggle with the notion of a peaceful home for one group of people depending on the dispossession of another. The "dead and gone generations" include not only Anglo-Abegweit-born people, but generations of Mi'kmaq too. When I now reread *Anne* and note the themes of the renaming and reclaiming of land, place, and space, I wonder how contemporary Mi'kmaq people feel about this canonical text. In attempting to challenge contemporary Western discourses of belonging and ownership, I want to understand the need to authenticate a "white" belonging to place. With my own ancestry and culture being a tangled, hybrid, tense, and uneasy mix of the Indigenous/colonized and the European/colonizer, *Anne of Green Gables* represents to me not only the power of white possession of the land but also the imagined belonging to that land that is shared and loved by so many. In relation to narratives that naturalize "settler" voices, the only certainty I have at the moment is that the voices of the dispossessed need to be heard too. We are reminded that postcolonialism is not just a linear temporal framework within which colonialism is a product of the past; rather, we must engage with its continuities and the power inequities that related to the ongoing "control and containment of many Indigenous peoples" in Canada that Cecily Devereux has discussed.[5]

The colonial grand narrative attempted to mask and silence the presence of First Nations peoples. Daniel N. Paul explains how Africans and First Nations peoples were demonized by European and Euro-American colonizers because of dominant ethnocentric attitudes, especially in Anne Shirley's birthplace of Nova Scotia: "Because of the way it badly mistreated both the Mi'kmaq and the Africans, Nova Scotia has been deemed by many as among the most racially discriminatory jurisdictions on the continent."[6] *Anne of Green Gables* allows an insight into the pervasiveness of colonizing national tendencies of the time, which can be traced into the twenty-first century. The narrative's lack of any acknowledgment or awareness of a non-Western civilization and history of the land is a result of the colonizing intent to silence, deny, and exclude. Clare Bradford makes a pertinent comment: "Dominant discourses can always be contested by alternative, questioning voices, and many texts, even those produced in the heyday of colonialism, exhibit ambivalence and uncertainty about imperialism. Thus, the argument that writers merely reproduce the ideologies of their time and place is far too deterministic, treating writers simply as transcribers of cultural norms."[7] *Anne of Green Gables* has been praised for the many ways in which it not only questioned dominant white Canadian society but contributed to it as well.

A discerning, extraordinary reader might find that as a beloved nation-child, Anne possesses the power to either perpetuate colonizing discourses or provide an insight into how they are constructed and presented. The book describes some excluded peoples and types explicitly. Marilla, for instance, says:

> There's never anybody to be had but those stupid, half-grown little French boys, and as soon as you do get one broke into your ways and taught something he's up and off to the lobster canneries or the States. At first Matthew suggested getting a "Home" boy. But I said "no" flat to that. "They may be all right – I'm not saying they're not – but no London street Arabs for me," I

said. "Give me a native born at least." There'll be a risk, no matter who we get. But I'll feel easier in my mind and sleep sounder at nights if we get a born Canadian.[8]

The "native" Canadian is not here a First Nations member but rather an Anglo-European, white Canadian. Arun Mukherjee argues: "But being just 'Canadian' is a privilege only white people enjoy ... It is we non-whites who are seen as deviants from the norm ... I am always conscious of being non-white and how that fact determines my whole life experience."[9] While Anne might wrestle with the confines of her social position and gender, she has no need to question or even consider her "race." The characters of Jerry Buote, Mary Joe, and the German Jew (peddler) signify recognition of cultural and ethnic difference, and cultural and ethnic inferiority, cementing the colonial enterprise. (Their language, as Caroline Jones explains in this volume, also is a signifier of class difference.) Anne and her fellow Canadians situate themselves comfortably within the centre of a white, nationalist identity and maintain "a particular vision of the English-Canadian nation as a racially constituted community, a branch of the imperial racial organization of 'Saxondom.'"[10] To borrow from Fredric Jameson, the political unconscious is complete:[11] absence, silence, and denial are the colonial solution to First Nations presence. The idea of being "native," of belonging to place and therefore innately possessing certain national qualities, has left no space for the first "natives" of Canadian soil.

Irene Gammel speaks to the complexity of this political unconsciousness: "When it came to the domains of temperance, prohibition, Sunday school, politics, suffrage, culture, and race, emotions ran high, and sometimes Maud, a creature of her own upbringing, was guilty of the same prejudices that she would mock in her fiction."[12] While my intention is not to establish dichotomies of innocence and guilt in colonizing practices, it is apparent that the narrative, while also contributing to the construction of Canadian children's literature, perpetuated and maintained certain colonizing discourses. As clearly outlined by Gammel, the text "satirizes the parochial xenophobia of Mrs. Lynde, who assumes orphans will bring mayhem and destruction to Green Gables. According to Mrs. Lynde, the foreign orphan may suck eggs, or poison the well with strychnine. Yet the novel's humour also relies on some of its own cultural stereotyping, for example, concerning the Italians ... the Jewish people ... and the Irish."[13] The ability and power of the characters of Avonlea to gaze at, judge, and present "other" peoples is heightened by their racial power to simply overlook and fail to see or acknowledge the First Nations peoples of Canada.[14] Racial hegemony is naturalized in the text: representations of what is acceptable and the norm, of who belongs to the centre and what knowledge is valued, are "managed through Eurocentric normative ideals."[15]

From the moment the text opens with the image of Rachel Lynde sitting at her window, keeping watch over the business of Avonlea, the power of the colonial gaze is apparent: "not even a brook could run past Mrs. Rachel Lynde's door without due regard for decency and decorum."[16] The implication is that the land has been tamed by the qualities of the Euro-American society that views place and space through a colonialist lens, determining who is included and excluded. Clare Bradford argues that strategies of elision and romanticization "enact a repression of memory concerning colonization, a manifestation of what Freud and Lacan describe as *Verdrangung*, the process of censoring and so forgetting a painful past redolent with violence and conflict."[17]

Anne's ability to read her landscape, to create meaning from it, and to develop her identity around local sites creates a map of nationality within the text. The narrative's emphasis on local, regional, and national importance strengthens (white) Canadian nationalism and patriotism, while also inverting (white) Canadian history and presence. The need to create meaning from the land, to develop a sense of belonging and history for local place and knowledge, also inadvertently reveals the colonizer's need to deny that which is already developed and present. Charlotte Cote employs Homi Bhabha and Tom Nairn's examination of modern nations as Janus-faced constructions: "That is, on the one hand, they claim to speak for all those within their borders but, at the same time, they suppress those voices that do not adapt to, or assimilate into, the nation's dominant culture."[18]

Montgomery's description of "her" island inscribes these attitudes. Her love of place reveals a national attachment to place, but it also exposes non-Indigenous indoctrination into colonizing societal, cultural, and historical purposes:

> It is the sea which makes Prince Edward Island in more senses than the geographical. You cannot get away from the sea down there. Save for a few places in the interior. It is ever visible somewhere, if only in a tiny blue gap between distant hills, or a

turquoise gleam through the dark boughs of spruce fringing an estuary. Great is our love for it; its tang gets into our blood: its siren call rings ever in our ears; and no matter where we wander in our lands afar, the murmur of its waves ever summons us back in our dreams to the homeland. For few things am I more thankful than for the fact that I was born and bred beside that blue St. Lawrence Gulf.[19]

Montgomery's use of "*our* lands" (my italics) is symptomatic of a history of colonization that pervades twentieth-century colonial (that is, non–First-Nations) representations of land, place, and belonging. It excludes any acknowledgment of previous or contemporaneous Mi'kmaq owners and perpetuates colonizing discourses of denial, which are clearly signified by the ability of both the colonizers, and then later Anne, to rename and claim land.

During their trip "home," Matthew and Anne pass through the "Avenue," which Anne claims anew as the "White Way of Delight." The colonial ability to map and claim land relied on the denial of Indigenous occupation of, and association with, land, while the power to rename emphasized the colonialist desire to transform and cultivate. "The 'Avenue,' so called by the Newbridge people, was a stretch of road four or five hundred yards long, completely arched over with huge, wide-spreading apple trees, planted years ago by an eccentric old farmer. Overhead was one long canopy of snowy, fragrant bloom. Below the boughs the air was full of a purple twilight and far ahead a glimpse of painted sunset sky shone like a great rose window at the end of a cathedral aisle."[20] The Newbridge people's naming of the "Avenue" excludes pre-existing Mi'kmaq knowledge and naming of the land. The wide-spreading apple trees were planted by a farmer years ago, and imply both a cultivation of the land by and an associated history for the colonialists. And the resemblance of the viewscape to a cathedral focuses the reader's gaze through specific cultural allusions. Gammel has argued that these are also an example of how Montgomery's double discourse works – that there is an overt conventional discourse and a more subversive discourse that challenges the status quo: she states that that Anne's multi-sensory engagement with the landscape (rather than the expected "Kantian 'disinterested' aesthetic engagement") allows the reader to employ an "ecological aesthetic or embodied landscape aesthetic."[21] However, both methods of surveying the landscape rely on a colonialist lens to organize, understand, and define land according to Western notions of beauty, cultivation, and value.

During a later incident in which Anne meets Diana for the first time in the Barrys' garden, Gammel argues, while Anne is too preoccupied to "deconstruct the garden as a cultured space of delineated boundaries" to open it "as a multi-sensuous nature landscape,"[22] it is still a cultivated, constructed, colonial garden – not the natural landscape. It is hard not to attach Anne's naming of "The White Way of Delight" to the notion that "white" is right. The only natural, "untouched" landscape, perhaps closest to its pre-colonized state, is the forest of "The Haunted Wood," which can strike fear into young (white) hearts and that Anne imagines is full of "otherness."

Recent theory of children's literature has examined the ways in which literature for children positions and constructs the idea of the child as both the colonized subject and the future colonizer. Such criticism, while acknowledging the parallel objectification of the child and the "other" (both inexperienced and in need of educational and social guidance), often fails to include the continued colonizing influence of this literature; that is, the historical experiences of colonization are overlooked in favour of often-romanticized and Western-valued experiences and qualities. The purpose of children's literature was, and commonly still is, to instruct and prepare future colonizers for their place in a national identity and history. As Bradford argues, "Such a combination of discourses, in which colonial tensions co-exist with the imperative of socialising children readers, makes for a peculiarly potent mix of ideologies."[23] The child remains positioned as both powerful and powerless. He or she represents the potential that the (white) nation aspires to, while also remaining constrained by the experience and knowledge of the adult. "What good would she be to us?" Marilla asks Matthew soon after Anne's arrival, to which Matthew responds, "We might be some good to her."[24] Later Marilla admits that she sees the need to keep the child Anne as "a sort of duty," finally stating that she will "make it [her] business to see she's trained to be [useful]."[25]

Included in Marilla's idea of becoming useful is an education. Western notions of getting an education to signify awareness and growth are implicit throughout the text. For Anne, education provides opportunity: her ability to wield the English language is perceived as a tool for empowerment. For the traditional occupants of the land, the arrival of the English language and the attached institution of Western education was a tool of disempowerment, as Paul instructs: "Although available on paper, education was all but denied until recent times [to First Nations peoples]. This unwritten requirement of White society – 'You may have an education, but only if you agree to assimilate and accept the eventual extrication of your culture' – plus the racism encountered by students attending White schools made an education practically unattainable. Mi'kmaq children were forbidden to speak their language at schools and discouraged to do so in many other public places."[26] The process of colonization also strongly involves the colonizer's belief in the need to Christianize and civilize the "natives." First Nations Canadians have been presented, defined, and acknowledged by the colonizers according to Western ideas of religion, spirituality, and civilization. In *Anne of Green Gables* the "colonized" subject, that is the (White) child Anne, is enabled not only to question but to subvert the restraints of institutionalized religion. The narrative continues to emphasize the "parallels" between the (white) child and the primitive "man," by allowing the child – with her innocence and imagination, her communication with nature – to feel a spirituality that is evoked by nature, rather than by the Church and what it represents. It is telling that such "heathen" beliefs were not allowed among the "heathens," regardless of their apparent knowledge and spirituality.

In response to Anne's critiques of a church service, "Marilla felt helplessly that all this should be sternly reproved, but she was hampered by the undeniable fact that some of the things Anne had said, especially about the minister's sermons and Mr. Bell's prayers, were what she herself had really thought deep down in her heart for years, but had never given expression to. It almost seemed to her that those secret, unuttered, critical thoughts had suddenly taken visible and accusing shape and form in the person of this outspoken morsel of neglected humanity."[27] Anne is further positioned as the colonized child: she speaks from a repressed subject position, but in doing so she speaks for a potential and intended national identity and future nationalist readers.

The subversive elements of the text that critics such as Gammel have noted need to be dismantled even further to reveal how the colonialist gaze can be inverted to make visible the discourses of normalization. Anne explains her time at the asylum by expressing her empathetic relationship with the "orphan trees," yet the same sense of displacement could be extended to First Nations and Acadian subjectivities:

I just love trees. And there weren't any at all about the asylum,
only a few poor weeny-teeny things out in front with little
whitewashed cagey things about them. They just looked like
orphans themselves, those trees did. It used to make me want
to cry to look at them. I used to say to them, "Oh, you poor
little things! If you were out in a great big wood with other trees
all around you and little mosses and Junebells growing over
your roots and a brook not far away and birds singing in your
branches, you could grow, couldn't you. But you can't where you
are. I know just exactly how you feel little trees." I felt sorry to
leave them behind this morning.[28]

Genevieve Wiggins articulates Anne's position: "She is the rebel, the
nonconformist, the independent spirit who appeals to the child reader
who chafes at adult strictures or to the adult who sometimes feels re-
stricted by society's expectations."[29] If we apply a decolonizing approach,
however, the idea that Anne is a nonconformist, rebel, and independent spirit needs to be understood within the framework of colonizing
discourses. She can only rebel and resist conformity according to, and
as allowed by, imperial, Western, and colonial power. The centre from
which Anne rebels remains the centre. The independence Anne reveals
is independence allowed only to someone of her race, gender, and cultural positioning. If we are then to consider the intended reader Wiggins
mentions, to what extent does this readership or perceived readership
include – even allow for – First Nation Canadians? The intended reader
of *Anne of Green Gables*, at the beginning of the 1900s, would have been
very much defined by colonization and imperial discourses – whether
the reader was Canadian or not, the assumed, implied, intended reader
was never First Nations Canadian.

As we proceed into the twenty-first century, can First Nations readers now be included? Can Anne's experiences of confinement, restraint,
and non-conformity be correlated with the actual experiences of the
colonized? Gammel argues that "Green Gables was built on national,
literary, and aesthetic ideals of home that would resonate with readers
who felt uprooted in a modern world of flux. That tension could be felt
underneath the peaceful surroundings of Green Gables."[30] What does it
mean to extend that tension to now include, acknowledge a space for,
and listen to what resonates with First Nation presences and readers?

I return to Montgomery's evocative descriptions of place:

Sometimes I have thought it was the touch of austerity in an
Island landscape that gives it a peculiar charm. And whence
comes that austerity? Is it in the dark dappling of spruce and
fir? Is it in the glimpses of sea and river? Is it in the bracing tang
of the salt air? Or does it go deeper still, down to the very soul
of the land? For lands have personalities just as well as human
beings; and to know that personality you must live in the land and
companion it, and draw sustenance of body and spirit from it; so
only can you really know a land and be known of it.[31]

The respect and love for the land apparent in Montgomery's quotation
as well as in the narrative of *Anne of Green Gables* are examples of the
colonizing struggle to appropriate and possess Indigenous land that excludes Indigenous presence, yet at the same time emphasizes a "native"
connection to it. In this effort to "possess their homeland imaginatively"[32] non–First Nations Canadians claimed the landscape physically
and attached meaning to it in much the same way that Anne reads and
possesses her landscape.

Imagination and landscape shape the character of Anne, the construction of Green Gables, the narrative, and the intended reader.
Anne's need to name, rename, translate, and transform frames the
narrative. Throughout the text, Anne's ability to "read" the countryside
contributes to her characterization, as well as to the depiction of nation,
place, and identity. Her positioning in society as an orphan female (not
lower class) child allows her to be both the imperial child and the colonial child. She retains the power to name, translate, and transform her
landscapes, but she is also located as a site of naming, translation, and
transformation.

Marilla says of Anne, "Matthew Cuthbert, it's about time somebody
adopted that child and taught her something. She's next door to a perfect heathen. Will you believe that she never said a prayer in her life
till tonight? ... I foresee that I shall have my hands full. Well, well, we
can't get through this world without our share of trouble. I've had a
pretty easy life of it so far, but my time has come at last and I suppose
I'll just have to make the best of it."[33] Marilla describes Anne as a site
of colonial expansion, and the narrative reminds us of ideologies of the
time that described the child as closer to nature (which is also where the

"primitive" was positioned) and therefore also in need of civilizing and Christianizing. The need to protect and control First Nations peoples involved policies and processes of "civilizing," "Christianizing," absorbing, and assimilating:[34] the imperial understanding was that Indigenous peoples were childlike and in need of the colonizers' guidance. Anne is empowered to see, name, and claim the landscape because she is a white child endowed with the qualities of imagination and innocence. Jacqueline Rose argues that the concept of childhood innocence relates to the idea of timelessness, "an older form of culture (nature or oral tradition), but the effect of this is that this same form of culture is infantilised. At this level, children's fiction has a set of long established links with colonialism which identified the new world with the infantile state of men."[35] The (white) child is treated and constructed like a primitive, "as a subject-in-formation, an individual who often does not have full legal status and who therefore acts or who is acted against in ways that are not perceived to be fully consequential."[36] The child/primitive trope reveals colonial instability: there is a need to conquer and control, but at the same time there is a need to appropriate and mimic that which is conquered and controlled. Anne has the power to read the landscape in ways that adults cannot – she is the imperial child who can conquer and control; yet at the same time, she is restrained and controlled by societal expectations influenced by gender, class, age, and education. The narrative becomes a colonialist lens for the "real" reader: it clears the landscape of any Indigenous presence and, through the gaze of the imaginative white child, claims and locates a sense of belonging to place.

As a white child, Anne, represents imperialist values while also emphasizing colonial difference. The narrative upholds children's literary frameworks and conventions of the time while also emphasizing the "national" – specifically, local and regional uniqueness. The narrative often aligns the child with the expectation that children remain indoors, while outdoors the spirit of adventure and the imagination run free. In *Anne of Green Gables* landscape is a potential *tabula rasa*. It is perceived through the colonial gaze as empty, young, and lacking in history, but therefore available for manipulation – some would say for Christianizing and civilizing. However, the land was not empty and devoid of history; it was not young and devoid of civilization. The countryside that Anne and those around her claimed as theirs and their nation's had long, complex, and intricate histories.

While *Anne of Green Gables* represents the local landscape, the text also creates it, transforms it, and attaches meaning to it. The relationship between landscape, spirituality, and imagination in the narrative establishes local/national identity and history as the lens through which colonial meaning is viewed. Mavis Reimer writes: "privilege is reproduced in and by children's literature and one of the terms through which privilege is discursively encoded is that of imagination, a notion closely aligned both with children and with fiction itself."[37] While Anne's scope for imagination is privileged and cements her power within the colonial and imperial centre, *Anne of Green Gables* and its power over the national imaginary needs to be revisited and reinterpreted, so that its established social and cultural paradigms are also read with a discerning eye and the awareness that colonizing mindsets can continue to manifest into the twenty-first century.

## NOTES

1   A version of this paper was presented at the 2008 conference "L.M. Montgomery and the Idea of the Classic" in Charlottetown, Prince Edward Island. I acknowledge the traditional custodians of the land on which the paper was presented, the Mi'kmaq people and their descendants. I also thank the Australian Academy of Humanities for the fellowship that enabled me to attend the conference.

2   Zeegers, "Cultural Explorations," 140.

3   hooks, *Black Looks*, 3–4. Linda Tuhiwahi Smith's *Decolonizing Methodology* is also essential to this paper's understanding of decolonization.

4   Montgomery, "Prince Edward Island," 19.

5   Devereux, "Are We There Yet?," 184.

6   Paul, *We Were Not the Savages*, 257.

7   Bradford, *Reading Race*, 20.

8   Montgomery, *Anne of Green Gables*, 7.

9   Mukherjee, "The 'Race Consciousness,'" 10.

10   Devereux, "'Canadian Classic' and 'Commodity Export,'" 12.

11   See Jameson, *The Political Unconscious*.

12   Gammel, *Looking for Anne*, 124.

13   Ibid., 130.

14   Petzold, "Multiculturalisms in Canadian Children's Books," 178. See also Paul, *We Were Not the Savages*, 50.

15   Saldanha, "Bedtime Stories," 265.

16   Montgomery, *Anne of Green Gables*, 1.

17 Bradford, "The Homely Imaginary."
18 Cote, "Historical Foundations of Indian Sovereignty," 15.
19 Montgomery, *The Alpine Path*, 11.
20 Ibid., *Anne of Green Gables*, 21.
21 Gammel, "Embodied Landscape Aesthetics," 228–47.
22 Ibid., 234–6.
23 Bradford, "Saved by the Word," 89.
24 Montgomery, *Anne of Green Gables*, 57.
25 Ibid., 57–8.
26 Paul, *We Were Not the Savages*, 258.
27 Montgomery, *Anne of Green Gables*, 98.
28 Ibid., 19.
29 Wiggins, *L.M. Montgomery*, 26.
30 Gammel, *Looking for Anne*, 138.
31 Montgomery, *The Alpine Path*, 11.
32 Gammel, *Looking for Anne*, 167.
33 Montgomery, *Anne of Green Gables*, 63.
34 Paul, *We Were Not the Savages*, 61.
35 Rose, *The Case of Peter Pan*, 50.
36 Slemon and Wallace, "Into the Heart of Darkness?" 20.
37 Reimer, "Making Princesses," 13.

## BIBLIOGRAPHY

Bradford, Clare. "The Homely Imaginary: Fantasies of Nationhood in Australian and Canadian Texts." In *Home Words: Discourses of Children's Literature in Canada*, edited by Mavis Reimer, 177–94. Waterloo, Ontario: Wilfrid Laurier University Press, 2008.

– *Reading Race: Aboriginality in Children's Literature*. Carlton South: Melbourne University Press, 2001.

– "Saved by the Word: Textuality and Colonization in Nineteenth-Century Australian Texts for Children." In McGillis, *Voices of the Other*, 89–110.

Cote, Charlotte. "Historical Foundations of Indian Sovereignty in Canada and the United States: A Brief Overview." *The American Review of Canadian Studies* (spring/summer 2001): 15.

Devereux, Cecily. "Are We There Yet? Reading the 'Post-Colonial' and The Imperialist in Canada." In *Is Canada Postcolonial?: Unsettling Canadian Literature*, edited by Laura Moss, 177–89. Waterloo, Ontario: Wilfrid Laurier University Press, 2003.

– "'Canadian Classic' and 'Commodity Export': The Nationalism of 'Our' Anne of Green Gables." *Journal of Canadian Studies* vol. 36.1 (spring 2001): 11–28.

Gammel, Irene. "Embodied Landscape Aesthetics in *Anne of Green Gables*." *The Lion and the Unicorn*, vol. 34:2 (2010): 228–47.

– *Looking for Anne: How Lucy Maud Montgomery Dreamed Up a Literary Classic*. Ontario: Key Porter, 2008.

hooks, bell. *Black Looks: Race and Representation*. Toronto: Between the Lines, 1992.

Jameson, Fredric. *The Political Unconscious: Narrative as a Socially Symbolic Act*. Ithaca, New York: Cornell University Press, 1981.

McGillis, Roderick, ed. *Voices of the Other: Literature and the Postcolonial Context*. New York: Garland, 2000.

Montgomery, L.M. *The Alpine Path: The Story of My Career*. Halifax: Nimbus, 2005.

– *Anne of Green Gables*. New York: Penguin, 1994.

– "Prince Edward Island." In *The Spirit of Canada, A Souvenir of Welcome to H.M. King George VI and H.M. Queen Elizabeth*, 16–19. Canadian Pacific Railway, 1939.

Mukherjee, Arun. "The 'Race Consciousness' of a South Asian (Canadian, of Course) Female Academic." In *Talking about Identity: Encounters in Race, Ethnicity and Language*, edited by C.E. James and A. Shadd, 212–18. Toronto: Between the Lines, 2001.

Paul, Daniel N. *We Were Not the Savages: A Mi'kmaq Perspective on the Collision between European and Native American Civilizations*. Halifax: Fernwood, 2000.

Petzold, Dieter. "Multiculturalisms in Canadian Children's Books: The Embarrassment of History." In McGillis, *Voices of the Other*, 177–92.

Reimer, Mavis. "Making Princesses, Remaking *A Little Princess*." In McGillis, *Voices of the Other*, 111–34.

Rose, Jacqueline. *The Case of Peter Pan, or the Impossibility of Children's Literature*. London: Macmillan, 1984.

Saldanha, Louise. "Bedtime Stories: Canadian Multiculturalism and Children's Literature." In McGillis, *Voices of the Other*, 165–76.

Slemon, Stephen, and Jo-Ann Wallace. "Into the Heart of Darkness? Teaching Children's Literature as a Problem in Theory." *CCL: Canadian Children's Literature*, vol. 63 (1991): 20.

Smith, Linda Tuhiwahi. *Decolonizing Methodology: Research and Indigenous Peoples*. London: Zed Books, 1999.

Wiggins, Genevieve. *L.M. Montgomery*. New York: Twayne, 1992.

Zeegers, Margaret. "Cultural Explorations of Time and Space: Indigenous Australian Artists-in-Residence, Conventional Narratives and Children's Text Creation." *Papers*, vol. 16:2 (2006): 138–44.

*Anne* and After: The Local and Global
Circulation of the Classic Text

# Teaching and Reading *Anne of Green Gables* in Iran, the Land of Omar Khayyam

GHOLAMREZA SAMIGORGANROODI

When I was teaching *Anne of Green Gables* in Iran, I never imagined I would one day visit Prince Edward Island. Like Anne Shirley, I had "always heard that Prince Edward Island was the prettiest place in the world, and I used to imagine I was living [t]here, but I never really expected I would. It's delightful when your imaginations come true."[1] After arriving at the airport, I "pinched myself so many times" but it was "real";[2] I was now in the land of Lucy Maud Montgomery.

I travelled from Iran, formerly known as Persia, the country of Zoroaster, the Magi, Cyrus the Great, Darius, Xerxes, the princess Shaherezad, and the poets Ferdousi, Rumi, Hafez, and Omar Khayyam, and home to one of the oldest civilizations in the world. As I was flying to Charlottetown to attend the centenary conference to mark the hundredth year since the publication of *Anne of Green Gables*, I had a few distinctive images in mind. First of all, I thought I might appear to the people I met as the "London street Arab"[3] that Marilla mentions in *Anne of Green Gables*. (I am not an Arab, but rather a Persian, but I expected people in this part of the world probably wouldn't know the difference.) Another image I had of myself was that of a pilgrim, as I was coming from the Iranian city, Kashan, which lies 260 kilometres south of the Iranian capital and is the city from which the Magi came, as some would claim.[4] I thought of myself as a Magi pilgrim, coming to Prince Edward Island to pay homage to a great work of literature.

As I more recently learned, there exists another quasi-biblical connection between Prince Edward Island's Montgomery and Iran. Annie Montgomery and Charlotte Geddie Montgomery, who were relatives of L.M. Montgomery, worked in Persia for many years as Presbyterian missionaries. Annie Montgomery travelled there in 1886 and stayed for thirty-five years, while her sister lived in Persia between 1886 and 1905.[5]

I was also thinking of Omar Khayyam and Montgomery's admiration for this Persian poet. This image appeared to me like a chiasmus: Montgomery read Omar Khayyam,[6] and now Omar Khayyam's children (that is, my Iranian students) are reading Montgomery. I wanted to tell people about the admiration of Khayyam's countrymen and countrywomen for L.M. Montgomery, and how Khayyam and Montgomery's powerful pens have connected our people to one another in a way that reveals our common humanity. Khayyam and Montgomery have outlived transitory life and have transcended time through their literature. As Khayyam said and Montgomery often quoted: "The Moving Finger writes, and, having writ, / Moves on; nor all thy Piety nor Wit / Shall lure it back to cancel half a Line."[7]

I love *Anne of Green Gables*, and this is the reason it is on the reading list of my literature courses. I teach this story because Iran loves this novel. I am very disappointed when I find that my daughter and her classmates who go to school here in Canada are more interested in Junie B. Jones and Harry Potter than in such classics as *Anne of Green Gables*. But Iran is different, and Iranian students still read classical works of fiction that depict a serene and slow-paced life, and they admire them immensely. Is this because Iran still has a traditional social structure and values? So Andrew O'Malley indicates in his reading of *Anne*'s reception in Iran; he suggests that the book's appeal there "seems to come from the close familial and community bonds [Anne] forges and maintains in her new environment."[8] Regardless, it is clear that Iranians are in love with *Anne of Green Gables*. It is well known that Anne is beloved in Japan, as Yoshiko Akamatsu outlines in this volume, but few people in Canada know that millions of Iranians watch the film and animation adaptations of *Anne of Green Gables*, and that the story is widely read, particularly by students such as my students of English literature, who are fascinated by what Mark Twain once called "the most lovable" heroine.[9] (My students do not agree with the second part of Twain's statement, "since the immortal Alice," for they say they could never identify themselves with *Alice in Wonderland*.)

The many translations of *Anne* available in Farsi, the Persian language, illustrate the extent of this novel's popularity in Iran. These translations carry titles such as "Aannie the Green Dream" ("Anne" is always pro-nounced with a long vowel "aa" at the beginning, because "Anne" with a short vowel means "poo" in Farsi), "Aannie in Avonle," and "Aanne Shirley." It has now become a catch phrase in Farsi, at least among the people I know, to call a girl with a powerful imagination "Anne Shirley." When a professor wants to hold a quiz or announces next week's exam, my students all say to each other, "That's the most tragical thing that has happened."

What happens when a fictional work is read in a country other than the one in which and for which it was written? West German critics of Gunter Grass's story *Ballad of a Badgerdog* viewed it unfavourably as a literal depiction of political events in their own country, while Amer-ican readers read this story as a parable of domestic political events in America.[10] George Orwell's novel *1984* is said to be based on his trau-matic, brutalizing childhood experience at a Sussex prep school.[11] But people who live under oppressive regimes read this work as a political allegory about their own country. The Burmese believe Orwell wrote *1984* about their country and call him "the prophet" who predicted the emergence of the ultimate oppressive regime in Burma.[12] In fact, in this kind of reader-based approach to literature, the process of reading be-comes the process of identification with the text and its reconstruction. As many reader-response critics argue, an actual reader's responses are inevitably coloured by his or her accumulated private experiences.[13]

Stanley Fish uses the phrase "interpretive community" for different interpretations generated by different groups of readers with similar "identity themes."[14] What I wish to share with Montgomery scholars is the reading of *Anne of Green Gables* of my interpreting community. I want to show how *Anne of Green Gables* transcends its immediate con-text, generates readings in a totally different cultural and geographical context, and creates a kind of fellow-feeling among people who come from diverse backgrounds to connect them globally.

Teaching literature in a foreign language is not an easy task. Foreign literature is sometimes seen as something remote and far removed from real-life situations. Unfamiliar foreign customs and situations some-times hinder reading in a foreign language. The study of literature in-volves a considerable amount of meta-language, a grasp of critical con-cepts, and a knowledge of conventions.

In order to overcome these difficulties I always try to connect for-eign literature with my students' lives. When they are given a choice, students love to read. They actively participate in their education and go beyond memorizing information for a test if they really love the text they read. I believe students learn what they live. They learn when learning becomes meaningful to them and is related to real-life situ-ations. Jane Austen's *Pride and Prejudice*, for instance, is a historical novel that nonetheless engages students in discourses on familiar social issues such as commoditized human relations, marriage as a market, and the problem of inheritance for women.

For the past few years I have been giving my students a list of novels I think might arouse their curiosity and interest in literature, asking them to read through the novels on their own and choose the one(s) they find relevant to their lives for further analysis and discussion in class. Among these novels are *Gulliver's Travels, Alice's Adventures in Wonderland*, and *Anne of Green Gables. Anne of Green Gables* has al-ways been at the top of the list of the students' favourite stories. While reading *Anne of Green Gables*, students are never conditioned to make limited judgments but are left free to make all kinds of possible infer-ences. Montgomery's novel is so interactive and expansive that it gen-erates multiple responses and interpretations. The process of reading it becomes the process of creating meaning when students integrate their own understanding with the story. Students bring different back-grounds, personal experiences, and emotional baggage to their reading, and still it becomes meaningful to them. This, I think, is the mark of an enduring classic.

Interestingly, students in Iran can readily identify with Anne Shir-ley; they match their unique identities to Anne. Interpreting the novel becomes an act of "identity," and they read the novel to find a symbol of themselves. As Norman Holland has shown in his case studies of particular readers and their experience of reading and free associating with specific poems and stories, reading is a function of the reader's identity, and readers actually internalize the literary text and shape their literary experiences according to their personalities. According to Holland, when readers read a text, they process it in accordance with their identity themes, and that why different readers read the same text differently.[15]

In my classes in Iran, *Anne of Green Gables* has always encouraged students' involvement and offered ample opportunities for them to contribute and share their own experiences, perceptions, and opinions. My students are so fascinated by *Anne of Green Gables* that it almost becomes an obsession. They dramatize the story and act it out in class, translate it into Farsi, write poems about it, relate it to their own lives and situations, and read it to replicate themselves.

When asked, "Why did you pick *Anne of Green Gables* as your favourite story?" my students came up with some interesting answers.[16] One wrote about how she loves "Anne's liveliness of character, the theatrical way she makes her apology to Mrs. Rachel, and the flowery language she uses, and the way she changes things which are annoying to things which can be enjoyable." Another student expressed her admiration in relation to inner beauty: "It shows us things can be pretty when you are pretty in your mind. The story gives you hope that even if you are not that beautiful, your beauty of mind and character can lead you into success and your dreams can come true." Some of the responses revealed how closely students identified their situation with the situations in the book: "I love *Anne of Green Gables*," wrote one student in her journal, "because it is a story that is never boring. To me Anne is not an abstract entity or a fictional character. She is a real person, and I can establish a connection between her and my life. Some years ago, one of my friends lost both her parents in an accident. After a long period of suffering, she decided to combat all her problems, financial and mental. She worked hard and studied at the same time. She is now a student of electronic engineering and also a professional guitar player and has a happy and wonderful life." The student concluded with a poem of her own in Farsi: "Life is beautiful, you who love beauty / Only people with lively minds can attain things pretty."

My students often like to connect the literature they read in English with Persian/Farsi works of literature. One day, a student described Anne in the words of the Persian poet Rumi, as a girl "born with potential," "born with goodness and trust," "born with ideals and dreams," "born with greatness," and "born with wings"; a girl who could not "crawl through life."[17] After reading about Anne, another student was reminded of the twentieth-century Persian poet Parvin Etesami, who wrote a satirical poem called "An Orphan's Tears" about orphans and social injustice.[18] I myself once tried to describe Anne's scope for imagination in class with the aid of a poetic phrase by Khayyam as a mind having a "banquet of delight."

Other students also constructed and articulated their personal responses to my question. One wrote that she loved Anne because she identified with her loneliness: "I understand her because I lost my father and went through a lot of difficulties after that." Another girl in my class admired Anne for her go-getting spirit and optimism despite all the adversity in her life: "Anne is so lively and so full of hope. We should see 'Anne Shirley' as an entry in the *Dictionary of Literary Allusions* for hope, optimism, success, and talkativeness." One student remembered the time when she was a little girl and hated her curly hair and dreamed of having straight hair: "I was twelve when I watched *Anne of Green Gables* on TV and I noticed we had something in common."

When I examined the students' responses, I realized why *Anne of Green Gables* struck such a resonant chord among these young people. One reason for the novel's popularity was its abundance of imagery and the quality of its language. *Anne of Green Gables* is rich in natural imagery and embellished with figures of speech. Poetic language of this sort is also characteristic of Farsi language and Persian literature, which are often laden with figures of speech and tropes. Farsi "has such a roll to it,"[19] to use Montgomery's words. It sounds a lot like poetry. It is full of circumlocutions and poetic phrases. The way people greet each other in Iran and the formalities and social etiquettes are theatrical and poetic. In fact, Persian literature is so full of rich and glorious imagery that it captivated the hearts of writers such as Goethe, Matthew Arnold, Alfred Lord Tennyson, Lord Byron, Emerson, Thoreau, and, interestingly enough, Lucy Maud Montgomery. After reading the students' impressions, I noticed that the imagery in *Anne of Green Gables* reminds these "teachable little things"[20] of the spectacular imagery in Persian literature with which they are familiar. Anne's fresh look at life reminds many students of the twentieth-century Persian poet Sohrab Sepehri's verse which reads, "We must wash our eyes and look at life differently."[21]

The idyllic world of Anne Shirley also reminds the students of their own villages and towns. Most of them come from the country to the cities to study, and they always long to go back to their beautiful and peaceful towns and villages. Persians have a great taste for scenic representations and relish what nature has bestowed on them. The natural splendour of Prince Edward Island reminds my students of the lush and bucolic Caspian coastal region, the pastoral landscapes, the breathtaking forests, the rivers, caves, and waterfalls, and the beauty of the famous Persian gardens. One student presented a photograph of her native village in Iran with a caption that read, "Our Persian 'White Way of Delight'" and tried to draw a parallel between the beauty of her village and that of Avonlea. Another student told the class about her native town's "Lake of Shining Waters."

During the devastating, eight-year Iran–Iraq war (1980–88) which came with great loss of life and tremendous economic damage, nearly all Iranian families were affected, losing either their homes, their belongings, or a member of their family; one in every four students lost a family member in the war. All students have seen close relatives or friends from school or their neighbourhood grow up as orphans, struggling to find their place in society. People in Iran can relate their situation to that of Anne Shirley because they have experienced Anne's problems first hand.

Anne Shirley lives in her dream world. Her powerful imagination comes to her rescue. This is a gift my young Iranian students also possess. They resort to dreams when reality becomes too burdensome. Dreaming is a force that no government in the world can control. They can put you in jail, but you can always pass over the walls through your imagination, "drifting luxuriously out on a sea of daydreams."[22] Your "lively fancy"[23] comes to your rescue when your life is a "graveyard full of buried hopes."[24] In effect, "Adventures wonderful and enthralling happen to you in cloudland," "adventures that always turn out triumphantly" and never involve you in "scrapes like those of actual life."[25] In your dreams, your spirit can fly away to "some remote airy cloudland, borne aloft on the wings of imagination."[26] You "get a passport to the geography of fairy land."[27]

From my students, I also realized that Iranians see *Anne of Green Gables* as a success story. Success stories become popular when there is economic depression in a country. In the 1930s, for example, mass-circulated magazines showed an "obsessive concern with questions involving success."[28] Biographies of successful people and "how-to-succeed" guidebooks and literatures became popular.[29] They replace the seamy sides of reality with the bromides of success. There are many similarities between those Great Depression days and present-day Iran, a country suffering under many crippling economic sanctions. Double-digit unemployment, severe financial problems, and inflation have taken their toll on ordinary people and are wreaking havoc on a once-prosperous nation. In a situation like this, inspirational stories of people who rise from obscurity to eminence and distinction become popular and attractive. There are many translations of "How-to-Succeed" books and success stories in the present-day Iranian book market.

But above any other reason, Anne Shirley has captured the hearts and minds of my Iranian students because she follows her heart against all odds. She does not allow life to make her a victim of circumstances. No obstacles can thwart her imagination and her dreams. She is feisty, lively, energetic, romantic, and stubborn. The students see themselves reflected in Anne; they do not like to be pitied and never let anyone make them a victim. The women, particularly, associate themselves with Anne Shirley. Just like Anne, and despite all the restrictions they are under, they are active, progressive, and self-protective. They are eminently the doers, the creators, and the discoverers. One of my students, who came from an Iranian nomadic tribe, gave me a photograph of an Iranian nomadic woman and, using Montgomery's words from *Anne of Green Gables*, described the "unyielding stubbornness looking out of" her face.[30]

Some of my students come from the Caspian Sea region where women work in paddy fields, and some from the mountainous regions and the deserts where women weave the famous Persian carpets. Young women who live in the cities do various activities that some might regard as "unwomanly," but they are strong and very determined women. One of their favourite games is polo, a game invented in Persia. These women are involved with sports such as track and field, car-racing, golf, horse-riding, soccer, cycling, rugby, ice-skating, and skiing. Women drive heavy trucks, sing in choirs, and become film directors and firefighters. When you see them in the streets, you can almost hear them say: "I am going to do it. I am sixteen years old, and I'm as stubborn as you are." As Montgomery phrased it: "Whatever comes into [my] head to say or do ... [I] say or do it without a moment's reflection."[31] If Montgomery were alive, she would probably wonder at the resemblances between her Anne and her female Iranian fans and ask the familiar question, "Is this *my* Anne?"[32]

Iranian students' love for *Anne of Green Gables* stems from an interest in and an ability to identify with the main character, an interest and ability that might be lacking among some young readers in other parts of the world. Anne Shirley has elicited a surprising degree of identification from female Iranian readers and offered them a fictional medium through which they can see their images and aspirations projected.

Although Omar Khayyam does not share the optimism of Montgomery in his poetry, like Montgomery and her creation, Anne, he is interested in the joys of life. In a world such as ours, which is built on greed and war, such poetic celebration of life and rejection of death and destruction become ever more important. Anne Shirley takes joy in life and thrives in the beauty of nature, reminding us of Khayyam, who wrote:

> Be happy, for the anguish Time
> Still has in store is infinite;
> But in the skies this blessed night
> The planets sing in perfect chime.[33]

Is it not interesting to see Iranian readers who can identify themselves with Anne Shirley and respond experientially to her world, despite living in a country whose culture and world is essentially different from those of the author of the novel? Could Montgomery have ever imagined that her story would one day transcend its context and reach people in such far-away lands as the land of her beloved poet Omar Khayyam?

## NOTES

1  Montgomery, *Anne of Green Gables*, 16.
2  Ibid., 22.
3  Ibid., 8.
4  Popular legend and even contemporary tourist guidebooks suggest Kashan as a starting point of the Bible's "Three Wise Men." The Magi were Zoroastrian priests.
5  Whytock, "Annie and Charlotte Montgomery."
6  Montgomery, *Selected Journals* 1:286–7, entries for 12 April 1903, 286; 11 March 1916, 180; and 28 August 1927, 352.

7   Rubio, *Lucy Maud Montgomery*, 118.
8   O'Malley, in Gammel, O'Malley, Hu, and Banwait, "An Enchanting Girl," 169.
9   Mark Twain was quoted in a letter written by his secretary to L.M. Montgomery, 3 October 1908. His comments were later quoted in L.C. Page's advertising for *Anne of Green Gables* in *The Publisher's Weekly*, 5 December 1908.
10   Hanne, *Power of the Story*, 30.
11   Orwell, "Such, Such Were the Joys."
12   Larkin, *Finding George Orwell in Burma*.
13   See Holland, "Unity Identity Self Text."
14   Fish, *Is There a Text?*
15   Holland, "Reading and Identity."
16   All student responses were gathered and translated, when necessary, by me.
17   This poem by Rumi is frequently quoted among inspirational quotations with its translator and source uncredited. For example, see http://www.enlightenedbeings.com/rumi.html.
18   Etesami, "Ashk e yatim."
19   Montgomery, *Anne of Green Gables*, 52.
20   Ibid., 43.
21   Sepehri, *Hasht Ketab*.
22   Montgomery, *Anne of Green Gables*, 62.
23   Ibid., 230.
24   Ibid., 39.
25   Ibid., 230.
26   Ibid., 35.
27   Montgomery, *The Alpine Path*, 47.
28   Hearn, *The American Dream*, 59.
29   Ibid., 60.
30   Montgomery, *Anne of Green Gables*, 116.
31   Ibid., 152.
32   Ibid., "Is This My Anne?"
33   Khayyam, *Rubaiyat*, no. 148.

## BIBLIOGRAPHY

Etesami, Parvin. "Ashk e yatim" ["An Orphan's Tears"]. http://iranonline.com/literature/etesami/ashk-e-yatim.html (accessed 20 December 2011).
Fish, Stanley. *Is There a Text in This Class? The Authority of Interpretive Communities*. Cambridge, Massachusetts: Harvard University Press, 1980.
Gammel, Irene, with Andrew O'Malley, Huifeng Hu, and Ranbir K. Banwait. "An Enchanting Girl: International Portraits of Anne's Cultural Transfer." In *Anne's World: A New Century of Anne of Green Gables*, edited by Irene

Gammel and Benjamin Lefebvre, 166–91. Toronto: University of Toronto Press, 2010.

Hanne, Michael. *Power of the Story*. Providence: Berghahn Books, 1996.

Hearn, Charles R. *The American Dream in the Great Depression*. Westport: Greenwood Press, 1977.

Holland, Norman. "Reading and Identity." 1998. http://www.clas.ufl.edu/users/nnh/rdgident.htm (accessed 20 December 2011).

– "Unity Identity Text Self." *PMLA*, vol. 90.5 (1975): 813–22.

Khayyam, Omar. *Rubaiyat of Omar Khayyam*. Edited and translated by Arthur J. Arberry. Persian-English-French edition. Tehran: Jaanzaadeh, 2008.

Larkin, Emma. *Finding George Orwell in Burma*. New York: Penguin, 2005.

Montgomery, L.M. *The Alpine Path: The Story of My Career*. Don Mills, Ontario: Fitzhenry & Whiteside, 1975.

– *Anne of Green Gables*. New York: Penguin, 2008.

– "Is This My Anne?" *Chatelaine* (Jan. 1935): 18–22. Reprinted (abridged) in *The Lucy Maud Montgomery Album*, compiled by Kevin McCabe, 333–5. Toronto: Fitzhenry & Whiteside, 1999.

– *The Selected Journals of L.M. Montgomery*. Vol. 1, 1889–1910; Vol. 2, 1910–1921; Vol. 3, 1921–1929. Edited by Mary Rubio and Elizabeth Waterston. Toronto: Oxford University Press, 1985; 1987; 1992.

Orwell, George. "Such, Such Were the Joys." 1953. http://orwell.ru/library/essays/joys/english/e_joys (accessed 20 December 2011).

Rubio, Mary H. *Lucy Maud Montgomery: The Gift of Wings*. Toronto: Doubleday, 2008.

Sepehri, Sohrab. *Hasht Ketab*. 16th ed. Tehran: Tahavori, 2006.

Whytock, Jack C. "Annie and Charlotte Montgomery: Teachers and Evangelists in Persia." Unpublished manuscript. 1–18. http://www.csph.ca/papers/CSPH/2011 - Jack Whytock - draft.pdf (accessed on 10 July 2012).

# Reading *Anne of Green Gables* in Montevideo

DORELEY CAROLINA COLL

When I first read *Anne of Green Gables* as an eleven-year-old in Montevideo, Uruguay, it gave me a sense of pure joy. On cold south-Atlantic nights, in my mother's bedroom, the only one with a fireplace, I could cuddle under thick quilts with my book, to be transported in no time to Marilla's kitchen, the smell of fresh-baked bread, and the "Snow Queen" in all her luminous and fragrant splendour. Being an eleven-year-old reader, I was less impressed by Anne's feisty spirit, her imagination, and her gift with words than by the warmth and humanity of her personality, the adventures she embarked on, and the vitality of the other characters in the novel. But what really captured my imagination was Montgomery's description of the ice cream available at the Sunday school picnic. In Montevideo, we could only get smooth, velvety, sweet gelato in stores; the kind available at home was as sharp as glass, pinching your palate with every spoonful. And while the south-Atlantic winds at my home in Montevideo whipped up an ice storm outside, I would sleep with images of ice cream dancing in my head: strawberry ice cream, chocolate ice cream, walnut ice cream swirling as the ice pellets tapped on the window panes. Ice cream at a picnic? Surely the Prince Edward Island described in *Anne* was an enchanted place!

The community of scholars and admirers of L.M. Montgomery's writing would not be shocked to find *Anne of Green Gables* sharing company with *Little Women* and *Huckleberry Finn* in a grade-six reader for elementary school students in Montevideo.[1] After all, since the publication of *Anne of Green Gables* in 1908, the red-haired, freckled heroine has entranced readers worldwide as translations have made her story available to the international community.[2] In this volume alone, we see how Anne has made her way to places as diverse as Australia,

Turkey, Sweden, Japan, and Iran. What may be surprising for Montgomery scholars is to find the cheerful, imaginative Anne appropriating and disseminating the idiologeme[3] of the red-haired woman in Western literature and art through her influence on the Uruguayan teacher, educator, and writer Armonía Somers.

As a teacher, Armonía Somers was the person responsible for including *Ana de las tejas verdes* in the Uruguayan curriculum and therefore making it possible for my eleven-year-old self to encounter Anne and her ice cream. The fictional world of Armonía Somers, the writer, was distinctly influenced by Montgomery's heroine, as is evident particularly in the way Somers used the image of a red-haired protagonist whenever she needed a rebellious, adventurous female who would change the course of events in the diegesis of the plot. Just as Anne brings renewal to moribund customs in Prince Edward Island, Somers's red-haired women also challenge the cultural modes in provincial Uruguayan society at the time.

Armonía Somers, born Armonía Etchepare de Hernesterosa, achieved unprecedented recognition as an outstanding educator and audacious writer who became a prominent voice in Uruguayan literature in the latter half of the twentieth century. She grew up in an intellectual household where her father kept a library well supplied with the world's literary classics, among them Montgomery's books. Like Montgomery, Armonía was a lonely child and an avid reader; she spent most of her time reading in the library. She obtained her teaching degree in 1933 at the age of nineteen. As a young, recently graduated teacher, Somers was sent to teach in the most underprivileged neighbourhoods in Montevideo. In those classrooms she came face to face with the miseries of humankind. Soon, she became a sharp observer of class differences and the impact they had on education. She published extensively on education and delinquency. In 1961 she became director of the Pedagogical Museum of Uruguay. From 1962 to 1971 she served in many different positions with the Ministry of Education and with education agencies in various countries in Europe and North America. Throughout her life, and like her father before her, Somers is known to have kept a collection of Montgomery's books in her personal library.[4]

Like L.M. Montgomery in her time, Somers in the mid-twentieth century was a modern, educated, financially independent, and rebellious woman. She kept separate her two public personas, teacher and writer, a decision she felt was necessary in the traditional Montevideo of the 1950s. This survival strategy proved wise, considering the reception the literary establishment gave her first novel, *La mujer desnuda* (*The Naked Woman*, 1950). The novel caused a sensation in literary circles. Its overt sexual content was considered scandalous; it was not thought possible that the book could be the creation of a woman. The local literary community attributed it variously to a male writer, a degenerate, a learned German or English author, a homosexual, or an anonymous sex maniac.[5] The allegoric tale in *La mujer desnuda* follows red-haired beauty Rebecca Linke's rebellion upon reaching her thirtieth birthday. Presented lyrically and set in a nebulous atmosphere, the story emphasizes the protagonist's anguished search for freedom. At the novel's climax, Rebecca parades naked through the village, igniting the men's sexual desires after long years of indolence. The village church burns to the ground as Rebecca walks by with her red, waist-long mane. Nathaniel, the old village forest keeper, hears her whisper in his ear that she is Eva, the primary and universal woman.

In the novel, Somers explores a scapegoat's capacity to unite groups in hatred and the price paid for nonconformity, a *leitmotif* also found in Montgomery's narrative, although Montgomery's focus is not on sexuality. In Somers's novel, the deep needs and sexual frustrations of an entire village emerge before a nude woman, described as naked in purity and innocence, who serves as a catalyst for their unacknowledged inadequacies. The men awake, longing for a virility they no longer have, for wives in whom they no longer see what they once loved. The women are envious of the red-haired naked woman for arousing their men. Angry and frustrated because they can no longer feel or elicit such emotions, the villagers join forces to destroy the woman whose crime was to have exposed their hidden desires.

Somers's originality rests in her unusual presentation of themes: a blend of realism, fantasy, and absurdity written in symbolic and poetic language. Her world is always polemical, with touches of humour and keen sarcasm; also, like Montgomery, she understood the purposes of satire. Somers's fiction is a chaotic quest for a radical new meaning for humankind. The darkness and unexpected violence found only covertly in Montgomery's world transform into a sordid, overtly nightmarish one in Somers's. Her characters are marginalized and come from all walks of life, but more often than not they are murderers, rapists, psychopaths, drifters, drunkards, or orphans – maladjusted individuals trying to survive in a hostile universe.

Like L.M. Montgomery, Somers was sidelined by the literary establishment, but for different reasons. Somers's problem was not that her books were considered too conventional in their adherence to a genre: in fact, quite the opposite was the case. Somers tried to fend off criticism of her work with her particular sarcastic humour, but her feelings of rejection are evident in her comments about the reception of *The Naked Woman*:

> In general the novel made its way into the hands of the intellectuals because they were the ones who bought the arts magazine where it was published. The general public didn't read it. The intellectuals formed two groups, those who repudiated the novel (I never knew why, perhaps because they sensed themselves to be identified with some character) and those who felt hypnotized by the novel. I had the privilege of attending a round table discussion on *La mujer desnuda* in the home of a painter. I went, not as the author, but as "Woman X," even though the painter knew it was my book. I remember how cold it was that night as we sat around the wood stove, and finally we ran out of logs. The discussion continued as they tore me to shreds, and the painter began to burn picture frames to keep the studio warm. One man, who was the most vicious slanderer of them all (afterwards I realized that he had seen himself reflected in one of the characters), referring to the woodsman whose wife is old and passionless, said, "How can a man be so cruel as to abuse the woman after having worked and fought at her side?" Then I, who was not Armonía Somers, but rather Woman X, said, "Maybe because the woodsman was dead, the way you are, until the naked woman aroused him, and no one knows what will happen when he is awakened." The brief but suggestive answer was, perhaps, one of the ways in which later I was discovered to be the author.[6]

After *The Naked Woman*, Somers continued publishing short stories and novels that portrayed orphans and prostitutes, their characters intertwined with iconoclastic themes. In 1966, in the novel *Only Elephants Encounter Mandrake*, Somers created a heroine close to Anne

Shirley in appearance and personality. Sembrando Flores, a name that literally means "sowing flowers," is a defiant, intelligent, indomitable, red-haired adolescent questioning the conventions of her everyday world as she comes of age. A painter illustrating the description of Sembrando Flores in the book could trace on the canvas an image of the perfect twin of Anne Shirley. In addition to her appearance, Sembrando Flores shares with Anne a love for books, nature, and solitude, a curious intelligence, a sense of justice, an abundant humour, a quick temper, a marvellous imagination, and a gift with words. Somers seduces the reader with the fresh, wild character of the teenager as she prepares her metamorphosis into a woman. By deploying a playful freckled teenager and describing her development in the tradition of the *bildungsroman*, Somers builds the reader's feelings and emotions toward the "horizons of expectations" she wants them to have when the adult protagonist continues the narrative. Eighty pages later, when the child has become an independent, feminist warrior, the reader welcomes Sembrando Flores's willingness to confront society's restrictions and wage battles against gender inequality.

In Somers's work, when she needs to reinvent and transcend the norms of society, she uses the image of the red-haired woman, knowing that it will tap into the readers' cultural code. Montgomery may also have drawn on the pervasive symbolism of the passionate red-haired woman. (Jennie MacDonald, in this volume, also traces plural meanings of red hair for Anne and her readers.) Both Somers's Sembrando Flores and Montgomery's Anne Shirley walk in the historical footprints of Adam's first wife, Lilith, the first insubordinate red-haired woman in Judeo-Christian cosmology to disrupt the well-thought-out plans of our patriarchal forefathers. Julia Kristeva[7] reveals that eighty-five per cent of Renaissance paintings show a black-haired Eve until she trespasses the threshold of the Garden of Eden and bites from the apple the serpent offers her. After her transgression, Eve is frequently depicted with red hair. According to Kristeva, the red-haired woman subverts patriarchy's collective imaginary; she is believed to possess the non-desirable traits in traditional binaries: she is passionate, rebellious, chaotic, anarchical, unruly, outspoken, and disobedient. Furthermore, in some cultures, red hair denotes a voracious sexual appetite; it is the phallic mother or the *vagina dentata*, always threatening the symbolic order of the Law of the

Father. A red-haired heroine is a pluri-meaningful sign decoding the dialogical conversation with the intertextuality inherited in the text and its context.

Although Somers's provocative red-haired protagonist may seem a far stretch from cheerful, innocent Anne, intertextuality shows Montgomery's influence in Somers: inspiration from Montgomery extends the space of her fictional work. It is evident that Somers admired the Canadian author because, beyond the dialogical aspect of the fictional work where influence is there for people to see it or not, it was Somers who introduced *Anne of Green Gables* into the grade six curriculum in Uruguayan schools. Somers had most likely read all of the Montgomery books contained in her library, including the English ones and the few volumes in Spanish that were translated at the time.

Somers the writer clearly responded to the symbolic power of a red-haired protagonist. What did Somers the educator think children could gain by reading about Anne, this animated child in a far-away land? Somers described in an interview how she foresaw that the classes she taught could benefit: "I worked in places that taught me a great deal ... Because I was sent to schools in poor neighbourhoods, such as La Teja, where children came to school with fingers in their mouths to warm them, since they slept in shacks, places where rats cross the floor. Only literature could offer them escape in the here and now. It has the potential to change their horrible destiny by boosting their self-esteem and confidence and allow[ing] them to dream."[8]

Perhaps when Somers considered the lives of the underprivileged students she taught, and when she had deciphered what she thought would be of value for these students, she was determined to introduce a success story, and *Anne of Green Gables* remains, fundamentally, a success story. (Samigorganroodi, in this volume, finds success to be an important element of Anne's appeal in Iran.) In Anne, we find an underdog, a person whom nobody wanted, a child considered of no value to society because she was an orphan and a girl. By speaking her mind and standing up for herself, Anne rises beautifully above the limiting stereotypes that are imposed upon her because of her gender and class. Somers's students from impoverished communities were considered "trash" by society because of their humble origins. Perhaps Somers saw in *Anne of Green Gables* a connection to them and a message of hope.

If there was a path out of the shantytowns for these children, literature would pave the way, and as a literary travelling companion, Anne would cheer them and imbue them with strength of character.

Armonía Somers's powerful influence as a pedagogue and her decision to share her love of L.M. Montgomery's work shaped my childhood. Not only were the impoverished children of Montevideo encouraged to dream of and imagine fabulous places, but also middle-class eleven-year-olds like me travelled far beyond their everyday worlds, savouring delicious ice cream in the make-believe. As a writer, Somers wrote bravely against the conventions that she saw stifling the dreams of children and adults in Uruguay. In her novels set in Prince Edward Island, Montgomery revealed the limitations of conformist society more gently, expanding "scope for the imagination" beyond rigid expectations based on gender and class. Reading their books with attention to intertextuality demonstrates the differences as well as the similarities of the writers' approaches. Whether these two authors were conditioned to create rebellious red-haired heroines by the idiologeme of the red-headed woman in Western literature and art, or their choices were provocative attempts to manipulate readers' responses, their heroines' fiery red tresses generate the sparks good literature creates and kindle in readers of many places and many times imagined visions of how the world may be.

## NOTES

1 I attended the "Escuela Experimental," a pilot project for elementary schools implemented in 1927. The pedagogy in the schools was based on the Belgian Decroly method of teaching. There were only three in Uruguay. It was at this experimental school that *Anne of Green Gables* was included in the reader. In 1980, because of the high cost involved in running the schools, all the Escuelas Experimentales reverted to regular schools.

2 The first translation of *Anne of Green Gables* in Spanish was published in 1951.

3 This term belongs to Julia Kristeva's conception of "idiologemes" and "idiolects." Kristeva draws from Mikhail Bakhtin's study of intertextuality in the novel and Michel Foucault's reflection on the "episteme." She weaves these concepts together, and coins the neologisms "ideologeme" and "idiolect." (See Kristeva, *La Révolution du langage poétique*, 200.)

4 Campodónico, "Diálogo," 225–45.

5  Visca, "Un mundo narrativo fantasmagórico y real," 11–15.
6  Risso, "Cronología," 256, my translation.
7  Kristeva, "The Annunciation to Anna, The Betrothal of the Virgin," in *Desire in Language*, 229–31.
8  Campodónico, "Diálogo," 245–55, my translation.

## BIBLIOGRAPHY

Bakhtin, Mikhail. *Problems of Dostoevsky's Poetics*. Ann Arbor: Ardis, 1973.
Campodónico, Miguel Ángel. "Diálogo." In *Armonía Somers, papeles críticos*, 225–45. Montevideo: Librería Linardi y Risso, 1990.
Foucault, Michel. *The Archaeology of Knowledge*. London: Tavistock, 1972.
Kristeva, Julia. *Desire in Language: A Semiotic Approach to Literature and Art*. Edited by Leon S. Roudiez. New York: Columbia University Press, 1980.
– *La Révolution du langage poétique*. Paris: Seuil, 1973.
Montgomery, L.M. *Anne of Green Gables*. Toronto: McClelland & Stewart, 1992.
Risso, Álvaro. "Cronología." In *Armonía Somers, papeles críticos*, 256. Montevideo: Librería Linardi y Risso, 1990.
Somers, Armonía. *La Mujer desnuda*. Montevideo: Clima No 2–3, 1950.
– *Solo los elefantes encuentran mandrágora* [*Only Elephants Encounter Mandrake*]. Argentina: Legasa, 1986.
Visca, Arturo Sergio. "Un mundo narrativo fantasmagórico y real." In *Armonía Somers, papeles críticos*, 11–15. Montevideo: Librería Linardi y Risso, 1990.

# Teaching *Anne* and *Antonia* in Turkey: Feminist Girlhood in L.M. Montgomery's *Anne of Green Gables* and Willa Cather's *My Antonia*

TANFER EMIN TUNC

Lucy Maud Montgomery scholars have frequently remarked upon the transnational applicability of her works, which stems primarily from the fact that texts such as *Anne of Green Gables* (1908) possess qualities that transcend time and place through strong protagonists who appeal to generation after generation of readers. While the *Anne* series has had extraordinary success in the United States, Japan, and Western European countries such as the United Kingdom and Sweden, it has only recently begun to be appreciated in parts of Eurasia such as Turkey. Although American literary texts entered the Turkish university curriculum during the mid-twentieth century, preceded by a few decades by British texts, it is only in recent years that Canadian, Australian, and other anglophone works have begun to receive serious academic and critical attention.[1] One of the reasons Canadian literature, in particular, has been marginalized is that the definition of "American" literature that exists in Turkey consists very narrowly of works produced in the United States, about the United States, or by U.S. citizens.

The first step toward remedying the marginalization of Canadian literature would therefore be to expand the Turkish interpretation of "American" literature to include all of North America, and not just the United States. A second step would be to integrate well-known works of Canadian literature, such as those by Lucy Maud Montgomery, into the Turkish university curriculum through courses taught in the dozen or so departments of American Culture and Literature that exist in Turkey. In Montgomery's case, this inclusion would enable serious scholarly consideration of the relatively unknown Canadian author: the only exposure most Turkish students have had to *Anne of Green Gables* is a short-lived 1980s cartoon series, which those born in the 1990s do not remember. The text itself was only translated into Turkish in 1983, and is still virtually unknown within the academic community.[2] While younger students have encountered abridged versions of *Anne of Green Gables* in their introductory English language classes, the great majority of university-level students have never read the novel's full text.

Inspired by conversations with international scholars at the Eighth International L.M. Montgomery Conference, held in Prince Edward Island in June 2008, I decided to incorporate *Anne of Green Gables* into my teaching program, specifically into my Women and Literature course, thereby becoming the first scholar in my department (and possibly in all of Turkey) to include the text in a university-level syllabus. After a great deal of thought, I concluded that the best way to frame the novel would be to teach it as a classic of Western women's literature, with protagonists and antagonists who could readily be compared and contrasted with other characters found in United States literature (that is, the "canon" with which students in my department are most familiar). I decided to focus on the gender roles expressed in the novel, as well as Anne's pervasive feminist voice, and began with a discussion of the work's place in the historiography of North American children's literature.

Lucy Maud Montgomery (1874–1942) and her U.S. contemporary Willa Cather (1873–1947) were both early twentieth-century writers who rescued female protagonists from the realm of the fairytale and transplanted them into authentic scenarios where they could have a voice that challenged patriarchal authority. Because Cather's novel *My Antonia* (1918) is often included in the canon taught in Turkish departments of American Culture and Literature and shares many similarities with *Anne of Green Gables*, this text serves as a natural point of comparison with Montgomery's work. The female protagonists – Antonia Shimerda and Anne Shirley – created by these authors provide girls and young women with realistic role models who act, react, and think like adolescents making the difficult transition from childhood to adulthood. More important, their actions in the face of tragedies such as death, adoption, and personal loss show these adolescent protagonists to be independent, intelligent, and personally empowered – characteristics that Turkish students have mostly encountered in the male-centred *bildungsroman*.[3] *Anne of Green Gables* and *My Antonia*, however, convey to students that girls can also be protagonists of classic literature –

girls who, through their feminist behaviour, successfully transgress rigid socially constructed definitions of masculinity and femininity to carve out their own roles in early twentieth-century North American society.

Because Turkish American Culture and Literature students acquire a basic knowledge of Western feminism and the history of feminism in the United States through courses such as American Cultural Concepts, Gender Studies, and American History, framing *Anne of Green Gables* and *My Antonia* as feminist works of children's fiction is a strategy that readily places these novels in their social contexts. This classification not only deepens students' analysis and understanding of the respective protagonists but also adds to their knowledge of the authors themselves. Although neither Montgomery nor Cather publicly aligned herself with turn-of-the-twentieth-century women's movements, both formulated feminist protagonists who, by actively questioning North American womanhood, convey the power inherent in the expression of "alternative girlhoods." Throughout the novels, Anne and Antonia not only negotiate the difficult position of being children in an adult world but, through their rebellious transgression of gender expectations such as female passivity, dependence, weakness, impracticality, and domesticity, also resist patriarchal and matriarchal authorities who attempt to dictate the place of young girls in society. Using their burgeoning feminist sensibilities (which, incidentally, mimic the admirable qualities of the traditional boy-hero – honesty, trustworthiness, bravery, resourcefulness, rationality, and resilience), they successfully illustrate that female inferiority is culturally constructed. Their messages of acceptance, empowerment, and individuality – all of which are still relevant to today's readership – also provide valuable insight into the fabric of U.S. and Canadian society, especially for foreign students of North American culture and literature.

In order for students to appreciate the feminist messages conveyed in *Anne of Green Gables* and *My Antonia*, they must understand the sociopolitical contexts of Montgomery's and Cather's respective worlds. Even though Montgomery lived during the peak of the early women's movement, "she often strove to establish a distance between herself and [activist] women."[4] Her desire to avoid feminists, especially the "New Women" who participated in the suffrage movement, stemmed from "her strong sense that women should not, in fact, have any career other than wife and mother unless they could accomplish their work, like she herself did, without interrupting, or in any way adversely affecting, what she clearly saw as the first responsibility of women: to home and family."[5] Montgomery was clearly conservative with respect to many issues affecting women; nevertheless, it is also clear that gendered power relations were at the centre of her novels. This paradox suggests that even though she did not identify herself as such, Montgomery was influenced by maternal or domestic feminism, which posited that women, as wives and mothers, could carve out a niche of power for themselves in society – namely by exposing the inequalities inherent in the private sphere, and by critiquing the patriarchy from within. This strategy allowed women to assume influential roles not only in their households but also within their communities.

While this analysis may sound essentialist in that it reifies socially constructed gender roles for women, this brand of domestic feminism complemented turn-of-the-twentieth-century Canadian values because it was not based on theory but was "steeped in realism," which suited a nation that was still trying to forge an identity.[6] As Erika Rothwell suggests, Montgomery was "an astute social historian ... who kept her finger upon the pulse of Canadian women's experiences ... [In her works], Montgomery ... recreates the tapestry of maternal feminism in Canada. The strands of her works tell the story of Canadian women's lives in relation to the changing social and political circumstances of Canadian society in the first half of the twentieth century."[7] Rather than challenging society overtly, she "played the literary game with superb finesse, remaining within the confines of genteel female respectability, while incorporating serious social criticism into her novels."[8] Thus, it is through this lens that contemporary readers – and especially readers in Turkey, where domestic feminism is still arguably the most pervasive and accepted form of women's activism – can access a complex world of gender relations and feminist resistance in *Anne of Green Gables*.

Like Lucy Maud Montgomery, Willa Cather did not identify herself with the turn-of-the-twentieth-century women's movement. Nevertheless, Cather spent most of her life "defining herself against the culturally-prescribed female identity roles [of wife and mother]."[9] She rejected "external signs of womanhood," and as a child wanted to pursue a career in the male-dominated profession of medicine. At certain points in her life, she even assumed the identity of "William Cather, MD," cross-dressing in male clothing, sporting shortly cropped hair, and expressing "her contempt for the masses of ordinary women who devoted themselves to respectable domesticity, [or what she called] 'the world of babies and salads.'"[10] Moreover, "as a college student, she formed intense friendships with women and cut a 'disturbingly androgynous figure'; as an adult, she maintained her commitment to female friendships, while challenging traditional gender/power arrangements in her fiction."[11] Unlike Montgomery, Cather did not maintain that women's primary calling in life should be marriage and motherhood. Yet, her works do celebrate matriarchal power and place value upon women's participation in the traditionally male activity of nation-building. Thus Cather provides an interesting point of comparison with Montgomery, both in terms of her personal philosophy and the way her characters resist traditional female gender roles.

As students observed and literary critics convey, Anne Shirley is a feminist figure because unlike most nineteenth-century female protagonists, she "deconstructs behavioral codes and exacts positive change from her community. With a vivid imagination and limitless energy, Anne contests the limited perspectives of her caretakers and friends, inspiring transformation and growth in the stuffiest of her elders."[12] As Temma Berg notes, "the feminism of the novel is present in a variety of ways: in its portrayal of Anne as an independent, creative [yet practical], and strong-willed heroine; in its emphasis on her extraordinary imaginative powers and on the way imagination can empower women; and in its forward-looking view of the dialectic that exists between men and women, and within each human being."[13] Anne's behaviour is "inspired by personal feeling, not by Divine, human, or [parental] command."[14] In other words, she presents a "rational approach" to the adolescent girl who, using independent judgment, is able to reject female gender roles. Moreover, her adoption of an "assertive, individualistic subjectivity" positions her as a transgressive force in a mostly traditional town.[15] Thus, she "provides a fascinating example of [a] subversive heroine [who] challenges gender stereotypes and [social] conventions ... [In doing so, she] breaks the mold of patriarchal tradition and provides insight [into] the grand narrative of 'Her-story.'"[16]

The students in my class (the great majority of them female) were able to relate to Anne's need to prove her worth as a girl – a psychosocial phenomenon that still exists in patriarchal societies such as Turkey, where male offspring, especially in the eastern/rural parts of the nation, are considered more valuable than female children. Soon after arriving in Avonlea, Anne discovers that the Cuthberts originally intended to adopt a boy and that she was sent to them in error. Although the Cuthberts eventually grow to love their daughter, deriving great pride from her numerous accomplishments, Anne's promise to Marilla – "to do and be anything you want, if you'll only keep me" – seems to inform her adolescent development.[17] Anne decides to substitute herself for a boy, which in itself assumes that boys and girls are interchangeable and not divided by inherent, essentialized differences. Her strategy is to adopt a "plucky girl" persona in order to reassure the Cuthberts that they made the right decision in keeping her, and to negate the supposition that being female implies inferiority. As Nancy Goulden and Susan Stanfield delineate, in classic "girls'" literature, "plucky girl" protagonists often function as replacements for male heroes, rejecting traditional female passivity and substituting masculine activity. Like their male counterparts, plucky girls "do things":

> They leave the house; go into the natural world; take journeys; have adventures. They create; solve problems; show bravery and leadership; and impetuously leap into one "scrape" after another. They do not repress their emotions, but actively express them ... To step outside of society's norms and [transgress gender roles] ... requires that a character be strong, self-confident, independent, stubborn, resilient, intelligent, and individualistic ... [These traits are often manifested] through behaviors such as being competitive ... refusing to conform to or abide by social norms, showing an explosive temper, being dramatic in expression, and, above all, being faithful to one's beliefs and self.[18]

In a word, by being "Anne."

As students noted, Anne's feminism is primarily conveyed through her hot temper, stubborn streak, impulsiveness, and purported "wickedness" as a plucky girl. When Anne feels under attack, she does not remain silent: she bravely voices her opinion and is ready to deal with the consequences. She thus functions as an admirable role model for young girls. When Marilla Cuthbert's neighbour, Rachel Lynde, insults Anne by calling her "skinny and homely," with "hair as red as carrots," Anne retorts: "How dare you call me skinny and ugly? How dare you say I'm freckled and redheaded? You are a rude, impolite, unfeeling woman! ... How would you like to be told that you are fat and clumsy?"[19] While Anne ultimately apologizes to Mrs Lynde and asks forgiveness for being a "wicked and ungrateful girl,"[20] her dramatic apology only endears her to Rachel and Marilla because they each see something of themselves – especially their desire to control their environment – in her. Anne's outspokenness appeals to Turkish students precisely because it transcends both time and place. As they observed, its underlying form and function are still relevant, especially in a world that marginalizes the voices of women, and girls in particular, as unimportant and insignificant.

As Marilee Lindemann notes, Willa Cather urged parents to deconstruct gender boundaries by shifting their focus from "girls'" and "boys'" books, to "gender neutral" books that all children could read.[21] With its strong gender-transgressing female protagonist, *My Antonia* is certainly one prominent example of literature that can be enjoyed by all children, adolescents, and young adults, especially girls and women seeking to escape from a patriarchal world. An immigrant to the United States from Bohemia (now the Czech Republic), Antonia Shimerda is, like Anne Shirley (who is a migrant from Nova Scotia), an adolescent in search of a new home and identity.

Although she is not an orphan in the traditional sense, Antonia also suffers from feelings of abandonment, displacement, restlessness, and rebellion. It is this state of liminality – of drifting somewhere between two cultures and not belonging to either, speaking English with an accent – that provides Antonia with the ability to transgress social boundaries and claim agency, mostly out of self-preservation. Rather than behaving like a "demure" child, she, like Anne, "talks back" and expresses her thoughts to both adults and her peers, and in the process attains self-awareness, self-confidence, and self-worth. As Jim Burden, the narrator of the novel and Antonia's childhood companion, conveys, she is "bright as a new dollar" with hair that is "curly and wild-looking," and a deep, "husky," and commanding voice which, like Anne, she often uses to recount stories.[22] The pinnacle of "alternative girlhood," she also constantly asks questions and has "opinions about everything."[23] Not only did Antonia's willingness to speak English despite her strong accent and poor vocabulary inspire my students, but her courage to do so in an atmosphere that is hostile to the voices of girls and women also helped them appreciate the power of self-expression.

Although Jim, as a representative of the white male Anglo-Saxon Protestant patriarchal hegemony, tries to curtail Antonia's "plucky" independence and rejection of essentialized female qualities, to his chagrin, she challenges his masculine authority by refusing to obey his directives.[24] Instead, she attempts to dominate him, rendering him both emasculated and ineffectual. As he states, "Much as I liked Antonia, I hated the superior tone that she sometimes took with me ... I was a boy and she was a girl, and I resented her protecting manner."[25]

Jim selfishly, and rather egotistically, assumes that by subjectifying Antonia as "My" Antonia, he will be able to restrain and possess her.[26] However, as students remarked, Antonia, like Anne, cannot be "owned," even by her potential love interest. In the end, it is Jim who, like Gilbert Blythe, assumes the "traditional" role of female passivity. Antonia is never possessed by Jim, just as Anne never really "belongs" to Gilbert. Thus, despite their shared fate of domesticity (both ultimately choose marriage and motherhood over other pursuits), Anne and Antonia remain "plucky," independent, and opinionated, successfully resisting patriarchal ownership. They use their imaginations to distinguish themselves from other characters in the novels, and in the process, (re)invent their own identities. Both protagonists even undergo a process of (re)naming that parallels their place in the world: Anne reminds us that her name is spelled with an "e," then prefers to be called Cordelia (though she also toys with Geraldine and Elaine), and eventually becomes "Anne of Green Gables," while Antonia becomes "Tony."

The novels concentrate mainly on the adventures of children. This focus not only encourages the formation of a subversive space in which both characters can create their own independent identities, but also allows student readers to enter Anne and Antonia's relatively unsupervised worlds by inserting themselves into their permeable landscapes.[27] Most students identified with Anne and Antonia's alienation, loneliness, and *difference*, as well as their struggles to "belong" in new environments. As social "outsiders," adolescents and first-year university students often face the same issues. Temma Berg observes that in her own case, "just as Anne's reading gave her models, patterns, and ways to interpret her experience, Anne and her books gave me models, patterns, and ways to interpret and validate my experience."[28] Moreover, because they are not under constant adult control, Anne and Antonia are able to experiment and explore "alternate modes of behavior," which prove to be successful strategies in eliding society's conformative drive to produce "predetermined personalities."[29] As Anne explains to her "bosom" friend and kindred spirit, Diana Barry: "There's such a lot of different Annes in me. I sometimes think that is why I'm such a troublesome person. If I was just the one Anne, it would be ever so much more comfortable, but then it wouldn't be half so interesting."[30]

Anne and Antonia's status as self-sufficient, ambitious, strong-willed, assertive, and even angry (as illustrated through Anne's "slate" scene with Gilbert) feminist girls nevertheless deprives them of many of the simple joys of childhood. Both are forced to mature beyond their years in order to survive, and both perceive competition and arguing, especially with Gilbert Blythe and Jim Burden respectively, as a means of expressing maturity and intelligence. Rather than being interested in domestic work, Anne is fascinated by the literary world (she frequently recites poetry and performs scenes from classic literature), while Antonia is deeply ensconced in the world of male labour. While, on the surface, Anne's fascination adds to the frivolity of her character by portraying a type of impractical escapism, and Antonia's choices reinforce her otherness in U.S. society as an Eastern European Catholic immigrant, Anne's eloquence and erudition and Antonia's ability to save her family from starvation through physical work ultimately challenge the socially constructed gender roles that posit men as aggressive and powerful and women as passive and weak.[31] Anne and Antonia are able to defy expectations about how "good girls" should act and win their respective power struggles mainly because they are "women in children's bodies" (or, as Anne first appears to Matthew, a "stray woman-child"), who are not only "seen" but also "heard."

By "joining men during times of struggle and mimicking masculinity, [Antonia] not only illustrates the constructedness of gender roles, but also challenges the traditionally-male occupation of nation building ... As Cather illustrates ... [this subversion] undermines male hegemony by portraying the 'masculine' immigrant pioneer woman as an active participant in nation building, while the 'effeminate' pioneer man remains a passive observer."[32] As students noted, on the one hand, Jim writes poetry; on the other hand, "rough" Tony is hired out "like a man," and draws her strength from the earth. She becomes "merged with the land,"[33] transforming the new "nation" from a wilderness, through her own physical effort and perspiration.[34] As Antonia asserts, "School is all right for little boys. I help make this land one good farm ... I not care that your grandmother say [farming] makes me like a man. I like to be like a man."[35] As Jim notes – perhaps with a sense of envy – Antonia is "too proud of her [own] strength."[36] However, he does not acknowledge that her pride is a defense mechanism – one that provides her with the strength to overcome poverty, starvation, and her father's suicide. Like Anne, Antonia is forced to forego her education not because of preference, but out of familial responsibility.

Despite Jim's bucolic, mythic, and even epic descriptions of the American frontier, *My Antonia* shatters the romance of the West by validating the brutality, violence, physical labour, and emotional turmoil involved in nation-building.[37] *Anne of Green Gables*, in contrast, elides these discourses through Anne's imaginative, romantic, pastoral, almost transcendental portrayal of the flora and fauna of her idyllic homeland. Nevertheless, like Cather, Montgomery conveys that children – whether they be male or female – are an integral part of nation-building, whatever form it might take. (In this volume, Collins-Gearing problematizes the nation-building child on "stolen land.") Anne shares Antonia's pioneering ethos; however, she does not participate in nation-building in the same overtly gender-transgressive manner. Throughout the novel, Anne engages in the multi-tasking associated with farms, and thus through the microcosm of Green Gables sustains a civilized oasis in the Canadian "wilderness." Anne's pioneering spirit is not expressed through a physical "ploughing of the land" because, as Elizabeth Helen Thompson conveys, her "frontier is social rather than physical."[38] She pushes the boundaries of acceptable behaviour for young women in Avonlea not through bodily prowess but through intellectual expression. When "financial disaster [the failure of Abbey Bank and the loss of the Cuthbert family savings], Matthew's death, and Marilla's failing eyesight mean that Green Gables is threatened, [Anne] decides to set aside her dreams and accepts her responsibilities."[39] Rather than attending Redmond and becoming a "world-renowned" writer, she assumes the admirable task of teaching future generations of Canadians – the local Avonlea children.

While critics have read this sacrifice of the public sphere for the private as anti-feminist – an example of how Anne's "horizons had closed in"[40] – this interpretation assumes that choices that involve the family (or the private sphere in general) are "feminine" and thus automatically inferior. In the context of nation-building, Anne's decision is significant because personal sacrifice and power drawn from the private sphere often serve as the bedrock of a country. The mere fact that she comes to her final choice looking forward to that adventurous "bend in the road"[41] makes it, if anything, a "heroic" maternal feminist decision.[42] Moreover, Anne's "substitution for the expected male laborer," and her succession of Matthew as "breadwinner," which essentially reverses the adult/child relationship in the Cuthbert household, reinforces her individual power and the notion that patriarchal "authority ... is not needed to create a happy family."[43]

Like Antonia, Anne also undergoes a series of adolescent physical, emotional, and moral transitions. In both novels, these transformations come with new gender codes that complicate the definition of what it means to be a "good girl." Initially, Anne and Antonia's prepubescent bodies resemble each other – both are lanky and without gender markers – in effect, almost indistinguishable from the bodies of boys of the same age. However, each takes a radically different course, with numerous consequences. While Antonia embraces her masculinity, Anne seeks to "feminize" herself by acquiring conventional, socially sanctioned, female attributes that will – superficially, at least – allow her to perform/imitate prescribed gender roles. However, Anne is unsuccessful in her acts of conformity, thereby becoming a nonconformist. She "wickedly" dyes her hair, with the hope of transforming it from the perpetually problematic red to a "raven black." Anne also attempts to mimic adulthood by putting her hair "up" and coveting what she believes to be mature (yet romantic) clothing.[44] Her mimicry of womanhood also extends to her behaviour, which has moral consequences when she hosts a private tea party for Diana. In an attempt to impress Diana, Anne decides to serve Marilla's famous raspberry cordial. Mistakenly, she retrieves the wrong bottle from the pantry and pours her guest currant wine instead. Diana becomes inebriated, and Anne is punished for the mishap, becoming, as students noted, a victim of the physical, psychological, and emotional mismatch that often occurs in adolescence.

Gender transgressions in Avonlea "are not simple failures to fulfill a role; they are viewed as moral derelictions that are punishable ... Anne's failure to succeed at feminine tasks – [such as] baking a cake [or] entertaining a friend at tea – [requires Marilla's corrective intervention]. [Anne] is held accountable to standards of femininity even when she does not fulfill them,"[45] an irony that explains why her guardians, from time to time, at least for appearance's sake, subject her to various forms of discipline. After Anne romantically decorates her hat with wild-flowers, Marilla scolds: "All I want is that you should behave like other little girls and not make yourself ridiculous."[46] However, even though Anne's misbehaviour reinforces the notion that a girl with a mind of her own is, as Mrs Barry comments, a "thoroughly bad, wicked little girl,"[47] the reader is left with the impression that Marilla does not really believe that Anne requires punishment. Marilla's attempts to discipline Anne seem to be the result of social pressures that require mothers to teach their daughters how to "behave like a proper young lady" – that is, to perform their female gender roles – and not a response to any genuine "wickedness" on Anne's part. At worst, Anne is a "strong-willed" child, who "unites practical ability through aesthetic sensibilities."[48] Some-times Anne daydreams as she completes chores, and on one occasion even mistakenly adds liniment to cake batter; but mostly her "wicked-ness" involves dispensing with facade in favour of direct action and expressing her opinions without paying attention to the social mech-anisms designed to limit women's voices (which is what Marilla and Rachel also do in varying degrees). Because these women are united in their transgression, Marilla's scoldings come across as almost tongue-in-cheek satires of adult authority. Thus, Anne is able to elide the shameful label of "wickedness" without much effort, and in the end reveals that it is not she who is "wicked," but rather the social rules that attempt to stifle female imagination, creativity, and intelligence.

Antonia's movement out of adolescence also involves the same sorts of struggles, however with far more violent consequences. While Anne's body eventually matures into a desirable adolescent slenderness which even Mrs Lynde admires, Antonia's body takes a decidedly masculine course of development – one that simultaneously makes her vulnerable to criticism and sexual danger.[49] Farmhands sneer at Antonia's mascu-linity, making her the target of (what we presume are vulgar, sexual) jokes. Moreover, she narrowly escapes being raped by her employer, Wick Cutter, whose misogyny manifests itself in violence toward An-tonia's unruly body.

Despite the fact that *Anne of Green Gables* and *My Antonia* were written approximately a century ago, their messages of acceptance, empowerment, individuality, self-reliance, and, above all, survival are still relevant to today's readership. This continued relevance, combined with the fact that these works seem to transcend time and place and are teachable globally, is what makes them and their female protagonists true literary "classics." Through their transgression of gender roles and unusual precocity, Anne and Antonia are able to stretch the boundaries of and provide alternatives to what it meant to be an adolescent in late-nineteenth- and turn-of-the-twentieth-century North America. Through "fearless, imaginative communication, Anne breathes life into the Avonlea community, challenging authority and offering creative alternatives ... She is able to exceed the gendered expectations of her caretakers and community, and alter their environment with profoundly positive effects."[50] Similarly, Antonia makes a significant impact on her environment by transforming it from barren prairieland into a habitable homestead, thereby conveying the resounding message that women, even as adolescents, have the capacity to shape society.

Even though they are unable to eradicate the artificial gendered constructs that dominate their worlds, these protagonists successfully illustrate that there is far more to be gained from diversity than conformity and that harmony can be found amid conflicting worlds. Both are able to transform from dependent children to self-sufficient, dutiful young women, with or without patriarchal figures waiting in the shadows.

## NOTES

1  See Raw and Gültekin, "Towards a Pedagogy," and Pakin, "American Studies in Turkey."
2  The first Turkish translation of *Anne of Green Gables* is *Yuvasız Çocuk* (1983). Its 185-page length suggests that it has been abridged.
3  See Kornfeld and Jackson, "The Female Bildungsroman."
4  Devereux, Introduction.
5  Ibid., 26–7.
6  Rothwell, "Knitting Up the World," 135.
7  Ibid., 142–3.
8  Epperly, *The Fragrance of Sweet-Grass*, 7.
9  O'Brien, "'The Thing Not Named,'" 580–1.
10  Ibid.
11  Carden, "Creative Fertility," 279.
12  Davis, "Mistress Mary," 42.
13  Berg, "*Anne of Green Gables*," 125.

14  Foster and Simons, *What Katy Read*, 160.

15  Ibid.

16  Davis, "Mistress Mary," 42.

17  Montgomery, *Anne of Green Gables*, 97.

18  Goulden and Stanfield, "Leaving Elsie Dinsmore Behind," 193–4.

19  Montgomery, *Anne of Green Gables*, 112.

20  Ibid., 120.

21  Lindemann, "'It Ain't My Prairie,'" 116–17.

22  Cather, *My Antonia*, 4, 23, 171. Critics have often associated Jim's last name, Burden, with the oppressive, racist, and patriarchal "White Man's Burden." See Irving, "Displacing Homosexuality," 98.

23  Cather, *My Antonia*, 29.

24  Irving, "Displacing Homosexuality," 91–2.

25  Cather, *My Antonia*, 41.

26  Peck, *The Imaginative Claims*, 128.

27  This notion of "becoming Anne Shirley" is echoed in the writings of numerous readers of the *Anne* series, including literary critics/authors such as Temma Berg and Margaret Atwood. See Berg, "*Anne of Green Gables*," and Atwood, Afterword.

28  Berg, "*Anne of Green Gables*," 125.

29  Davis, "Mistress Mary," 43.

30  Montgomery, *Anne of Green Gables*, 200.

31  For more information on the status of nineteenth-century Eastern European (Czech) immigrants in U.S. society, see Prchal, "The Bohemian Paradox."

32  Tunc, "Nation-Building," 214.

33  Saposnik-Noire, "The Silent Protagonist," 177.

34  Cather, *My Antonia*, 133.

35  Ibid., 118, 133.

36  Ibid., 121.

37  For more information on Cather's pastoral, yet violent, description of the American landscape in *My Antonia*, see Saposnik-Noire, "The Silent Protagonist," and Tellefsen, "Blood in the Wheat."

38  Thompson, The Pioneer Woman, 82.

39  Dawson, "Literary Relations," 42.

40  Montgomery, *Anne of Green Gables*, 332.

41  Ibid., 334.

42  Kornfield and Jackson, "The Female Bildungsroman," 74.

43  Davis, "Mistress Mary," 53; Daniher, "From Green Gables to Shangri-L.A."

44  For more on Anne's fashion sensibilities, see chapter 11 in Gammel, *Looking for Anne*, and MacDonald in this volume.

45  McQuillan and Pfeiffer, "Why Anne Makes Us Dizzy."

46  Montgomery, *Anne of Green Gables*, 131.

47  Ibid., 170.

48  Thompson, *The Pioneer Woman*, 82.
49  Carden, "Creative Fertility," 289.
50  Davis, "Mistress Mary," 52–3.

## BIBLIOGRAPHY

Atwood, Margaret. Afterword to *Anne of Green Gables*, by L.M. Montgomery, 331–6. Toronto: McClelland & Stewart, 1992.

Berg, Temma F. "*Anne of Green Gables*: A Girl's Reading." *Children's Literature Association Quarterly*, vol. 13.3 (1988): 124–8.

Carden, Mary Paniccia. "Creative Fertility and the National Romance in Willa Cather's *O Pioneers!* and *My Antonia*." *Modern Fiction Studies*, vol. 45.2 (1999): 275–302.

Cather, Willa. *My Antonia*. 1918. Edited by Charles W. Mignon, Kari Ronning, and James Leslie Woodress. Lincoln, Nebraska: University of Nebraska Press, 1994.

Daniher, Colleen. "From Green Gables to Shangri-L.A.: Uncovering the Path of Feminism in Adolescent Literature." http://www.uwo.ca/wcwi/essay-award/2005.htm (accessed 23 January 2013).

Davis, Shannon. "Mistress Mary, Quite Contrary: Transformational Anger in the Heroines of Children's Literature." *Explorations* (2005): 39–55.

Dawson, Janis. "Literary Relations: Anne Shirley and Her American Cousins." *Children's Literature in Education*, vol. 33.1 (2002): 29–51.

Devereux, Cecily. Introduction to *Anne of Green Gables*, by L.M. Montgomery, 12–38. Peterborough, Ontario: Broadview Press, 2004.

Epperly, Elizabeth R. *The Fragrance of Sweet-Grass: L.M. Montgomery's Heroines and the Pursuit of Romance*. Toronto: University of Toronto Press, 1993.

Foster, Shirley, and Judy Simons. *What Katy Read, Feminist Re-Readings of "Classic" Stories for Girls*. Iowa City, Iowa: University of Iowa Press, 1995.

Gammel, Irene. *Looking for Anne of Green Gables: The Story of L.M. Montgomery and Her Literary Classic*. New York: St Martin's Press, 2008.

Goulden, Nancy Rost, and Susan Stanfield. "Leaving Elsie Dinsmore Behind: Plucky Girls as an Alternative Role Model in Classic Girls Literature." *Women's Studies*, vol. 32.2 (2003): 183–208.

Irving, Katrina. "Displacing Homosexuality: The Use of Ethnicity in Willa Cather's *My Antonia*." *Modern Fiction Studies*, vol. 36.1 (1990): 91–102.

Kornfeld, Eve, and Susan Jackson. "The Female Bildungsroman in Nineteenth-Century America." *Journal of American Culture*, vol. 10 (1987): 69–75.

Lindemann, Marilee. "'It Ain't My Prairie': Gender, Power and Narrative in *My Antonia*." In *New Essays on "My Antonia,"* edited by Sharon O'Brien, 111–36. New York: Cambridge University Press, 1999.

McQuillan, Julia, and Julie Pfeiffer. "Why Anne Makes Us Dizzy: Reading *Anne of Green Gables* from a Gender Perspective." *Mosaic: A Journal for the Interdisciplinary Study of Literature*, vol. 34.2 (2001): 17–32.

Montgomery, L.M. *Anne of Green Gables*. Edited by Cecily Devereux. Peterborough, Ontario: Broadview Press, 2004.

– *Yuvasız Çocuk*. Translated by Ipek Öngun. Istanbul: Altin Çocuk Kitapları, 1983.

O'Brien, Sharon. "'The Thing Not Named': Willa Cather as a Lesbian Writer." *Signs*, vol. 9.4 (1984): 576–99.

Pakin, Esra. "American Studies in Turkey during the 'Cultural' Cold War." *Turkish Studies*, vol. 9.3 (2008): 507–24.

Peck, Demaree C. *The Imaginative Claims of the Artist in Willa Cather's Fiction*. Selinsgrove, Pennsylvania: Susquehanna University Press, 1996.

Prchal, Tim. "The Bohemian Paradox: *My Antonia* and Popular Images of Czech Immigrants." *MELUS*, vol. 29.2 (2004): 3–25.

Raw, Laurence, and Gonca Gültekin, "Towards a Pedagogy for 'Adapting America' in the Language Classroom." In *The Theme of Cultural Adaptation in American History, Literature, and Film: Cases When the Discourse Changed*, edited by Laurence Raw, Tanfer Emin Tunc, and Gülriz Büken, chapter 15. Lewiston, New York: Edwin Mellen, 2009.

Rothwell, Erika. "Knitting Up the World: L.M. Montgomery and Maternal Feminism in Canada." In *L.M. Montgomery and Canadian Culture*, edited by Irene Gammel and Elizabeth Epperly, 133–44. Toronto: University of Toronto Press, 1999.

Saposnik-Noire, Shelley. "The Silent Protagonist: The Unifying Presence of Landscape in Willa Cather's *My Antonia*." *Midwest Quarterly*, vol. 31.2 (1990): 171–9.

Tellefsen, Blythe. "Blood in the Wheat: Willa Cather's *My Antonia*." *Studies in American Fiction*, vol. 27 (1999): 229–44.

Thompson, Elizabeth Helen. *The Pioneer Woman: A Canadian Character Type*. Montreal: McGill-Queen's University Press, 1991.

Tunc, Tanfer Emin. "Nation-Building and American National Identity in Willa Cather's *My Antonia*." *Çankaya University Journal of Arts and Sciences*, vol. 6 (2006): 205–21.

# The Continuous Popularity of *Red-haired Anne* in Japan: An Interview with Yoshiko Akamatsu

YOSHIKO AKAMATSU

*This interview came about following Yoshiko Akamatsu's presentation titled "The Powers of Text, Translaion, and Transformation: Rethinking the Continuous Popularity of* Red-haired Anne *in Japan," given at the 2008 L.M. Montgomery International Conference on 26 June 2008. Intrigued by the variety of Akamatsu's ideas about "translations" of the text in Japan, the editors initiated an email conversation to uncover more about the linguistic and technological innovations that have transformed the text into multiple media in contemporary Japan.*[1]

EDITORS: How would you explain the continuous popularity of *Anne of Green Gables* in Japan?

AKAMATSU: In Japan, L.M. Montgomery's *Anne of Green Gables*, known as *Akage-no-An* or *Red-haired Anne*, is universally recognized as a Canadian classic. *Red-haired Anne* has not been out of print since its first translation in Japan in 1952. One generation has passed it to the next, and this inheritance continues. Almost all school and public libraries have copies of *Anne of Green Gables* in Japanese, which means that this Canadian novel has become part of Japan's "cultural capital," the unconscious knowledge cultivated by one's parents, education, and society.[2] Although most young Japanese readers today have never read a Japanese translation of *Anne of Green Gables*, they certainly know her name and can easily recognize her image, made popular by the famous animation series adaptation of 1979. In 2008 Japan joined the world in celebrating Anne's centenary. As a result of the many events and celebratory projects, Anne's exposure again spread through Japan, touching many who had never even read the book.

EDITORS: What are the key aspects of the novel that have drawn readers to Montgomery's books through the years in Japan?

AKAMATSU: Anne's forward-looking attitude and her philosophy of making the most of life have always attracted Japanese readers. Many readers also remember the scene in *Anne of Avonlea* in which Anne and Gilbert are talking about life. Anne says, "I'd like to add some beauty to life ... I'd love to make [people] have a pleasanter time because of me ... to have some little joy or happy thought that would never have existed if I hadn't been born."[3] To which Gilbert answers: "I think you're fulfilling that ambition every day."[4] The *Anne* books' attention to beauty – the aesthetic – is also hugely appealing to readers. For example, in chapter 21 of *Anne of Green Gables*, Anne shows her artistic talent by decorating the tea table with roses and ferns for Mr and Mrs Allan. As the couple praise the table's loveliness and Marilla recognizes its beauty, this episode shows that a suitably decorated table setting can be both an art and a symbol of hospitality. Later, in chapter 36, when Anne, who has now graduated from Queen's Academy, returns to Green Gables, she finds Marilla "set a flowering house rose on the window sill"[5] for Anne. This suggests Anne's influence on Marilla, who did not previously realize the value of such decorations. These scenes suggest ways of enjoying beauty in everyday life, and Japanese readers relate to aesthetic values.

Anne's tendency to name beautiful places and things is another way of finding beauty in everyday life. For instance, she calls the cherry tree outside her bedroom "Snow Queen" because it is so white in full bloom. As she says, "one can imagine that it is [always in blossom]"[6] owing to its name. Anne preserves the beauty of an object in its name and makes objects more accessible that so everyone can understand them. But there are a number of other features of the text that have made it universally appealing. First, there is its protagonist, Anne Shirley. Her personality, full of imagination, observation, and expression, has had enduring appeal. Also appealing to Japanese readers are the literary quotations and allusions that bring depth to the text. Representations of gender have also been important to Japanese readers. These can be seen in Anne's failure to embody the feminine ideal despite her striving to do so (as Tanfer Emin Tunc's essay in this volume shows) and in Montgomery's well-written descriptions of women's culture, such as the interest in fashion (which Jennie MacDonald's essay in this volume discusses).

The book's depiction of the innocence of adolescence, when young adolescents have limited interest in the opposite sex, and the delicate descriptions of nature, which relate to Anne's growth, are subtle themes not lost on Japanese readers. Finally, Japanese readers appreciate that the story is one of wish-fulfillment and that the richness of the reality portrayed is based on the author's experience. All these elements come together to create the power of this text, the most important of which is Anne's personality.

EDITORS: Hanako Muraoka's enchantment with *Anne of Green Gables* and her heroic efforts to translate the book during wartime in Japan are of special significance when we think of the novel and its classic status. Could you discuss Muraoka's translation?

AKAMATSU: In *Anne of Green Gables*, there are elements of metaphorical translation. Anne is a girl "from away" and, struck by the beauty of Prince Edward Island, after having heard that it is "the prettiest place in the world,"[7] she begins to rename places as she drives to Green Gables with Matthew Cuthbert. "The Avenue" of apple trees is christened the "White Way of Delight"; "Barry's Pond" becomes the "Lake of Shining Waters." In a sense, she translates the places she sees into her own "language." By the end of chapter 20, her re-naming is complete and not only Anne, but also other people of Avonlea have come to accept and use the new names she has given them.

Anne's power of "translation" – namely, the power of her poetic sense – captured the heart and mind of Hanako Muraoka (1893–1968), the first Japanese translator of *Anne of Green Gables*. Muraoka, who was a poet as well as a translator, encountered *Anne* for the first time in 1939 when she received a 1908 copy of the book from her Canadian missionary friend, Loretta Shaw (1872–1940). Shaw gave the book to Muraoka as a token of their friendship when Shaw was forced to leave Japan because of the fierce conditions of the Second World War. Immediately taken by the power of the text of *Anne of Green Gables*, Muraoka began translating it as bombs rained down upon Tokyo. Muraoka's poetic sensibility was drawn to Anne and to Montgomery's artistic use of words, and she succeeded in catching the spirit of *Anne of Green Gables*, which she entitled *Red-haired Anne*. The book was first published in Japan in

1952, when Japan had regained peace after its unconditional surrender, and Muraoka wanted children to have access to positive and uplifting books. In the next seven years, Muraoka went on to translate all the sequels, and their publication has contributed to the first book's ongoing popularity.[8]

EDITORS: Despite the success of this translation among readers, it remains controversial among scholars. What is the source of their criticism of Muraoka's work?

AKAMATSU: Recently, some scholars and readers have criticized Muraoka for having omitted parts of the original from her translation.[9] Muraoka's *Red-haired Anne* is missing portions of the dedication, the epigraph from Robert Browning's poem, and some parts of the latter chapters, as chapters 36, 37, and 38 are abridged. One of the possible reasons for these omissions is that the publisher requested them because of the shortage of paper after the war, but the true reason remains a mystery. Muraoka may have had a chance to revise her translation when postwar conditions stabilized, but she didn't do so. However, since the main role of Japanese literary translations immediately after the war was simply to introduce Western stories to Japan, not to reproduce them strictly in their original form, it is unfair to be too critical of Muraoka, especially in light of her achievement.[10]

EDITORS: Have there been other translations into Japanese?

AKAMATSU: Since Muraoka's death in 1968, more than thirty translators have completed new versions of *Anne of Green Gables*; almost all of them used *Red-haired Anne* as their title, and many of them used the same Japanese words as Muraoka when they translated such Anne-isms as "bosom friend" and "Lake of Shining Waters." The first translation is the touchstone for all the others. Subsequent translators have tried to come up with their own translations, but Muraoka's still has the charm of her poetic expression.

Since then, times have changed and today's Japanese readers can easily access the original text through books and the Internet. Therefore, translators of the twenty-first century have to find ways to attract modern readers. In early 2008 we saw new and different strategies offered to promote new translations by translators Yuko Matsumoto and Mie Muraoka.

First, a three-month-long English conversation program called *To Anne's World* aired on television.[11] Yuko Matsumoto, a translator of *Anne*, was the host, and the program contained a lot of footage of Prince Edward Island. This program was very popular and was soon scheduled for rebroadcast later that same year.[12] Matsumoto used the program primarily to guide viewers to the original text, and also to attract readers to her 2000 revised translation of *Anne of Green Gables*. Her translation, first published in hardcover in 1993, has many notes and is targeted toward adult readers. Matsumoto also published two sequels, *Anne of Avonlea* in 2001 and *Anne of the Island* in 2008, in the same fully annotated style, under the same Japanese titles as Muraoka's. She also published by-products of her translation, such as the backstory of her translation, *Red-haired Anne's Translation Story* (1998) and *Shakespeare Hidden in Red-haired Anne* (2001), and has continued advertising her translations on her Web site. It can be said that the differences between Muraoka's translation and Matsumoto's are time and technology.[13]

Another recent translation is by Hanako Muraoka's granddaughter, Mie Muraoka. If Matsumoto's translation uses time and technology to do something new with the translation, then Mie Muraoka can be said to collapse time with hers, to close the gap between generations. Mie published a revised translation of her grandmother's work in February 2008, remaining true to Hanako's style, adding the omitted parts, and modernizing some of the language to make it more accessible to today's readers. Mie did not want her own name printed on the cover of the books but preferred instead to pass on the legacy of her grandmother's work; she has since completed her revision of all ten translated *Anne* books. Cleverly, the publisher offered an essay contest, the first prize of which was a trip to Prince Edward Island. This strategy was sure to guarantee that many people would participate in the contest and read the revised translation. Mie's younger sister, Eri Muraoka, also published their grandmother's biography, called *Anne's Cradle*, in 2008 and explained how Hanako devoted herself to capturing Anne's appealing use of language in the original text. Eri's book also played the role of supporting her sister's revised translation, allowing readers to understand how the original text stimulated Hanako Muraoka's "scope for imagination," and how her granddaughter breathed new life into Hanako's translation of *Anne of Green Gables*.[14]

EDITORS: You have mentioned that while young people may not be reading the novel, they are accessing *Anne* through other means, such as the animated television series. Tell us about these strategies.

AKAMATSU: The 1979 animated version of *Anne of Green Gables* had a tremendous influence on Japanese culture, especially on children. It was part of a series called "World Classics Theatre" on television from 1975 to 1997.[15] *Anne* and other works such as *Heidi* and *Little Women* were animated and broadcast on Sunday evenings from 7:30 to 8:00. They were like classics being read at public libraries for the whole family to enjoy. The production staff used a brand new translation of *Anne* by Taeko Kamiyama (1973), and they went to Prince Edward Island to make their work more visually authentic. As the series has fifty episodes in contrast to the thirty-eight chapters of the original book, additional scenes were added, mostly as background to already established scenes. In spite of these additions, this animation is said to be very faithful to the original text.

Although many devout Anne-fans had their initial doubts about the series, this animation was highly esteemed and has been rebroadcast many times. It was even broadcast in Italy in 1980 under the Italian translation of the Japanese title, *Red-haired Anne*.[16] As a devout Anne-fan myself, I was at first hesitant to watch this program for fear that the visualization might spoil the mystery of Anne's imaginary world for me. However, when I later had the opportunity to see the series for the first time, I regretted having lost the chance to see it when it was originally broadcast. One of my favourite scenes is Anne and Matthew's drive to Green Gables, which portrays Anne's rich imagination well. An adapted episode in the animation, in which Marilla scolds Anne for trying to make Diana persuade her parents to let her enter Queen's Academy, gave me new insights into Anne and Diana's relationship that I had not thought of when reading the original text. There are also some scenes in the animation that I do not like; for example, there is unnecessary expansion of the character of Minnie May, Diana's younger sister. Overall, however, the animated *Anne of Green Gables* is successful in widening the scope of the story over fifty episodes rather than the original thirty-eight chapters.

The animation of *Anne of Green Gables* made Anne a recognizable icon in Japan to a whole new generation of young people. Since then, there have been countless products bearing her image – little moveable plastic dolls, stuffed dolls, stationery items, jigsaw puzzles, memorial plates, and so many more. In celebration of the centenary of *Anne of Green Gables* in 2008, memorial stamps of Anne were issued in Japan, as they were in Canada, and the Japanese designs are those of the animated *Red-haired Anne*. The ten stamps show Anne coming of age with her new family and friends. The same company that produced the original animation series, Nippon Animation, made a new animation based on *Hello, Anne*, the Japanese translation of Budge Wilson's *Before Green Gables*. The translation was published in 2008, and the animation aired in 2009. The character of this younger Anne is reminiscent of the Anne in the 1979 version and gives a second life to the animated character of Anne Shirley which is familiar to most Japanese people. Although some may say such visual manifestations of the text have the tendency to limit one's imagination, these transformed versions do have the positive function of leading people back to the original text.

EDITORS: You have been involved in "Anne-centred exhibitions" in Japan. Can you describe these?

AKAMATSU: Before the centenary, the Fukuyama Literary Museum held an exhibition called "*Anne of Green Gables*: Journey to Prince Edward Island," in 2004. This museum is situated in Hiroshima Prefecture in western Japan, in Fukuyama City. As a co-producer and adviser, I invited the co-operation of my friends who belong to Buttercups, a Montgomery fan club of 130 members,[17] and we held this exhibition to express our love for Anne and Prince Edward Island. People from all over Japan loaned us their Anne-inspired treasures. Some of the handicrafts included a big dollhouse of Green Gables, tapestries, hats, Anne-dolls, and apron dresses. One housewife had planted the same flowers as those in *Anne of Green Gables* and made panels of photos of them to share. In the months leading up to the exhibition, all the participants experienced the truth of Anne's declaration, "Oh Marilla, looking forward to things is half the pleasure of them."[18]

Although it was the first time the museum had focused on a Canadian novel with no direct connection to Fukuyama City, this exhibition was a great success, attracting the fourth-highest number of visitors the museum had ever had. The enthusiastic response showed not only Japanese readers' admiration for Western culture but also their desire to include it in their daily life in the twenty-first century. As fewer and fewer people read books these days, literary museums play an important role in giving people the chance to discover the pleasure and happiness of reading books.

Four years later, from December 2008 to February 2009, the Fukuyama Museum of Literature hosted an exhibition called "Montgomery's Winter Tales: The Worlds of Anne and Emily" under my supervision. We analyzed *Anne of Green Gables* and *Emily of New Moon* from the viewpoint of Canadian life shifting from winter to spring. Although Montgomery did not describe many winter scenes in Anne's story, Anne's presence leads Matthew and Marilla to remember their youth and changes their colourless life into an exciting one. Anne shows us the magic of imagining spring during winter.[19] Following a close reading of the text, we tried to reproduce the world of Montgomery in Japan. Just before the exhibition's opening, Kate Macdonald Butler, the granddaughter of L.M. Montgomery, visited the Fukuyama Museum of Literature. Her visit received full coverage in newspapers and contributed to the promotion of this exhibition. This second Anne exhibition was also a great success and broke another record for the museum, making it the third-most-visited exhibition in its history. Not only citizens of Fukuyama, but people from all over Japan visited the museum.

From June 2008 to June 2009, department stores around Japan hosted a touring exhibition honouring Anne's centenary. This exhibition was called "*Anne of Green Gables*: Montgomery's Beloved Prince Edward Island." Montgomery's manuscripts were exhibited outside Canada for the first time, some scenes from the book were reproduced, and photos of Prince Edward Island, Hanako Muraoka's biography, Prince Edward Island products, and, of course, items inspired by the animated series were available for sale. As Margaret Atwood mentions in her essay "Nobody ever did want me," the Japanese are a souvenir-obsessed people![20] Since it is a journey of over fifteen hours from Japan to Prince Edward Island, these exhibitions offered a rare chance for Japanese people to buy products made in Prince Edward Island and Canada. It is reported that more than 200,000 Japanese people visited the department store exhibitions.[21]

Some would claim that exhibitions such as these are purely money-making schemes, and they certainly are that. However, I believe that they also offer people an opportunity to encounter Anne "first hand," so to speak, generating interest in Montgomery's works and her beloved home, Prince Edward Island, hopefully leading some to visit the original text for the first time.

EDITORS: What is it about these "first-hand" encounters that is valuable to Japanese Anne enthusiasts?

AKAMATSU: As Mary Rubio wrote in *Lucy Maud Montgomery: The Gift of Wings*, Montgomery emphasizes the natural beauty of Prince Edward Island in *Anne of Green Gables*, capturing "the province's desire to develop tourism in the 1903–1907 period."[22] The original text inadvertently serves as a guidebook of Prince Edward Island. Japanese Anne enthusiasts want to see "the prettiest place in the world," remembering Anne's words from chapter 2. As most Japanese Anne fans understand the world of Anne through translation, information not translated into Japanese is inaccessible to them. In particular, information about L.M. Montgomery's life, including most of her journals, is still unknown to Japanese readers. When the Japanese audience has the opportunity to learn about the author through "first-hand" encounters such as exhibitions, they express their desire to read Japanese translations of all of the *Selected Journals of L.M. Montgomery* and new Anne-related books published in English-speaking nations. If Japanese publishers recognize the demand for the translations, they may be more willing to explore the writings by and about Montgomery outside Japan.

As a consequence of technology, it is increasingly possible to create Anne-centred "exhibitions" that are accessible in Japan. Another practical and useful way to send "first-hand" information from Prince Edward Island to the world, including Japan, is the Internet. "Picturing a Canadian Life: L.M. Montgomery's Scrapbooks and Book Covers,"[23] written in English, French, and Japanese, is a good example. An increase in such sites will boost Japanese readers' interest in Montgomery-related books, locations, and research.

EDITORS: It is fascinating to hear about how new media and technologies are introducing *Anne of Green Gables* to the younger generations who may not have read the book. What is the significance of these developments, and what might they mean for the classic novel?

AKAMATSU: Some people may criticize the Japanese ways of enjoying *Anne of Green Gables* as being transformations of the original, but the power of these Japanese adaptations makes the Canadian story an intimate classic, very much alive in twenty-first century Japan. In 2008 Japanese people celebrated the centenary of *Anne of Green Gables* as well as the millennium of *Genji Monogatari* (*The Tale of Genji*) (1008) by Murasaki Shikibu, or Lady Murasaki (c. 973–c. 1014 or 1025). Both are part of the cultural capital of Japan, which can be shared by people all over the world. Classics are books that allow for multiple interpretations, and *Anne of Green Gables* is no exception. As a result of encountering the animated version of *Anne of Green Gables*, or one of the Anne-centred exhibits, both children and grown-ups who seldom read books may find some interest in *Anne of Green Gables* and stretch out their hands to the bookshelves of libraries or bookstores. Permitting various means of access to the story will allow *Anne of Green Gables* to survive long into the future.

## NOTES

1 Akamatsu expresses her sincere thanks to her colleague and friend, Lyn Swierski, and to Kate Bowes, who patiently assisted her in preparing for the conference presentation.
2 Bourdieu and Passeron, *Reproduction*, 73–4.
3 Montgomery, *Anne of Avonlea*, 53.
4 Ibid.
5 Montgomery, *Anne of Green Gables*, 230.
6 Ibid., 35.
7 Ibid., 18.
8 Hanako Muraoka published her translation of the *Anne* series from *Anne of Green Gables* (1952) to *Rilla of Ingleside* (1959). For more information see Akamatsu, "Japanese Readings."
9 See Izawa, "The Problems Stemming from Truncation," 59–71.

10  See Sato, "Various Translations."
11  See Nippon Hoso Kyokai, *To Anne's World*.
12  For example, the April issue of this program sold more than 135,000 copies,
    according to Online Diary, April 2008, Yuko Matsumoto's Homepage, 30 April
    2008. http://homepage3.nifty.com/office-matsumoto
13  Yuka Kajihara-Nolan gave me useful hints for analyzing Matsumoto's attitude.
14  Muraoka [Revised by Mie Muraoka].
15  Nozawa, *Sekai Meisaku Gekigyo*.
16  At the 2008 L.M. Montgomery International Conference, Francesca Montushi
    explained how many children in Italy were introduced to *Anne of Green Gables*
    through this Japanese animation.
17  In 2008, Buttercups had about two hundred members.
18  Montgomery, *Anne of Green Gables*, 80.
19  See Akamatsu, "*Anne of Green Gables* as a Girls' Story and Adolescent Novel."
20  In her essay "Nobody ever did want me," Atwood describes Japanese tourists'
    enthusiasm for shopping as a mystery, but it is indeed a cultural trait.
21  "*Anne of Green Gables*: Montgomery's Beloved Prince Edward Island," 23
    March 2009. http://www.anne100th.com/
22  Rubio, *Lucy Maud Montgomery*, 257.
23  Available at http://lmm.confederationcentre.com

## BIBLIOGRAPHY

Akamatsu, Yoshiko. "*Anne of Green Gables* as a Girls' Story and Adolescent
    Novel." In [*World Classics We Would Like to Know More About*, Vol. 10: *Anne
    of Green Gables*], edited by Yuko Katsura and Sumiko Shirai, 41–50. Kyoto:
    Minerva Shobo, 2008.
–  "Japanese Readings of *Anne of Green Gables*." In *L.M. Montgomery and Can-
    adian Culture*, edited by Irene Gammel and Elizabeth Epperly, 201–12. To-
    ronto: University of Toronto Press, 1999.
[*Anne of Green Gables*: Montgomery's Beloved Prince Edward Island,] 23
    March 2009. http://www.anne100th.com/ (accessed 20 December 2011).
Atwood, Margaret. "Nobody ever did want me." *Guardian* [UK] 29 March 2008.
    http://www.guardian.co.uk/books/2008/mar/29/fiction.margaretatwood
    (accessed 20 December 2011).
Bourdieu, Pierre, and Jean-Claude Passeron. *Reproduction in Education, Soci-
    ety and Culture*. 2nd ed. London: Sage, 1990.
Confederation Centre of the Arts. "Picturing a Canadian Life: L.M. Montgom-
    ery's Personal Scrapbooks and Book Covers." 2002. http://lmm.confedera-
    tioncentre.com (accessed 20 December 2011).

Izawa, Yuko. "The Problems Stemming from Truncation: Muraoka Hanako's Truncations in Chapter 37 of *Anne of Green Gables*." *Miyagi Gakuin Women's College Annals of the Institute for Research in Humanities and Social Sciences* (Bulletin of Universities and Institutes), vol. 16 (2007): 59–71.

Matsumoto, Yuko, trans. *Akage no An* [*Red-haired Anne*]. By L.M. Montgomery. Revised edition, 1993. Tokyo: Shueisha, 2000.

– [Online Diary, April 2008, Yuko Matsumoto's Homepage]. 30 April 2008. http://homepage3.nifty.com/office-matsumoto (accessed 20 December 2011).

Montgomery, L.M. *Anne of Green Gables*. 1908. Edited by Mary Henley Rubio and Elizabeth Waterston. New York: Norton, 2007.

– *Anne of Avonlea*. 1909. Toronto: Bantam, 1998.

Muraoka, Eri. *An no Yurikago: Muraoka Hanako no Shogai*. [*Anne's Cradle: Biography of Hanako Muraoka*.] Tokyo: Magazine House, 2008.

Muraoka, Hanako, trans. *Akage no An* [*Red-haired Anne*.] 1952. By L.M. Montgomery. Tokyo: Mikasa Shobo; Tokyo: Shinchosha, 1954.

– *Akage no Anne* [*Red-haired Anne*.] By L.M. Montgomery. Revised by Mie Muraoka. Tokyo: Shinchosha, 2008.

Nozawa, Toru, ed. *Sekai Meisaku Gekigyo (World Classics Theatre): Akage no An*. [*Anne of Green Gables: Memorial Album*.] Tokyo: Kawaide Shobo Shinsha, 2005.

Nippon Hoso Kyokai [NHK], ed. *To Anne's World* (April, May, June, 2008). Tokyo: NHK Shuppan, 2008.

Rubio, Mary Henley. *Lucy Maud Montgomery: The Gift of Wings*. Toronto: Doubleday Canada, 2008.

Sato, Motoko. "Various Translations." In [*The Illustrated Dictionary of Children's Books and History of Translations*], edited by The Society for the Study of Children's Books and History of Translations, 16–19. Tokyo: Kashiwa Shobo, 2002.

Usagawa, Akiko, trans. *Konnnichiwa An* [*Hello, Anne*]. Translation of *Before Green Gables* by Budge Wilson. Tokyo: Shinchosha, 2008.

# "I experienced a light that became a part of me": Reading *Anne of Green Gables* in Sweden

## ÅSA WARNQVIST

*Anne of Green Gables* was first translated and published in Sweden as *Anne på Grönkulla* in 1909, the year after its original publication, making it the very first foreign-language translation of *Anne*. The novel has celebrated a century of success in the Swedish publishing industry and has long been established as a classic. The quotation in the title of this chapter comes from a Swedish reader's response to L.M. Montgomery's work. It captures the joy and fulfillment that the fictional world of Montgomery gave this reader in her youth. "I experienced a light that became a part of me" is her poetic way of describing the encounter with Montgomery's novel, and it is expressed much in the way Montgomery's heroine might have phrased it herself.[1] This reader is far from alone in describing a special bond between herself, the story, and the protagonist, Anne Shirley.

Montgomery's debut novel was published in Sweden as a story for youth, and it has been in print continuously since 1909. Few foreign-language books for youth have been in print consistently for more than a century in Sweden, and, to my knowledge, there is no other with a female protagonist. *Anne of Green Gables* is one of the best known and most influential foreign youth books in Sweden, and its century-long success calls for attention.

As Gabriella Åhmansson has put it, *Anne of Green Gables* is "as familiar to many Swedes as if it had been part of our own literary heritage."[2] What are the key factors in the novel's long-lasting fame in Sweden? How has Anne been regarded by publishers, critics, and readers during these hundred years? What impact did the story have on Swedish readers and writers during the twentieth century, and how do contemporary Swedish readers relate to the story of Anne? These are some of the questions that inform my research on the success and impact of Montgomery's work in Sweden. In this chapter, I outline some of my findings.[3]

From its first Swedish publication, *Anne på Grönkulla* was marketed as a story for young readers. The publishing house of C.W.K. Gleerups, known for its list of academic and religious works and textbooks, was the novel's first Swedish publisher. It was a large publishing house situated in Lund in the south of Sweden, with a strong connection to Lund University, one of Sweden's biggest universities, founded in 1666. Apart from its successful youth book series, C.W.K. Gleerups' Books for Youth series (C.W.K. Gleerups ungdomsböcker), the publishing house did not publish much fiction.[4] Its fiction list consisted largely of classic works such as the plays of Shakespeare and prominent works of ancient history. *Anne på Grönkulla* was adapted to fit into their youth book series.

Youth book series were quite common at the time, and C.W.K. Gleerups was just one of many Swedish publishing houses that published fiction for young readers. The series was popular, and many of its titles were reprinted multiple times. The first work in the series was published in 1899, and they kept adding new titles until the 1960s. *Anne på Grönkulla* appeared as Number 24. The last title carrying the book series name, a reprint of *Vår vän Anne* (*Anne of Avonlea*), was published in 1977, some years after the publishing house had been sold to the textbook publisher Liber.

The book series included a wide range of fiction, from stories about other parts of the world which were didactic or adventurous or both, to adaptations of Shakespeare plays. Initially it had a strong focus on adventure stories with male protagonists, like Herbert Strang's *Kobo, A Story of the Russo-Japanese War* and Baroness Emmuska Orczy's *The Scarlet Pimpernel*. *Anne på Grönkulla* was one of the first stories featuring a female protagonist and themes of classic girls' stories. The only record of C.W.K. Gleerups' decision to publish the novel is the letter of publisher Agne Gleerup (1872–1910) to the translator, Karin Jensen (1866–1928), in which he writes that both he and the introducer of the work appreciated *Anne of Green Gables* and that it "in our opinion is absolutely charming."[5] Since the work has motifs that touch the central topics of the publishing house's catalogue (education and religion), one can assume that they also considered it a fine contribution to their list. Girls' stories had also been a flourishing genre in Sweden, including Louisa May Alcott's *Little Women* (1866), which was translated and published in 1871, and Ethel Turner's *Seven Little Australians* (1894), published as early as 1895.

The translator Karin Jensen (née Lidforss) was married to the author and renowned translator Alfred Jensen and was the sister of Bengt Lidforss, a professor of botany at the University of Lund. Lidforss was long believed to have introduced *Anne* to Sweden. However, my research shows that it was Seved Ribbing (1845–1921), a doctor of medicine at Lund University and the president of the university from 1904 to 1907, who introduced the novel. According to correspondence between Agne Gleerup and Karin Jensen, it was Ribbing who brought the book to the publisher's attention.[6] Ribbing was a member of the board of the publishing house and an avid reader with a special interest in English literature. As an advocate of education, he would also have sympathized with the morals of the *Anne* story. No documents in the publishers' archives or Ribbing's personal archive provide specific information as to how Ribbing learned of the book's existence. Since Agne Gleerup ordered it in March 1909 from the British publisher, and at the same time asked after their terms for translation, one might surmise that Ribbing had become aware of it through British book advertisements, a review of the British edition, or a recommendation from an acquaintance with connections to the British Isles.[7]

Early correspondence between the publisher and Karin Jensen shows that C.W.K. Gleerups did not have the official rights to translate the novel into Swedish before Jensen was asked to begin her work. Agne Gleerup sent a letter to L.C. Page on 21 June 1909 inquiring about "what terms you are willing to grant me the right of translating 'Anne of Green Gables' by L.M. Montgomery into the Swedish language." In his letter Gleerup referred to the lack of agreement between the two countries when it came to copyright (no agreement was signed until 1911), and he indicated that he hoped therefore to pay less for the rights: "Althoug[h] no convention between United States and our country is existing, I find it more convenient to get the translation authorized, but the sum I have to pay must of course be a very little one."[8] On 26 June, four days before he received an answer from Page, Gleerup sent a letter to Jensen presenting the project and asking her to begin her translation as soon as possible so that the book could be released "well before Christmas."[9] There is no mention of the rights not being finalized in this or any other letter to Jensen, which suggests that Gleerup was either quite sure of a positive response from Page or was intending to publish the book regardless of the answer. Perhaps he wanted to act quickly before any other publisher got hold of it.

Page was willing to grant C.W.K. Gleerups the rights, but not for the moderate sum that Agne Gleerup had in mind. Most of the correspondence from Page to Gleerup has disappeared, and we therefore do not know precisely how Page responded. However, it is likely that Page not only enlightened Gleerup that *Anne of Green Gables* was published in England and therefore protected by copyright but also suggested a steep price for the rights. In his next letter, dated 14 July 1909, Gleerup stated that Page's conditions were "rather high" but agreed to them. Perhaps he did not dare to negotiate further, since he had already asked Karin Jensen to start working on the translation. Gleerup thus agreed to pay "a regular royalty of 10% of the publisher price, payment to be sent yearly in the month of June for copies sold last year."[10] A couple of months later, he sent the cheque for the advance (£10). However, no signed contract from Page showed up until 19 November, although the contract itself was dated 9 October.[11] By that time, Jensen would have completed her translation, and the novel would have already been sent to the printers. *Anne på Grönkulla* was released in mid-December.

One wonders if Gleerup had not expected a smoother process when dealing with Page. Correspondence concerning *Anne of Avonlea* indicates that he was not altogether pleased with the way things turned out, and that he did not wish to pay this "rather high" royalty for yet another book. The fact that he nevertheless continued to pay the same amount in royalty for each of the Montgomery books that Page had originally published suggests that he tried to renegotiate the terms of payment for the rights and failed.[12]

The C.W.K. Gleerups 1909 translation of *Anne of Green Gables* was a product distinctly shaped for the target group for which it was intended. Karin Jensen worked quickly to meet the publisher's deadline for the translation. She would have received the book in late June of 1909, and letters show that the translation was delivered piece by piece to the publishing house. Jensen probably finished and proofread the greater part, if not the whole of the book, before the end of October. This would mean that she completed the entire translation in little more than four months.

Several times in earlier correspondence with Karin Jensen, Agne Gleerup had indicated that the length of youth novels by writers from the English-speaking world was problematic. They were too long and often had to be abridged to fit the publisher's youth book series. *Anne of Green Gables* was apparently one of these too-lengthy books, for, along with the copy of the book, Gleerup sent Jensen notes from Seved Ribbing with suggestions of what could be omitted in the Swedish translation.[13] Neither these notes nor Jensen's reply have been kept, and we therefore do not know to what extent she followed Ribbing's suggestions. She did, however, make abridgments. As Cornelia Rémi has noted, "countless minor and major abridgements" occur in Jensen's translation. In chapters 25 and 26, for instance, the Swedish reader misses out on the scenes in which Matthew attempts to buy a dress for Anne in Carmody, and the formation of the Story Club. According to Rémi the more substantial omissions occur in the latter part of the novel, resulting in an emphasis on Anne as a child, a strategy that most likely sprang from the choice of target audience.[14]

Jensen not only made abridgments but also included changes and supplements to adjust the novel to the young audience. Both Gabriella Åhmansson and Cornelia Rémi have noted that Jensen adapted her translation to conform to a contemporary Swedish context.[15] Jensen let the people of Avonlea have coffee with their breakfast (as was customary in Sweden) instead of tea; she adapted botanical terms and food to the Swedish flora and cuisine, and changed literary references. For example, she replaced a canto from Walter Scott's "Marmion" with a more commonly known quote from Shakespeare's *Macbeth* and replaced a reference to *Ben-Hur* with one to *Uncle Tom's Cabin*, the latter being a well-known novel in Sweden at the time, having been adapted for children several times in the late nineteenth century. Apart from changes originating in socio-cultural differences, Jensen also seems to have had a didactic purpose when inserting additional explanations concerning, for example, baking preparations and needlework. "For a Swedish child not yet familiar with the habits and customs of other parts of the world, Jensen's translation provided ideal conditions to feel as close to Anne as if she were living on a nearby farm," concludes Rémi.[16]

In a later article, however, Rémi takes the analysis further and notes that Jensen, even if she reduced the impression of distance between heroine and reader, also kept elements that create geographical distances from the Swedish reader and anchor the work in its Canadian context. Jensen kept most of the Canadian place names, such as New-bridge, Bright River, and Carmody, and personal names such as Rachel Lynde, Matthew Cuthbert, and Gilbert Blythe – all challenges for young Swedish readers not familiar with English pronunciation. Because the scenery and climate of Prince Edward Island and Sweden are similar, Montgomery's descriptions of nature and seasonal changes are easily recognizable to Swedish readers. Had Jensen changed the Canadian place and personal names, it would indeed have been easy to look upon Anne as a next-door neighbour, but she chose not to. Thus, even if most of Jensen's changes strengthen the identification for young Swedish readers, both the exotic and the familiar are present in the work. This strategy, concludes Rémi, suits both readers who wish to discover the exotic and those seeking the familiar. The reader responses that I have collected support this conclusion. They show that it is not solely familiarity that has appealed to Swedish readers; quite a few emphasize the exotic elements of the story.[17] Both of these components seem to have been important in facilitating the novel's success.

When the Swedish translation came to be reviewed in 1909, Karin Jensen's translation was but one of many qualities critics appreciated. All the major newspapers reviewed the novel when it was released a few weeks before Christmas in 1909, and it is notable that all the critics praised it; negative remarks were few. Swedish critics warmly described Anne's story as funny, touching, and well written. For instance, *Svenska Dagbladet*, a leading Stockholm newspaper, compared *Anne på Grönkulla* with two other new novels aimed mainly at female readers in their early teens released at the same time, and concluded that "of these three, *Anne på Grönkulla*, is without doubt the best written, best translated, the funniest and also the most moving."[18] Montgomery's style and way of building an intriguing story were among the main reasons for the critics' high esteem. For instance, *Dagens Nyheter*, another Stockholm-based newspaper, wrote, "*Anne på Grönkulla* ... [is] by an author with a psychologically keen eye and unerring technique, not by a book manufacturer."[19]

The implicit expectation of female readership is likely the reason for the critics' emphasis on praising good morals and values in the story. For instance *Göteborgs-Posten*, a Gothenburg newspaper, suggested that "when it is so correct in morals and so God-fearing, any cautious mother can happily allow her young ones to become acquainted with red-haired Anne."[20] There is a general emphasis on Anne's educational struggles and ambitions, her "honest work, hopeful striving, and sincere friendship," and the way these, as well as the socialization and adaptation into a new society, foster her becoming a "useful and moral" citizen and a "good and moral woman." The story is consistently described as "wholesome" or "sound."[21] These values can be seen as complying with the criteria of a literary work directed toward upper- and middle-class girls. Thus, it well fulfilled the demands of a girls' story of the early 1900s. C.W.K. Gleerups' early editions of *Anne på Grönkulla* would have been read largely by girls of the middle and upper classes, partly because they were in fact intended for that audience, and partly because books were still not readily affordable at the beginning of the twentieth century.[22] Cheap books were becoming available in Sweden in the early 1900s, and the working class could eventually afford the luxury of books, but *Anne på Grönkulla* did not seem to be included in what the majority of the working class read. In a study of the 1920s and 1930s reading habits of the Swedish working class, few classic girls' stories were mentioned. The only one being widely read was Louisa May Alcott's *Little Women*.[23]

Things would soon change, however. In 1938, Eva von Zweigbergk (1906–1984), one of the most influential children's book critics at the time, was asked to mention the five books for young readers that she held in highest esteem. She chose *Anne på Grönkulla* as the second of these five, thus establishing the novel as one of life's "indispensible" books.[24] And, soon enough, the *Anne* series was widely embraced by readers.

In total, fourteen of Montgomery's novels and collections of short stories have been translated into Swedish, and several publishers have printed the *Anne* and *Emily* series in whole or in part during the last decades. *Anne på Grönkulla*, however, has had the most prominent and most lasting appeal. In 1988 the Sullivan TV series was broadcast and became a favourite that directed a new generation of readers to the books.[25] Thus, after more than a hundred years, this novel still finds an audience in Sweden. It has reached the status of classic and belongs on the prescribed reading lists of many university courses in children's literature.

Several studies of reading preferences in twentieth-century Sweden show that *Anne på Grönkulla* was well liked by young girls. The most famous of the early Swedish readers of Anne's adventures is Astrid Lindgren (1907–2002), author of the international classic *Pippi Långstrump* (*Pippi Longstocking*, 1945). Lindgren had a great love of *Anne på Grönkulla* and on several occasions delighted in recalling the impact of Anne on her young life. In a 1956 article on her childhood readings, she wrote: "Anne of Green Gables, oh, you my unforgettable; forever you ride in the buggy next to Matthew Cuthbert beneath the blossoming apple trees of Avonlea! How I lived with that girl! One whole summer I and my sisters played Anne of Green Gables in the big pile of sawdust up by the mill. I was Diana Barry and the dung puddle behind the barn was The Lake of Shining Waters."[26] The impact of Montgomery's writing on Lindgren's work has been the subject of several critical studies by scholars, and she is a good example of Montgomery's impact on Swedish writers and Swedish literary heritage.[27]

This impact carries into the present day. My research shows that Montgomery's books, despite the fact that they were marketed as books for youth, have not been read solely by children and young people in Sweden. Catherine Ross's study of North American readers, and Suvi Ahola and Satu Koskimies's results from collecting reading experiences from Finnish readers of Montgomery[28] support my conclusion that Montgomery's work crosses generational boundaries and becomes a link between generations. I found that new readers of Montgomery often become acquainted with Anne through their mothers, grandmothers, and other – generally female – relatives. Reader responses also show that readers tend to attribute power to the book as a physical object. Copies of *Anne på Grönkulla*, and quite often its sequels, are often passed along from one generation to another in a household; Montgomery's books are artifacts considered worthy of keeping in the family.[29]

The interesting question is *why* so many Swedish readers read and re-read *Anne på Grönkulla*, for it has proven to be a novel and a book series that people not only read once, but return to at different stages of their lives. In line with what Ross and also Ahola and Koskimies have noted, it is not uncommon for Swedish readers to re-read their favourite Montgomery books several times, sometimes every year.[30]

In my research, I collected experiences from Swedish readers through public libraries and the four major newspapers in Sweden. I received just over three hundred letters, and many of these readers start their accounts by expressing their joy at the fact that someone finally acknowledges their transformative experience of reading *Anne på Grönkulla*.[31] That kind of remark reappears so often that one has to conclude that the readers of Montgomery notice the lack of recognition given to their reading.

Almost all of the three hundred readers who shared their experience described their connection with Anne and her story as deep, heartfelt, and passionate. The principal source of the readers' emotional connection is above all Anne Shirley as a character, a girl and later a young woman to whom readers worldwide have been able to relate, regardless of culture, sex, age, social position, or education. One explanation is intimated by the wide range of adjectives with which readers described Anne, encapsulated in the following quotation from Eva Lindsten Nilsson (b. 1949), who wrote, "I was fascinated by Anne's personality, full of nuances and contrasts. Plus and minus interplaying gave charged energy – Avonlea met a girl who was skinlessly sensitive, exposed, labile *and* irrepressible, with defined limits, intact. Alone, 'ugly', rejected, *and* contact-seeking, captivating, charming. Destitute, homeless, underfed, *and* rich – a human being who in the impossible saw – or invented! – the possible. A mind's triumph over matter."[32]

The adjectives in this quotation are contradictory, a common trait in the material I collected, suggesting that there are a number of different ways to understand and embrace Anne as a character. As mentioned, Anne crosses both age and gender boundaries. The youngest readers who wrote to me were twelve years old, the oldest was ninety-two, and the majority of the readers were women. Regardless of their age, their first meeting with Anne generally took place at the age of eleven or twelve. The experience is often vividly remembered and described. For instance, Inga Mörkberg (b. 1932) described her memory of reading *Anne* at the age of twelve and recalled not only the story itself but also the physical experience of reading: "I'm sitting with my back against the stove, reading *Anne of Green Gables* and hoping that nobody will call for me, interrupt my stay with Anne in Avonlea … The stove is so warm against my back, the draught by the floor icy cold against thighs and legs. In that moment I am Anne and Anne is I."[33]

The last sentence of this quotation illustrates the kind of intimacy that readers experience when stepping into Montgomery's fictional world. Like the readers in Ross's study and Ahola and Koskimies's anthology, many identify with Anne and describe her as a "friend" or "kindred spirit." Jeanette Rosenberg (b. 1967), another Swedish reader, even writes, "I loved her like a sister."[34]

Several scholars have suggested that *Anne of Green Gables* played an important role for girls and women during the twentieth century. Before women had the right to vote, and before the Great War that gave women new opportunities in the labour market of the Western world, Montgomery created a heroine with strong ambitions and the will to become a writer, a female intellectual who competes with a boy and, among other things, questions why women were not allowed to become priests. Female Canadian writers, as well as Finnish readers, also appreciate Montgomery's heroine Emily Byrd Starr because of her great ambitions and desire to be a writer.[35]

In 1991 Gabriella Åhmansson was one of the first scholars to relate readers' responses to Anne's education and ambitions: "In my opinion ... Anne's intellectual tenacity and her ambitious mind have played a far greater part in maintaining her popularity among women than is generally acknowledged."[36] A year later, Mary Rubio pointed to Montgomery as "a powerful force in the empowerment of women in the 20th century" and described her as "a writer of international influence who had changed lives and affected the ways that people thought."[37] Montgomery's novels are regarded as works that can affect female readers profoundly and have power to emancipate women in patriarchal societies. Ahola and Koskimies state that several of the Finnish readers from whom they collected reading experiences, many of them journalists, scholars, teachers, authors, or in other careers working with text, had "relied on the books in choosing their occupations."[38] Other readers, like Eva Lindsten Nilsson above, claimed that their own personality had been coloured by their reading of Montgomery's fiction.[39] Various contributions to this volume also point to the cross-cultural significance of Montgomery's works.

The description of Anne Shirley as a female intellectual has, according to the readers' own statements, made her a role model. "Anne," says Gunilla Glans who read the series in the 1950s, "was different and original in ways which we did not dare to emulate in those days, but which we admired. Maybe this has influenced our adult lives, to dare to stand alone and become independent." Other female readers write, "Anne was one of our guiding stars" (Ellen Andolf-Steinwall, b. 1943), and "I saw a lot of myself in her and she was a kind of role model to me. I wanted to be like her" (Emma Björklund).[40] Anne has also been a "guiding star" in the same kind of key moments referred to by Finnish readers: "No doubt it was Anne's very devotion to her students that contributed to my own choice of profession,"[41] writes Helena Bergmann (b. 1950), a scholar and university teacher of English. Maria Gunnarsson Contassot (b. 1944) says that Anne "taught me to use literature as a compass in my life. I also know that she is directly an accessory to me choosing to become a teacher."[42] A further example is Margareta Swerre (b. 1951), who writes, "The book also encouraged me to believe in my own feeling and the importance of daring to dream about how I wished my life to be." She continues: "Up until the moment of writing, I hadn't realized that the books about Anne had had a greater influence in my life than I previously had been aware of myself. I made a similar choice of profession as Anne when I once studied to become a preschool teacher, and along with my family I have for 17 years provided a foster home for children and youth from disbanded families. Perhaps I have subconsciously in my work with the children been inspired by how Anne, with a feeling of being unloved, came to a home where she was accepted and loved, and how it changed her chances in life."[43]

The three hundred accounts from Swedish Montgomery readers show the power of her fiction in the lives of individuals, a power that probably goes beyond the imaginations of the first Swedish publisher and translator who adopted Anne and introduced her to their country's young people in 1909.

## NOTES

1  Warnqvist, *Besläktade själar*, 95.
2  Åhmansson, "'Mayflowers Grow in Sweden Too,'" 14.
3  In my research, funded by the Swedish Research Council, I collected 303 reading experiences from Swedish readers. In the notes, quotations from unpublished ones will be referred to as "Warnqvist, reading experiences." Quotations from reading experiences were translated by Stefan Warnqvist.
4  Svedjedal, *Bokens samhälle*, 60, 62, 325–6, 537, 607, 649–50, 775, 802–4.

5  Letter from Agne Gleerup to Karin Jensen, 26 June 1909, Lund University Library, 6:245.

6  Letters from Agne Gleerup to Karin Jensen 26 June 1909, Lund University Library, 6:245 and 25 September 1909, Lund University Library, 6:245. In the second of these letters, Gleerup explicitly declares Ribbing the "discoverer" of the book.

7  Letter from Agne Gleerup to Sir Isaac Pitman & Sons, Ltd., 16 March 1909, Lund University Library, 6:247; also Lund University Library, 6:245; and Persson, Seved Ribbing, 16.

8  Svedjedal, *Bokens samhälle*, 205–13; letter from Agne Gleerup to L.C. Page & Company, 21 June 1909, Lund University Library, 6:245.

9  Letter from Agne Gleerup to Karin Jensen, 26 June 1909, Lund University Library, 6:245.

10  Letter from Agne Gleerup to L.C. Page & Company, 14 July 1909, Lund University Library, 6:245.

11  Letter from Agne Gleerup to L.C. Page & Company, 29 November 1909, Lund University Library, 6:245. The signed contract can also be found in the Lund collection, but it is not yet catalogued.

12  Lund University Library, 6:235, 6:236, and 6:237.

13  Letter from Agne Gleerup to Karin Jensen, 26 June 1909, Lund University Library, 6:245.

14  Rémi, "Interactions with Poetry," 167–8, quotation from 167; see also Rémi, "From Green Gables to Grönkulla."

15  Åhmansson, "'Mayflowers Grow in Sweden Too,'" 18–19; Rémi, "Interactions with Poetry," 165–90.

16  Rémi, "Interactions with Poetry," 168.

17  Rémi, "From Green Gables to Grönkulla"; Warnqvist, reading experiences.

18  *Svenska Dagbladet*, 23 December 1909, Lund University Library, Serie Ö 1 B, Vol. 1, 1899–1920.

19  *Dagens Nyheter*, 22 December 1909, Lund University Library, Series Ö 1 B, Vol. 1, 1899–1920.

20  *Göteborgs-Posten*, 16 December 1909, Lund University Library, Series Ö 1 B, Vol. 1, 1899–1920.

21  See for instance *Svenska Dagbladet*, 23 December 1909; *Dagens Nyheter*, 22 December 1909; *Göteborgs Morgonpost*, 11 December 1909. Quotations from *Smålands-Posten*, 16 December 1909, *Nya Daglig Allehanda*, 15 December 1909, *Göteborgs Handels- & Sjöfarts-Tidning*, 11 December 1909, and *Svensk kommunal-tidning* 17 December 1909. Lund University Library, Series Ö 1 B, Vol. 1, 1899–1920.

22  Ørvig, *Flickboken och dess författare*, 15.

23  Kristenson, *Böcker i svenska hem*.

24  Interview with Eva von Zweigbergk, Lund University Library, Series Ö 1 B, Vol. 1, 1899–1920: Arkivkartong. No. 24, Vi 47–51: 1938.

25  Warnqvist, *Besläktade själar*; Warnqvist, reading experiences.
26  Lindgren, "Anne på Grönkulla och Mannen med stålnävarna," 244–5 (translated by Åsa Warnqvist and Åhmansson, "'Mayflowers Grow in Sweden Too,'" 14–15).
27  In my research project, Astrid Lindgren is the primary example in my analysis of Montgomery's impact on Swedish writers.
28  Ross, "Readers Reading L.M. Montgomery," 23–35; Ahola and Koskimies, "Love and Controversy," 239.
29  Ross, "Readers Reading L.M. Montgomery," 23–35, especially 29–30; Warnqvist, *Besläktade själar*.
30  Ross, "Readers Reading L.M. Montgomery," 29–30; Ahola and Koskimies, "Love and Controversy," 239; Warnqvist, reading experiences.
31  Warnqvist, reading experiences.
32  Warnqvist, *Besläktade själar*, 97.
33  Ibid., 57.
34  Ross, "Readers Reading L.M. Montgomery", 30; Ahola and Koskimies, "Love and Controversy"; Warnqvist, *Besläktade själar*, 65.
35  Ahola and Koskimies, "Love and Controversy," 239; Rubio, "Subverting the Trite," 6, 12.
36  Åhmansson, *A Life and Its Mirrors*, 115.
37  Rubio, "Subverting the Trite," 6, 12. See also Rubio, *Lucy Maud Montgomery*, 10.
38  Ahola and Koskimies, "Love and Controversy," 239.
39  Ibid.; Warnqvist, *Besläktade själar*, 95.
40  Warnqvist, reading experiences.
41  Warnqvist, *Besläktade själar*, 104.
42  Ibid., 114.
43  Ibid., 115–16.

## BIBLIOGRAPHY

Åhmansson, Gabriella. *A Life and Its Mirrors: A Feminist Reading of L.M. Montgomery's Fiction*. Vol. 1. *An Introduction to Lucy Maud Montgomery: Anne Shirley*. Studia Anglistica Upsaliensia 74. PhD diss. Uppsala: Uppsala University, 1991.

– "'Mayflowers Grow in Sweden Too': L.M. Montgomery, Astrid Lindgren and the Swedish Literary Consciousness." In Rubio, *Harvesting Thistles*, 14–22.

Ahola, Suvi, and Satu Koskimies. "Love and Controversy for Over Eighty Years: Anne, Emily, and Finnish Women; An Interview." In *Storm and Dissonance: L.M. Montgomery and Conflict*, edited by Jean Mitchell, 238–44. Newcastle, UK: Cambridge Scholars Press, 2008.

Kristenson, Martin. *Böcker i svenska hem. Om Carl Cederblads lit007atursociologiska undersökning 1928–31* [*Books in Swedish Homes: On Carl Cederblad's*

*Study Within the Field of Literature of Sociology, 1928–31*]. Litteratur och samhälle, vol. 23 (1987):1/2. Uppsala: Avdelningen för litteratursociologi, Litteraturvetenskapliga institutionen, Uppsala University, 1988.

Lindgren, Astrid. "Anne på Grönkulla och Mannen med stålnävarna" ["Anne of Green Gables and the Man with the Steel Fists"]. *Bokvännen*, vol. 10 (1956): 244–5.

Lund University Library, Manuscript Section, Gleerupska förlagsarkivet (catalogued):

6:235. Bokförlagets specifika kostnader. No. 2. 1904–12 [The Publishing House's Specific Costs no. 2. 1904–12].

6:236. Bokförlager. No. 3. 1913–18 [The Publishing House's Specific Costs no. 3 1913–18].

6:237. Bokförlager. No. 4. 1919–26 [The Publishing House's Specific Costs no. 4. 1919–26].

6:245. Kopiebok 4 1/5 1907–Aug. 1910 [Copy Book 4, 1 May 1907–August 1910].

6:247. Styrelsens för AB C.W.K. Gleerup protokollbok 13/1 1897–24/7 1925 [The Board for C.W.K. Gleerups' records 13 January 1897–24 July 1925].

Series Ö 1 B, Pressklipp och bokrecensioner av ungdomsböcker [Press Cuttings and Book Reviews of Youth Books]. Vol. 1, 1899–1920: Arkivkartong. Nr. 1–37.

Lund University Library, Manuscript Section, Gleerupska förlagsarkivet (uncatalogued):

Contract for the Swedish edition of *Anne of Green Gables* between L.C. Page & Company and C.W.K. Gleerups, signed 9 October 1909.

Ørvig, Mary. *Flickboken och dess författare. Ur flickläsningens historia* [*The Book for Girls and Its Writers: From the History of Girls' Reading*]. Skrifter utgivna av Svenska barnboksinstitutet, vol. 33. Hedemora: Gidlund, 1988.

Persson, Ola. *Seved Ribbing. Legendarisk Lunda-läkare, humanist och människovän* [*Seved Ribbing: Legendary Lund-Doctor, Humanist and Philanthropist*] Lund: Föreningen för äldrevård och gerontologi and Stiftelsen Ribbingska sjukhemmets minnesfond, 1990.

Rémi, Cornelia. "From Green Gables to Grönkulla: Anne's Arrival in Sweden." Presentation at international conference "L.M. Montgomery – Writer of the World," Uppsala University, Uppsala, 20 August 2009.

– "Interactions with Poetry: Metapoetic Games with Anne in Astrid Lindgren's *Madicken.*" In *100 Years of Anne with an "e": The Centennial Study of "Anne of Green Gables,*" edited by Holly Blackford, 165–90. Calgary: University of Calgary Press, 2009.

Ross, Catherine. "Readers Reading L.M. Montgomery." In Rubio, ed., *Harvesting Thistles*, 23–35.

Rubio, Mary. *L.M. Montgomery: The Gift of Wings*. Toronto: Doubleday Canada, 2008.

–, ed. *Harvesting Thistles: The Textual Garden of L.M. Montgomery, Essays on Her Novels and Journals.* Guelph, Ontario: Canadian Children's Press, 1994.

– "Subverting the Trite: L.M. Montgomery's 'Room of Her Own.'" CCL: *Canadian Children's Literature*, vol. 65 (1992): 6–39.

Svedjedal, Johan. *Bokens samhälle. Svenska Förläggareföreningen och svensk bokmarknad 1887–1943* [*Society of the Book: The Swedish Publishers' Association and the Swedish Book Industry, 1887–1943*]. Vol. 1–2. Stockholm: Svenska Förläggareföreningen, 1993.

Warnqvist, Åsa, ed. *Besläktade själar. Läsupplevelser av Anne på Grönkulla* [*Kindred Spirits: Reading Experiences of Anne of Green Gables*]. Lund: BTJ Förlag, 2009.

# Paratext and Aftertexts: Further Words on *Anne*

# "I just love pretty clothes": Considering the Sartorial in *Anne of Green Gables*

JENNIE MACDONALD

Writing about her own experiences, L.M. Montgomery embroiders her descriptions with sartorial metaphors. Upon receiving her copy of *Anne of Green Gables*, she eagerly writes, "As far as appearance goes the book is all I could desire – lovely cover design, well bound, well printed. *Anne* will not fail for lack of *suitable garbing* at all events."[1] Although less enthusiastic about her second novel, Montgomery describes *Anne of Avonlea* in similar fashion terms: "I liked its '*get-up*' and glanced over it with calm approval."[2] Central to both of these comments is an anxiety about acceptance that seems assuaged, in Montgomery's view, by the costuming of the texts in attractive and appropriate attire. Similarly, the *New York Times* adopted sartorial terms to describe the delay of the book's debut: "'Anne of Green Gables,' after many announcements, came this week from Messrs. L.C. Page & Company. The heroine, like many a real girl, was delayed by the dress question, a satisfactory cover not being easy to produce, but Mr. George Gibbs has made a portrait which really resembles the pleasing girl of the text, and does not look like all the other pretty girls on the book covers of 1908, so *Anne*, with her much-deprecated red hair, is now to be seen of men."[3]

Like Anne herself, the book *Anne of Green Gables* was seen to require lovely dressing in order to be publicly acceptable. Also like Anne, the book's appearance differs from that of "all the other girls" – that is, all the other books published for young women in 1908. Its "suitable garbing" in a printed form, ornamented with a romantic and up-to-date Gibson Girl cover, reflects and gratifies the text's emphasis on a desire for beauty in the form of beautiful clothing. To commemorate the hundredth anniversary of *Anne of Green Gables*, Penguin Canada in 2008 published a facsimile[4] of L.C. Page & Company's 1908 first edition. The Penguin edition faithfully replicates the debut edition and offers modern readers the opportunity to encounter the book in ways approximating the experience of its first audience. This essay focuses on a thematic trajectory suggested by the original's paratextual elements, particularly its illustrations with their emphasis on fashion and style.

By "paratextual" I mean the elements of a book that stand outside the main text itself, such as covers, front matter, and illustrations. Such elements have been identified by Gérard Genette as sites of exchange between the book (as a material and visual object) and the reader, which create certain expectations that inform the reading of the story.[5] The eight original illustrations by M.A. and W.A.J. Claus[6] are reproduced in the 2008 Penguin Canada edition. The frontispiece of the 2008 facsimile faces the table of contents. Rather surprisingly, for readers familiar with later editions that employ Anne's initial wincey-dressed appearance for their covers, this image portrays Anne's dressing for the concert at White Sands Hotel and is captioned with Diana's comment, "There's something so stylish about you, Anne." Because they precede the text, this image and the book's Gibson Girl cover by George Gibbs present a vision of fine beauty attained, enacting, on a paratextual level, Anne's imaginative vision of beauty bestowed by fine clothes. They hover before the reader's mind's eye – as Anne's visions of beautiful dresses appear in *her* mind's eye – as images that will be fulfilled when the text confirms, as the reader believes it must, that they are accurate representations of a character who in no way resembles them when the story opens. Indeed, the subsequent illustrations bear out the frontispiece's anticipation of Anne as a sartorially interesting figure whose outfits are depicted as increasingly attractive and stylish – from the familiar wincey asylum dress and cheap straw hat of the picture illustrating Marilla's reaction to Anne's arrival ("'Matthew Cuthbert, who's that?' she ejaculated"[7]) to the lovely gown and tastefully decorated hat of the final illustration showing Anne's meeting Gilbert on her way home from Matthew's grave ("Come, I'm going to walk home with you"[8]).

Anne Shirley's coming-of-age story recalls classic novels of the nineteenth century such as *Jane Eyre* and *Little Women*, in which a disadvantaged but determined girl encounters the difficulties of making her way in the world as she grows into a strong and independent woman. The premium Anne places on pretty clothes underlines her desire for transformation, the social acceptance she believes such transformation promises, and her will to participate bodily in the beauty of nature. Her very act of longing for a beautiful dress contributes to her perception of beauty just out of actual reach and thus all the more desirable. "Anne is an aesthete,"[9] after all, worshipping at the altar of beauty, an altar adorned with, among other things, images of beautiful clothing. Her desire for beautiful gowns reflects Montgomery's own love of fashion, reiterated throughout the author's journals and illustrated in the many fashion plates with which she adorned her scrapbooks.

Alison Matthews David and Kimberly Wahl have identified "fashion" as "a comforting and reifying presence in the novel," participating in the "girlhood rituals" of Anne and Diana's formative years in pastoral Avonlea.[10] It also, however, "serves a more subversive purpose as well, alluding to the modern world of ambition, evolution, and physical and intellectual transformation. So pervasive is the influence and power of modern fashion that it must be mediated for Anne in the text."[11] Such mediation is carried out by figures such as Marilla, Matthew, and Mrs Lynde, who "provide access and eventually sanction the presence of 'modern' fashion in Anne's world."[12] Not only is fashion mediated by other characters in the story, but it is also filtered through romantic language and symbolism, which together produce an iconic image of an unlikely heroine.

During the drive from the train station to Green Gables, Anne says, "I do hope that some day I shall have a white dress. That is my highest ideal of earthly bliss. I just love pretty clothes. And I've never had a pretty dress in my life that I can remember – but of course it's all the more to look forward to, isn't it? And then I can imagine that I'm dressed gorgeously."[13] In the 1908 edition of the book, the lovely white dress is pictured in the frontispiece, so the reader expects Anne's wish to come true. Though it is some time in coming, Anne finally wears such a dress for her performance at the White Sands concert years after her arrival at Green Gables. Both Anne and the reader must appreciate the benefits of delayed gratification.

Through the intervention of such unlikely fairy godmothers as Matthew and Marilla Cuthbert and Rachel Lynde, Anne is granted her desire for her first beautiful dress on the eve of the Christmas concert at Avonlea school. Surrounded by people she knows and who have come to love her, Anne can never effect a complete transformation into another person via her clothing; instead, the process of attaining her sartorial accoutrements contributes to her development as a complex creature nerved by desire and self-awareness. She knows what she wants when it comes to clothing, though what she believes she wants and what she actually gets are somewhat different things. Her articulation of her desires becomes a key mechanism driving many of the dramatic situations of her story.

Anne needs a beautiful dress not only to join in her community but also to transcend her life of deprivation. She must have a beautiful dress, in part because she loves beautiful things, but also because a dress is the only thing that she believes can make her appearance beautiful. Most important, she must have such a dress because she has envisioned it, and it is her due as a visionary.

Anne stands as literary and artistic heir not only to the heroines of nineteenth-century novels but also to those of Greek and Roman mythology, medieval legend seen through Romantic and Victorian poetry, pre-Raphaelite painting, and the contemporary Art Nouveau movement. In the course of the story, Anne grows from child to young lady, proceeding from her very first appearance through a sartorial landscape that she herself partly articulates into being and that involves characters around her in deeply meaningful evolutions of their own. Along the way, she acquires quite a wardrobe of beautiful dresses, coats, hats, and shoes. Montgomery is not, however, interested in a simple tale of wish-fulfillment. Anne's relationship with personal, social, cultural, and figurative ideas about clothing accompanies signature events in her life and connects her to the literary and artistic heritages to which she belongs and which she carries into the modern age.

The Gibson Girl and "stylish" Anne of the paratext of the first edition invite a reading of the narrative focused on Anne's romantic fashion sense. Early in the first chapter, "Rachel Lynde is Surprised," the narrator speaks of the "bridal flush" of the orchard,[14] an expression that anticipates and captures Anne's own voice heard shortly afterward, in her depiction of the cherry tree as a bride. In describing Marilla's response to hearing Anne's history for the first time, Margaret Doody, for example, has noted the narrator's use of "the device known as *style indirect libre*, in which the narrator's voice takes on the colour of a character's mind, [and] seems closer to that of the general narrator and the reader."[15] Although during the first arrival at Green Gables Anne is preoccupied by her anticipation of living in this beautiful new place, the narrator continues to supply clothing-related metaphors that reflect Anne's ongoing subconscious interest in fashion.

Anne's first textual appearance completely upsets this expectation of stylishness; she is assuredly not a young lady of exquisite style, but rather a little girl dressed in an appallingly unstylish and ugly dress and hat. Nevertheless, the narrator's sympathetic attitude offers the poplar leaves "rustling silkily" all around the yard at Green Gables when Matthew brings Anne home that first evening.[16] Elizabeth Epperly identifies "a blurring of the borders between imitation and commentary" that "encourages the reader, in chapter two, to recognize Anne's perspective in the narrator's poetic interpretations of sky and landscape ... The 'bridal flush' of the orchard [and] the hollows where wild plums shyly 'hung out their filmy bloom' all suggest the welcoming personality of the countryside and the season; Anne is due to arrive in a world that is more than ready for her."[17] It is a world that shares her language of romantic clothing. Along with Anne's desire for the "most beautiful pale blue silk dress"[18] and her rapturous description of the cherry tree "all white and lacy" like "a bride all in white with a lovely misty veil,"[19] such textual cues predict the presence of fashion and style somewhere in the book to validate the reader's expectation that little Anne will grow into the stylish young lady of the first edition's two initial visual images.

Interestingly, it is Diana, not Anne, who becomes the arbiter of taste in Avonlea fashion. The acquisition of fabrics, buttons, and patterns and the mechanics of dress production are not for Anne. Nor does she dictate others' fashion choices, as Diana does. Anne ultimately becomes the model of Avonlea fashion and, even before the story opens, its visionary and votary. Achieving her role as a romantic fashion icon is no easy task. True heroines must overcome terrible obstacles: the disagreeable reactions of others to wildflower-adorned hats, the pains of wearing unattractive if serviceable outfits, and a desire for beauty that is necessarily accompanied by delay and sometimes by disappointment. Along the way, Anne's sartorial journey involves her in the fashion debates of the late nineteenth century, reveals her problematic red hair as a site of celebration, and presents a complex reading of colour and style.

The creation of Anne's brown Gloria dress with puffed sleeves brings about a true partnership between Matthew and Rachel, allowing them both to assert a new approach in Anne's upbringing that Marilla has resisted. It results in deeply personal changes for Matthew, who crosses into the world of women for perhaps the first time in his long life; for Rachel, who makes the dress that materially represents her compassionate nature; and for Marilla, who must move into a modern way of dealing with fashion and a growing child. She does so successfully, not only to combat Rachel's intrusion into Anne's upbringing, but also because she comes to love Anne so dearly. Marilla and Anne's struggle over puffed sleeves reflects the late nineteenth-century fashion reform debate between tradition, practicality, and economy and women's emancipation, well-being, and style.

When Matthew gives Anne her long-dreamed-of dress with puffed sleeves for Christmas, she manages to articulate her overwhelming gratitude, but then adds, "I'm so glad that puffed sleeves are still fashionable. It did seem to me that I'd never get over it if they went out before I had a dress with them. I'd never have felt quite satisfied, you see."[20] It is clear Anne fully appreciates the fact that fashion changes rapidly and with relative finality. We never see her reading or talking about a fashion publication, though plenty of literary texts are read and referred to in the novel. Such a strategy fits with David and Wahl's belief that the actual inclusion of modern objects such as fashion magazines and activities such as window-shopping would detract from the novel's shaping as a pastoral tale: "Anne seems aware of what is fashionable, and yet there is a marked lack of any kind of material associated with mass or popular culture in the novel."[21] Anne has evidently been keeping up with the fashion news that in the late 1800s was becoming a more prominent element in the Canadian daily newspapers, but such activity is left off the page of her own story. That we don't see Anne actively engaged with such materials lends an air of mystery to her pronouncements regarding fashionable ideas, although most of these seem to arise from her encounters with Avonlea girls such as Diana, who wear up-to-date dresses, and public figures such as the lady elocutionist at the White Sands Hotel "in a wonderful gown of shimmering grey stuff like woven moonbeams, with gems on her neck and in her dark hair."[22] Part of what entices Anne about beautiful clothes is her romantic nature, echoed in the narrator's *style indirect libre* vocabulary, as it conjures imaginative phrases like "woven moonbeams." The language of fashion, for Anne, is poetic language.

Anne's views of fashion, however, are not solely romantic. Underlying them is an interest in practicality, a concern of the fashion debates of the later nineteenth century that play out at Green Gables.

Barbara E. Kelcey comments on contemporary views: "While there was some move towards clothing which reflected the new consciousness of women's need for emancipation ... fashion still projected the ideal of the fragile, feminine, delicate woman ... Problems developed because of weight, [lack of] cleanliness, and a lack of freedom in movement," due to multiple layers of petticoats, restrictive undergarments such as corsets, gathered waists, and an effort to conserve fabric that resulted in tight shoulders, sleeves, and wristbands.[23] At Green Gables, this view of fashion can be seen in the sleeves of the first three dresses Marilla makes for Anne, which are as "tight as sleeves could be."[24] The tightness of those sleeves, like Anne's tight wincey asylum dress, evokes the confining power of the past. Anne's desire for puffed sleeves suggests expansion, growth, and fashion. Despite Anne's romantic desire for puffed sleeves, she is also expressing one of the concerns of the dress reformers – to loosen women's clothing for the sake of their health and ease of movement. Her interest in fashion reflects "two different but overlapping branches of dress reform," distinguished by Barbara M. Freeman, "one seen as more feminist and practical, and the other as more aesthetic or artistic."[25] Feminist dress "tended to be plain, sensible, and bordering on the masculine"; "aesthetic dress was flowing and graceful," allowing for romantic details like "inset yokes of white muslin, or lace frills at the neck."[26]

Anne's imagination allows plenty of ornamentation and luxurious fabrics, subscribing to the appeal of aesthetic dress. Looking into the mirror the first night after Marilla tells her she may stay at Green Gables, Anne dictates a fantastic scene, telling herself: "I am tall and regal, clad in a gown of trailing white lace, with a pearl cross on my breast and pearls in my hair. My hair is of midnight darkness, and my skin is a clear ivory pallor. My name is the Lady Cordelia Fitzgerald."[27] Anne's fictionalizing taps into Montgomery's recollection of how she dressed her own "dazzlingly lovely heroines" as an impressionable child writer: "Silks – satins – velvets – laces – they never wore anything else! And I literally poured diamonds and rubies and pearls over them."[28] Anne's actual dresses seem to bridge feminist and aesthetic dress, accommodating practical and social concerns, as well as an interest in being up to date.

Marilla articulates a surprisingly imaginative and astute fashion metaphor about puffed sleeves: "The puffs have been getting bigger and more ridiculous right along; they're as big as balloons now. Next year anybody who wears them will have to go through a door sideways."[29] Likening the sleeves to balloons was something Montgomery had done when poring over her old scrapbooks in July 1905: "An old-time fashion plate with big sleeves! The big puffed sleeves are in again now. When I put on a new dress the other day with big sleeves it gave me the oddest sense of being a Dalhousie girl again [1895–96] – for that was the year they came to their fullest balloon-like inflation, stiffened out with 'fibre-chamois' etc."[30] David and Wahl note that "dresses with some form of puffed sleeve were almost constantly in fashion from 1890 to 1905, the period in which Montgomery herself came of age, conceived of, and wrote the novel."[31] Irene Gammel comments that "puffed sleeves were more than inhabitants of those dusty [scrapbook] pages; they were also the latest Edwardian style,"[32] as evident in Montgomery's comment that "big puffed sleeves are in again now."[33] Marilla's objection to puffed sleeves is that they are impractical and frivolous. She also seems surprisingly alert to the evolving state of fashion. As for Anne's desire for puffed sleeves, Marilla believes they cause vanity and lack of productivity, neither of which is acceptable in her household. Undermining Marilla's fears, though, the vision of her "lovely puffed sleeves," the "crowning glory" of her new dress, enables Anne to overcome stage fright at the Christmas concert, knowing that she "must live up to" them.[34] Later, when preparing for her visit with Diana to Miss Josephine Barry's house in Charlottetown, Anne offers a moral perspective to Diana, "It is ever so much easier to be good if your clothes are fashionable."[35] After describing her new hat, however, she equivocates: "Do you suppose it's wrong for us to think so much about our clothes? Marilla says it is very sinful."[36] Finally, she throws moralizing to the wind, happily admitting that clothing "is such an interesting subject, isn't it?"[37]

If Anne equates interest and goodness with fashion, bad things are often equated with her red hair. (For more on the complex cultural associations of red hair, see Doreley Coll in this volume.) Juliet McMaster identifies hair as "a site of intense conflict," as it is "the body substance that mediates between the individual and the culture."[38] Intense conflict arises for Anne during her first encounters with Rachel Lynde and Gilbert Blythe, when they comment on her hair colour, likening it to carrots, because, as McMaster rightly notes, "Anne instinctively seeks a reason for the world's rejection and locates it in her hair colour."[39] Rachel and Gilbert confirm Anne's impression of a world that she thinks would "keep her" if only her hair were "a glorious black, black as the raven's wing."[40] A comparison to the wing of a beautiful black bird in flight is far preferable to an association with carrots, a lowly vegetable that grows in the ground. In her journal, Montgomery records: "Anne's tribulations over puffed sleeves were an echo of my old childish longing after 'bangs' [which] came in when I was about ten. ... [and] were 'all the rage.'"[41] Although puffed sleeves and bangs represent the latest in fashion for character and author, respectively, Anne's own desire to change her hair colour is purely due to her romantic imagination.

Anne's red hair stands out in Avonlea and has been read by McMaster[42] and Gammel[43] as intimately connecting Anne to Prince Edward Island's red roads. Although likened to carrots, Anne's hair is still more deeply associated with the red soil of her new Island home. Appropriately, Anne's red tresses operate as roads leading to her relationship with Rachel, who becomes her first fashion benefactress. Importantly, her braids lead to her academic competitiveness with Gilbert, which results in her triumphant win of the Avery Scholarship and her graduation from college – Queen's College – and these are Anne's crowning achievements in this first book.

Long before commencement, though, Anne has been creating her own crowns, wreaths of flowers to adorn her hats and, more significantly, her hair.[44] As Doody observes, "Anne the flower-crowned is like a Greek maiden ... singing to herself in shadowy places and wreathing wildflowers in her hair."[45] Although unable to imagine her red hair away, Anne is perfectly oblivious to the fact that crowning it with flowers draws attention to her head. But as the focus of intense imaginative activity, Anne's hair becomes a site for adornment and celebration, literally and liberally garlanded on her first journey to church with yellow buttercups and pink roses, despite her assertion that people with red hair cannot wear pink. Her flower offerings to her own head confirm her rightful place as a votary of nature, a reincarnation of such classical Greek goddesses as Persephone, and a representative of the pre-Raphaelite and Art Nouveau movements, with their lovely red-haired women wreathed about with flowers.

Hats, wreaths, and hair ornaments are important to Anne, but none give greater delight or cause greater anxiety than the wedding veil with which she imaginatively dresses trees and which she envisions Diana wearing as a grown-up bride.[46] The white dress that is Anne's "highest ideal of earthly bliss"[47] does not necessarily equate to a bridal dress, but the association is difficult for modern readers to set aside.[48] Montgomery, in fact, takes pains to subvert this expectation. The one time Anne does wear a white dress is to the White Sands Hotel concert where she recites "The Maiden's Vow," a poem in which the maiden Reinette de Veer goes unwed to the grave rather than marry another after learning of her beloved's death.[49]

The dresses of Anne's desire are notable for their colours, those she can and can't wear, and for their ornamentation or style, as with the puffed sleeves. Like Montgomery, Anne "consciously [privileges] colour," as Elizabeth Epperly notes.[50] Although Anne admires the white raiment of the Snow Queen, her first imagined dress is pale blue silk, accessorized with "a big hat all flowers and nodding plumes, and a gold watch, and kid gloves and boots."[51] She later acquires at least three blue dresses: the "stiff print of an ugly blue shade,"[52] one of the three little-girl dresses Marilla makes for her, all based on the same pattern; the "navy blue ... made so fashionably"[53] for her sojourn with Diana to Charlotte-town; and the stiff blue-flowered muslin that Diana rejects on the evening of the White Sands concert.[54] Her beloved Mrs Allan wears "blue muslin with lovely puffed sleeves."[55]

Pink, of course, is for Anne "the most bewitching colour in the world. I love it," she says, "but I can't wear it. Redheaded people can't wear pink, not even in imagination."[56] As Gammel and David and Wahl have noted, Anne's recitation of prescriptive views on fashion echoes popular beauty guides such as *The Art of Beauty* (1878) by Eliza Haweis. More importantly, pink dresses throughout the book symbolize characters' close proximity to marriage, from which Anne in her role as virginal icon, in this first book at least, is barred. Prissy Andrews, whose romance with Mr Phillips is common knowledge, can wear "a new pink silk waist."[57] Mrs Allan, in her married state, dresses "in the sweetest dress of pale pink organdy, with dozens of frills and elbow sleeves [looking] just like a seraph."[58] The "stout lady in pink silk ... who was the wife of an American millionaire"[59] at the White Sands concert turns out to be one of Anne's admirers. Even Diana "was looking very pretty on [that] particular night in a dress of the lovely wild-rose pink from which Anne was for ever debarred,"[60] an ominous indication that Anne's vision of Diana as a bride will soon come true.

If neither blue nor pink seems to be Anne's predestined colour, she does have a powerful relationship with whiteness and its representation of joy and sorrow. Anne's joy at whiteness can be seen in her response to the White Way of Delight, blooming trees, a snowy Christmas, and white flowers. In her journal Montgomery writes, "The White Way of Delight is practically pure imagination,"[61] but Anne, enraptured, renames "that white place," in an act that linguistically binds it to her, because it "couldn't be improved upon by imagination."[62] This first naming functions cathartically, opening the door for subsequent renamings that dress objects and places with words, and equate whiteness with a blank surface awaiting inscription and enabling acts of creation.

However appealing whiteness initially appears as a site of joy, beauty, and creativity, it equally participates in situations involving suppression, pain, and death. The poor trees at the orphanage have "little whitewashed cagey things about them."[63] The whiteness of snow suggests freezing and decay. The "Snow Queen ... won't always be in blossom,"[64] and when Matthew dies, "the white majesty of death [fell] upon him and set him apart as one crowned."[65] The image of a white – especially a bridal – dress particularly invites ideas about death. Diana's "snowy"[66] bridal garments mean the end of her friendship with Anne. When Diana's mother effectively ends the girls' friendship after the raspberry cordial incident, Anne writes to Diana, signing it with the language of a wedding vow: "Yours until death us do part, Anne or Cordelia Shirley,"[67] reiterating the connection between marriage and death. The Haunted Wood is inhabited by "white things [that] reach out from behind the trees," including "a white lady" who "appears when there is to be a death in the family."[68] Rachel Lynde likens Anne to white narcissus,[69] the flowers Anne is holding when Matthew dies and lets fall to the floor as though she has died too; "it was long before Anne could love the sight or odour of white narcissus again."[70]

But after the sorrow, Anne will learn to love white narcissus again, and so whiteness, the colour of creation and destruction, also comes to symbolize resurrection: in the Snow Queen's blooming again, in Gilbert's picking up the white paper flower that falls from Anne's hair at the Christmas concert, and in the little slip of white Scotch-rose that she plants on Matthew's grave. The circular nature of whiteness and Anne's innate drive for wholeness are captured in her little pearl bead ring and the circlet of pearls Matthew gives her, which confirm their kindred spirithood. Both know without thinking or speaking that pearls are Anne's rightful jewels. She is, after all, a heroine who arrives from across the sea.

The dress Anne wears to the White Sands concert is "white organdie,"[71] which Diana describes as "so soft and frilly and clinging" it "seems as if it grew on you."[72] For ornaments, she ties Anne's braids with white bows, fastens a little white house-rose just behind her ear, and pronounces in favour of Anne's pearl beads.[73] The end result is the manifestation of the "white maid of Avenel" in "The Maiden's Vow," the incarnation of a virginal goddess dressed by her votary Diana in a temple of white, hung with curtains of "pale green art muslin."[74]

Marilla's criticism of Anne's dress restores a sense of reality. It "looks most too thin for these damp nights. Organdie's the most unserviceable stuff in the world anyhow, and I told Matthew so when he got it."[75] Even so, "Then Marilla stalked downstairs, thinking proudly how sweet Anne looked, with that 'One moonbeam from the forehead to the crown.'"[76] (Paul Keen's essay in this volume traces the auspicious origins of this quotation in Elizabeth Barrett Browing's *Aurora Leigh*.) Marilla's struggle to reconcile practicality with profundity recalls again the fashion debates of Montgomery's time. If, on the one hand, Anne seems to capture the reform dress idea of practical, looser-fitting dress for the sake of comfort, movement, and style, she also subscribes to aesthetic dress that "was flowing and graceful," often depicted as an adaptation of "the Greek dress with its empire line."[77] Anne delights in visions of flowing gowns that recall Romantic and medieval heroines, but she also embodies the goddesses of ancient Greece. Her white dress is simple and lovely, her act of recitation a profound moment of art. Though in this first book Anne is not yet the woman of letters she will become in the sequels, she is a worshipper at the altar of literature. Her dress would have been approved by no less an authority on style than Oscar Wilde, who wrote in 1882: "The literary dress should, in fact, be free, untrammeled and unswathed. As simple and as easily adjusted as Greek drapery, and fastened only with a girdle or a brooch. No stiff corselet should depress the full impulses of a passionate heart! ... Nothing to mind, nothing to care about; no bondage, through fashion or vanity, either on soul or body, should be the law of dress for literary women."[78] The image of Anne as literary icon flames only briefly in the first *Anne* book. It cannot be sustained because the story cannot contain such power for long within Anne's community.

So it is green that becomes Anne's emblematic colour, linking her to her new home at Green Gables, and to the rich green of Prince Edward

Island. Perhaps it is surprising that Anne never articulates a desire for a green dress when she is so enamoured of the other many colours she longs for in dresses.[79] Like her string of pearl beads, though, a green dress is her unspoken birthright. It marks her vivacity of spirit, her connection with nature, and her embodiment of the ancient earth gods. It need not be called forth, for Marilla – not the Marilla of old but the Marilla whose inner vision is expanding even as her physical sight is deteriorating – "one evening ... went up to the east gable with her arms full of a delicate pale green material ... [that is] made up with as many tucks and frills and shirrings as [Emily Gillis's] taste permitted"[80] and brought it down. "Anne put[s] it on one evening for Matthew's and Marilla's benefit, and recite[s] 'The Maiden's Vow' for them in the kitchen,"[81] an authorial move reiterating Montgomery's decision not to end this book with Anne as a married lady. Pale green marries the dreamy white of her early visions with the deep green of her adopted Island home and with Green Gables itself.

The second and final time Anne wears this dress is at the great moment of her triumph at the Queen's College commencement exercises. She has finished her teaching certificate at the top of her class, won the Avery Scholarship, and read the best essay.[82] Matthew and Marilla are both present, a fact that acquires deeper poignancy when they confirm to each other for the first time that they are glad they kept her, and when Matthew dies at the beginning of the next chapter. The sight of Anne is delivered from their distant perspective: they had "eyes and ears for only one student on the platform – a tall girl in pale green, with faintly flushed cheeks and starry eyes, who read the best essay and was pointed out and whispered about as the Avery winner."[83] Anne seems to be glimpsed at as if through a camera lens – remote, ethereal, and still, an iconic figure of glory, yet part of the green earth.

A pearl's mystical glow arises from the iridescence of nacre, the milky substance an oyster produces to protect itself from a foreign object. Like a grain of sand, Anne travels the sea to arrive in the oyster that is Prince Edward Island. It takes time for Anne to be clad in beauty. It makes sense that Anne, being a creature of imagination, of vision, should dream of dressing her world and herself in the fantasy of fashion, the most immediate and visual way of revealing one's inner self. Once in her new Island home, she travels through a sartorial landscape, covering both it and herself with imagined and real dresses of many shapes, materials, and particularly the colours one might discern in a pearl's iridescent surface: white lace, pale blue silk, pink organdy, brown Gloria, pale green. Hats, wreaths, hair ornaments, and veils contribute additional layers. On a metatextual level, one finds layers of the fashion debates of contemporary sartorial literature. At the centre is Anne, the little girl in the "yellowish gray wincey" dress who emerges in pale green as a visionary goddess, independent and triumphant.

## NOTES

1   Montgomery, *Selected Journals*, 1:355. Emphasis added.
2   Ibid., 358. Emphasis added.
3   *New York Times*, "Boston Gossip," 20 June 1908.
4   Quotations and references from the text of *Anne of Green Gables* are cited from this edition.
5   Genette's "Introduction to the Paratext" provides his basic tenets of paratextuality.
6   May Austin Claus (1882–?) and William Anton Joseph Claus (1862–1926). Christy Woster discusses the Clauses in her article, which recounts her discovery of George Gibbs as the artist of the book's Gibson Girl cover illustration.
7   Montgomery, *Anne of Green Gables*, 25.
8   Ibid., 297.
9   Gammel, *Looking for Anne*, 170.
10  David and Wahl, "'Matthew Insists,'" 47.
11  Ibid.
12  Ibid., 45.
13  Montgomery, *Anne of Green Gables*, 15.
14  Ibid., 4.
15  Doody, Introduction, 19.
16  Montgomery, *Anne of Green Gables*, 23.
17  Epperly, "Romancing the Voice," 245–6.
18  Montgomery, *Anne of Green Gables*, 15.
19  Ibid.
20  Ibid., 195.
21  David and Wahl, "'Matthew Insists,'" 46.
22  Montgomery, *Anne of Green Gables*, 261.
23  Kelcey, "Dress Reform," 230–6.
24  Montgomery, *Anne of Green Gables*, 78.
25  Freeman, "Laced In and Let Down," 306.
26  Ibid.

27  Montgomery, *Anne of Green Gables*, 62.

28  Ibid., *Selected Journals*, 2:64.

29  Ibid., *Anne of Green Gables*, 194.

30  Ibid., *Selected Journals*, 2:308. See also Epperly, *Imagining Anne*, 87.

31  David and Wahl, "'Matthew Insists,'" 41.

32  Gammel, *Looking for Anne*, 178.

33  Montgomery, *Selected Journals*, 1:308.

34  Ibid., *Anne of Green Gables*, 197.

35  Ibid., 224.

36  Ibid.

37  Ibid.

38  McMaster, "Taking Control," 60.

39  Ibid., 64.

40  Montgomery, *Anne of Green Gables*, 64.

41  Ibid., *Selected Journals*, 2:41. Montgomery (born 30 November 1874, died 24 April 1942) would have been "about ten" in 1884.

42  McMaster, "Taking Control," 63.

43  Gammel, *Looking for Anne*, 172–3.

44  Although Anne does not take an active role in making her dresses, she does create her own flower crowns and can later be seen "[gathering] some sprays of pale yellow honeysuckle and [putting] them in her hair." Montgomery, *Anne of Green Gables*, 287.

45  Doody, "Gardens and Plants," 436.

46  The white veil and dress, established as the ideal bridal attire by Queen Victoria who wore them for her own wedding, were not inseparable in the later 1800s. Brides often wore white veils with their best dresses, which were not always white dresses. Montgomery's mother was married in a green dress.

47  Montgomery, *Anne of Green Gables*, 15.

48  Montgomery's own wedding dress was "of white-silk crepe de soie with tunic of chiffon and pearl bead trimming – and of course the tulle veil and orange blossom wreath." See Montgomery, *Selected Journals*, 2:64.

49  See MacGregor. In "Mars La Tour, or, The Maiden's Vow: A Legend of 1870–1871," Reinette de Veer (like Anne, "not the fairest of maidens"), upon hearing of her betrothed's death in Lorraine, vows:

> Ne'er at the high altar the knee I will bow,
> As bride to another, but weep thee till death,
> Encircle my brow with a funereal wreath,
> And to another my troth I will plight,
> Or cease to forget the adieu of to-night.

50  Epperly, *Through Lover's Lane*, 14.

51  Montgomery, *Anne of Green Gables*, 15.

52  Ibid.

53  Ibid., 224.
54  Ibid., 257.
55  Ibid., 163.
56  Ibid., 39.
57  Ibid., 148.
58  Ibid., 174.
59  Ibid., 261–3.
60  Ibid., 257–8.
61  Ibid., *Selected Journals*, 2:40.
62  Ibid., *Anne of Green Gables*, 19.
63  Ibid., 17.
64  Ibid., 37.
65  Ibid., 284.
66  Ibid., 118.
67  Ibid., 134.
68  Ibid., 160.
69  Ibid., 240.
70  Ibid., 283.
71  Ibid., 256.
72  Ibid., 257.
73  Ibid., 258.
74  Ibid., 256.
75  Ibid., 258–9.
76  Ibid.
77  Ibid., Freeman, "Laced In and Let Down," 306.
78  Wilde, "The Suitability of Dress," 234. Wilde visited Nova Scotia and Prince Edward Island in 1882 and spoke on aestheticism in Charlottetown. See Gammel, *Looking for Anne*, 171–2.
79  Marilla does make Anne a dark green dress during the summer before the Entrance exams to Queen's College. See Montgomery, *Anne of Green Gables*, 243.
80  Montgomery, *Anne of Green Gables*, 265.
81  Ibid.
82  Ibid., 278.
83  Ibid.

## BIBLIOGRAPHY

David, Alison Matthews, and Kimberly Wahl. "'Matthew Insists on Puffed Sleeves': Ambivalence towards Fashion in *Anne of Green Gables*." In *Anne's World: A New Century of Anne of Green Gables*, edited by Irene Gammel and Benjamin Lefebvre, 35–49. Toronto: University of Toronto Press, 2010.

Doody, Margaret Anne. "Gardens and Plants." In Montgomery, *The Annotated Anne*, 434–8.

– Introduction to Montgomery, *The Annotated Anne*, 9–34.

Epperly, Elizabeth Rollins. *Imagining Anne: The Island Scrapbooks of L.M. Montgomery*. Toronto: Penguin, 2008.

– "Romancing the Voice: *Anne of Green Gables*." In Montgomery, *Anne of Green Gables*, 343–59.

– *Through Lover's Lane: L.M. Montgomery's Photography and Visual Imagination*. Toronto: University of Toronto Press, 2007.

Freeman, Barbara M. "Laced In and Let Down: Women's Fashion Features in the Toronto Daily Press, 1890–1900." In Palmer, *Fashion*, 292–314.

Gammel, Irene. *Looking for Anne of Green Gables: The Story of L.M. Montgomery and Her Literary Classic*. New York: St Martin's Press, 2008.

–, ed. *Making Avonlea: L.M. Montgomery and Popular Culture*. Toronto: University of Toronto Press, 2002.

Genette, Gérard. "Introduction to the Paratext." Translated by Marie Maclean. *New Literary History*, vol. 22 (1991): 261–72.

Kelcey, Barbara, E. "Dress Reform in Nineteenth-Century Canada." In Palmer, *Fashion*, 229–48.

MacGregor, Stafford. "Mars La Tour, or, The Maiden's Vow: A Legend of 1870–71." In Montgomery, *The Annotated Anne*, 481–2.

McMaster, Juliet. "Taking Control: Hair Red, Black, Gold, and Nut-Brown." In Gammel, *Making Avonlea*, 59–71.

Montgomery, L.M. *Anne of Green Gables*. Toronto: Penguin Canada, 2008.

– *The Annotated Anne of Green Gables*. Edited by Wendy E. Barry, Margaret Anne Doody, and Mary E. Doody Jones. Oxford: Oxford University Press, 1997.

– *The Selected Journals of L.M. Montgomery*. Vol. 1, 1889–1910; Vol. 2, 1910–1920. Edited by Mary Rubio and Elizabeth Waterston. Toronto: Oxford University Press, 1985; 1987.

*New York Times*, "Boston Gossip of Latest Books," 20 June 1908.

Palmer, Alexandra, ed. *Fashion: A Canadian Perspective*. Toronto: University of Toronto Press, 2004.

Wilde, Oscar. "The Suitability of Dress." 1882. In *The Rise of Fashion: A Reader*, edited by Daniel Leonhard Purdy, 232–8. Minneapolis: University of Minnesota Press, 2004.

Woster, Christy. "The Artists of *Anne of Green Gables*: A Hundred Year Mystery." *The Shining Scroll*. L.M. Montgomery Literary Society. 2007. http://home.earthlink.net/~bcavert/index.html (accessed 20 December 2011).

# Writing after *Anne*: L.M. Montgomery's Influence on Canadian Children's Literature

SUSAN MEYER

At the opening of Bernice Thurman Hunter's *As Ever, Booky* (1985), the teenage protagonist, Booky, is having an argument with her brother about literary greatness. Arthur, who is supposed to be doing his homework at the dining room table, staunchly maintains that Ralph Connor, Christian adventure novelist of the Western Canadian frontier, is Canada's greatest author. But Booky thinks differently. When Booky's sister opens the front door, Booky immediately turns to her for support. "Who's the most famous Canadian author, Willa?" Booky cries, to which Willa answers, without hesitation, "L.M. Montgomery."[1] Arthur groans and bangs his head on the table, but he is outnumbered. Booky, Willa, and their mother agree that the right answer is Montgomery. Even Booky's father, who doesn't "know much about books or authors" has heard of her.[2]

*As Ever, Booky* is set in the 1930s; nowadays, it would seem even less necessary to mention that a Canadian character, bookish or otherwise, had heard of L.M. Montgomery. Even those who condescend to children's literature recognize her stature. In the over one hundred years since the publication of *Anne of Green Gables*, L.M. Montgomery has cast a long shadow. But what is it like to be a Canadian author writing for children *after* L.M. Montgomery? How has she influenced subsequent generations of writers? How have they responded to or reacted against her work?

Harold Bloom, writing in the 1970s, posited a theory of literary influence as a family squabble between poets in which "strong" literary sons struggle against their powerful fathers, appropriating and aggressively misreading their work, "so as to clear imaginative space for themselves."[3] Feminist critics have since noted that Bloom's model of the "anxiety of influence" does little to describe the situation of women writers. Sandra Gilbert and Susan Gubar contend that for a woman writer, the central struggle is against the gender ideology of their powerful male precursors, an ideology that defines literary creativity as essentially male.[4] Most subsequent feminist criticism describes the relationship between women writers, on the other hand, as affirmative. Later women writers, feminist critics frequently maintain, are eager to find female literary precursors and are deeply appreciative of them. I tend on the whole to agree that there is far more affirmation in the relationships between women writers than in the model Bloom describes. Nonetheless, as I have demonstrated elsewhere using the example of the Brontë sisters, interesting tensions and rivalries as well as affirmations can and do exist between women writers, tensions that add an element of vitality and complexity to the women's literary tradition.[5]

But gender is not the only factor that distances writers from the Bloomian struggle. When writers are (for any of a variety of reasons) at a remove from the acclaimed centre of the literary canon, as children's writers, say, or as members of an ethnic group or nationality that has received little by way of literary acclaim, they are more likely to see earlier writers who resemble them as enabling precursors rather than as emasculating rivals. Celebration and contention are more likely to be mixed in such relations of literary influence. And to consider the way that later Canadian children's writers respond to L.M. Montgomery is to see such a mixture of homage and contention, of celebratory affirmation and aggressive revision.

Some Canadian children's authors imagine L.M. Montgomery as a powerful and overwhelming force, a figure to be struggled against. Tim Wynne-Jones's short story "The Anne Rehearsals" (1999) reveals the way that struggle can exist alongside or within literary admiration. "The Anne Rehearsals," as is characteristic of Wynne-Jones, is a light, deft story with serious undertones. It is narrated by Carmen, a young would-be writer and ardent admirer of L.M. Montgomery, who is devastated when her school plans a performance of the musical of *Anne of Green Gables*. Unlike her two best friends, who also admire Montgomery so much that they all make a green birthday cake in the shape of Prince Edward Island in her honour, Carmen has no talent as a singer or a scene-painter. Carmen can't figure out a way to participate in the musical, so she ends up grumpily on the sidelines instead, spending her time planning a pirate-themed birthday party for her annoying younger brother Sterling.

Despite Carmen's admiration for Montgomery, the story is about Carmen's experience of being excluded from artistic expression by *Anne of Green Gables* – and about the pain that exclusion causes because of the force of her admiration. "It's Anne this and Anne that all the live-long day," she explodes at her friends, to her own later astonishment.[6] Yet at one point in the story, Carmen prevails upon herself to visit a rehearsal, and there she finds herself transformed into a mouthpiece for L.M. Montgomery. When the teacher directing the musical refers to "Lucy Montgomery," Carmen cannot help herself. "I have a message from Maud Montgomery," she calls out, in a voice that has suddenly, without her volition, become "eerie and wavering": "she wants you to know, wants you *all* to know, she *hated* being called Lucy."[7] The ensuing derision from Carmen's classmates silences and excludes her even further. In bed at night, Carmen miserably ponders her lack of acting ability: "I try to figure out why I'm so good at telling stories and so hopeless onstage. It's not that I can't remember lines. Maybe ... I'm just horribly selfish and want to say only my own words."[8] Carmen is coming closer to the realization that will help her become a writer at the story's end. Praying to Maud for help, directly echoing her words, retelling her stories, or even, as in the eerie voice incident, channelling her voice – none of these strategies will allow Carmen to become a writer herself.

And Carmen's literary sensibility is perhaps not as close to Montgomery's as she thinks. Carmen scorns her younger brother because he is so unlike Montgomery in his tastes: "so unpoetical," she thinks, echoing one of Anne's favourite words.[9] But when Carmen creates a birthday party for Sterling, setting up the scenery and telling scary, fascinating pirate stories to him and his friends, it is an enormous triumph: "Very piratical," she thinks to herself, with satisfaction.[10] Because Sterling thinks so highly of Carmen's pirate stories, he suggests that she write about the school musical for the town newspaper. ("Isn't that how Anne started her career?" he surprises her by asking.[11]) And when Carmen allows her imagination to find its own path, letting the poetical mutate into the piratical, when she stops trying to channel or to replicate L.M. Montgomery, she finds her own voice as a writer ("I'm amazed how much pours out," she comments[12]) and she sees her first piece published.

Carmen's struggle, in Wynne-Jones's story, demonstrates the way that adulation for a past literary figure can be stifling. Carmen needs to accept the "horrible selfishness" of wanting to "say [her] own words." And through the irritating but perceptive younger brother Sterling in the story, Wynne-Jones suggests that Canadian boys also have a thing or two to say about Maud Montgomery's legacy.

Another Canadian author who struggles, yet more fiercely, with Montgomery as predecessor is Bernice Thurman Hunter. This might seem like a surprising claim, given what Hunter has said about her adoration of L.M. Montgomery and her books. At the age of fourteen, Hunter telephoned and wrote to Montgomery, and Montgomery kindly spoke and corresponded with her. Later, a schoolmate who lived next door to Montgomery wangled an invitation to tea there for the two young girls. They ate in the garden, and years later Hunter still remembered the menu: little pink-iced cakes and green-cheese pinwheel sandwiches! In an interview, Hunter spoke with appreciation of her youthful meeting with Montgomery in 1937. When asked, "Was L.M. Montgomery your favorite author?" she answered, "Oh, heavens yes. And you read her books not once but every one over and over and over ... You never get tired of them."[13] But she also explained that Montgomery, after reading some of Thurman's youthful writing, told her that higher education was essential for a writer: "you couldn't hope to be published unless you were a university graduate":[14] "In those days, and particularly in my class of people, you were lucky to stay in high school until you graduated with a diploma because it got you a job ... My mother knew that education was the key. But higher education – that was beyond us. My older sister should have gone to university, but there just wasn't the money."[15] Hunter recounts that her heart dropped when she heard Montgomery's words and that she then "just gave up the idea of being a writer."[16] She "got stuck on those well-meant words for many years," she writes.[17] It was only when Hunter became a grandparent and submitted the winning essay to a *Toronto Telegram* competition that she became a published author. Hunter then began rapidly producing novels and had written more than a dozen by the time of her death in 2002.

Hunter politely characterizes Montgomery's discouraging words as "well-meant." But in Hunter's fiction, Montgomery comes across as an adversary. In the third book of the highly autobiographical *Booky* series, her heroine, Booky, who aspires to becoming a writer, along with her classmate, is invited to tea with Montgomery (or Mrs Macdonald, as the girls use her married name). They eat the same cakes and sandwiches that the actual Montgomery served Bernice Hunter, and Mrs Macdonald offers Booky the same advice: "channel your energies into your studies."[18] Booky's reaction mirrors Hunter's: "The thought of all that higher education struck terror into my heart. And besides, I was dying to be done with school so that I could go out to work and make money to buy nice clothes like Gloria's."[19] After the tea, Booky receives a letter from Montgomery in which she repeats her advice. Deeply discouraged, Booky buries the letter and the story in the closet, not to look at them again for years.[20] She is melancholy for weeks afterward. On her birthday, school friends give her a diary, which "thrill[s] her to pieces"; but the wealthy classmate who had gotten Booky invited to Montgomery's home showily offers another gift that causes Booky tremendous pain – an autographed first edition of L.M. Montgomery's recently published *Jane of Lantern Hill*. "Now it just reminded me of my impossible dream," Booky says, "and I couldn't keep the pained look off my face. I didn't even trust myself to speak."[21]

The beautiful diary, filled with blank pages for Booky's own words, delights her with its invitation and promise; the novel by Montgomery – who has, inadvertently, told her she can never become a writer – wounds her and silences her. Later in the novel, Hunter gives her character authorial success, at a much younger age than she herself experienced it: the teenaged Booky wins a contest held by the *Toronto Telegram* and has her essay published (as Hunter herself did as a grandmother). Hunter displaces triumphant resentment at Montgomery onto Booky's mother. "I hope L.M. Montgomery sees it," Booky's mother cries, "rubbing her hands together gleefully."[22] Affirmed by this triumph, and by her brother, who surreptitiously reads her diary and then appeases her by telling her, "it was just like reading a real book," Booky determines to become a writer "no matter what."[23] Nonetheless, Booky does leave school after completing her commercial diploma, and begins work, as all her working-class friends are doing. She works at Eaton's department store, just as Hunter herself did as soon as she left high school, as she mentions in an epilogue appended to the novel.[24]

Toward the end of the trilogy, Hunter engages in a final act of subtle fictional retribution against Montgomery, by imagining what would have become of Montgomery's most renowned heroine if she had been situated in Bernice Thurman Hunter's social milieu. Did Hunter realize what she was doing? Perhaps not. But at Eaton's, working as an envelope-stuffer in the accounts office, Booky meets a girl named Anne – with an "e." She has red hair, green eyes, and – and this is the clincher, recognizable by anyone who knows Anne Shirley –"a nice neat nose."[25] She is a friendly, likeable girl, dissatisfied with her red hair, which she wishes she could trade for Booky's. But like the young adult Booky, and like Hunter herself as a young woman, she is neither pursuing a higher education nor writing. Hunter's "Anne with an e" does nothing more "poetical" all day than stuff bills into envelopes at Eaton's.

But if Hunter's literary relationship to Montgomery is surprisingly (if somewhat humorously) contentious, the allusions to Montgomery in the work of other Canadian children's writers are sometimes less confrontational than a reader might expect. A number of Carol Matas's powerful novels are about children and teens encountering the horrors of the Second World War, fascism, and anti-Semitism. Her Dear Canada novel, set in Winnipeg in 1941, *Turned Away: The World War II Diary of Devorah Bernstein* (2005) chronicles the efforts by Devorah's family to get visas from the Canadian government to allow Devorah's French aunt, uncle, and cousins entry into the country. Their agonizing struggle ultimately fails, and Devorah's relatives are left to the mercy of the Nazis occupying France. Matas's novel is a fierce indictment of the anti-Semitism of the Canadian government (Canada had a far worse record in admitting Jews during these years, she observes in the "Historical Note" than the restrictive United States, or even than Chile or Bolivia.)[26] Devorah begins to notice anti-Semitic comments by her schoolmates and even in the work of her favourite author, Agatha Christie. She writes Christie a sad letter criticizing the stereotypes of Jews in *And Then There Were None*, signing it "Your biggest fan."[27] Devorah then decides to reread *Anne of Green Gables* instead, for relief.

At this point in Matas's novel, I thought I knew what was coming. I expected Devorah to be brought up short by what is always for me a moment of painful disruption in the experience of reading the novel. After Anne accidentally dyes her hair green with the "raven-black" dye she bought from a peddler, Marilla scolds her, "Anne Shirley, how often have I told you never to let one of those Italians in the house!" to which Anne replies: "Oh, I didn't let him in the house ... I went out, carefully shut the door, and looked at his things on the step. Besides, he wasn't an Italian – he was a German Jew."[28] Anne completely and humorously misses Marilla's point. Inside or out – that makes little difference. Marilla means that she shouldn't listen to the peddler or let him display his wares. And an Italian or a German Jew – to Marilla, both are unreliable foreigners. The Jewish peddler has played upon Anne's ready sympathies, wheedling a child into buying hair dye (something he surely knows no child's guardian would want her to do) by speaking "so feelingly" of a wife and children whom he wishes to bring out of Germany. He convinces Anne that he has a kind heart by knocking down the price, and of course the dye itself is of poor quality. These are the oldest of tricks by a dishonest peddler – and in this case a peddler who is clearly identified in the novel as racially alien and deceptive. But Matas lets this episode pass. She doesn't show Devorah again feeling rejected, as a Jew by a literary text – here by *Anne of Green Gables*, the central, defining work of Canadian children's literature, to which she turns for comfort.[29] Perhaps Matas hadn't recently reread the novel and didn't remember – so Devorah never mentions experiencing the temporary alienation other Jewish readers have felt upon coming to this moment in *Anne of Green Gables*.

More than any of the other writers I consider in this essay, Jean Little engages most with the legacy of L.M. Montgomery in her fiction. In the course of her more than forty-year career, Little's novels repeatedly allude to Montgomery: from 1966, in *Spring Begins in March*, where Meg's grandmother reads her *Anne of Ingleside*; to 2007, in *Dancing Through the Snow*, where the abandoned child, Min, eavesdropping on a conversation about her destiny, like the orphaned Emily Starr, hears herself condemned in terms that echo the criticism Emily hears of herself. "She's sly," says Enid Bangs, just as Emily's Aunt Ruth does.[30] Similarly, in Little's *The Belonging Place* (1997), Elspet Mary's struggle with her adoptive mother over a kitten recalls Emily Starr's struggle with Aunt Elizabeth in Montgomery's *Emily of New Moon*. "Aunt Elizabeth," says Emily, with the fearsome "Murray look" in her eyes, "this poor little kitten is cold and starving, and, oh, so miserable ... It shall NOT be drowned again."[31] Here is Elspet Mary in Little's novel: "I looked my mother in the eye. 'This kitten is starving and hurt. He's coming with us,' I stated. 'He's mine.'"[32]

In *Brothers Far from Home: The World War I Diary of Eliza Bates* (2003), Little's protagonist, Eliza, has met L.M. Montgomery. The novel also alludes more subtly to Montgomery's *Rilla of Ingleside*: after Eliza's brother, Hugo, is killed in the war, she brings her mother a snowdrop in the spring because he always brought the first snowdrops to their mother – just as Walter brought Anne the first mayflowers.[33]

The frequent allusions to Montgomery in Little's fiction suggest not only admiration but something more complicated, something unresolved. Little's novels are compelling in their vivid and honest exploration of the emotional lives of children. Her protagonists are seen from time to time telling lies, being nasty to their siblings, cheating on tests, and deliberately smashing telephones with crutches. Little aggressively refuses to idealize – and it is in this respect that her work most engages with and revises Montgomery's.

In an essay published in *Canadian Children's Literature* in 1975, titled "But What About Jane?" Jean Little acknowledges the profound effect Montgomery's fiction had on her in her own childhood and both praises and criticizes L.M. Montgomery. Little writes appreciatively of Montgomery's deep understanding of children, yet bluntly criticizes her for sometimes mediocre writing and sentimentality. She expresses a strong preference for the imperfect, tall, awkward Jane (of *Jane of Lantern Hill*) over the "sweet-lipped" Anne Shirley or Emily Starr with her "little ears ... pointed just a wee bit to show that she was kin to the tribes of elfland."[34] Quoting the scene in which a humiliated Jane, startled and unable to reply to a sudden drilling in geography facts at her grandmother's table, knocks her fork onto the floor, Jean Little writes: "We all hope we possess that magic extra ingredient that sees Anne and Emily through, but underneath that hope lies the hard knowledge that we are fork-droppers."[35]

Similarly, the allusions to Montgomery in Little's fiction are both admiring and contentious, respectful and revisionary. Little's early novel, *Spring Begins in March* (1966), is (in part) about the relationship between a new girl writer and her powerful ancestress. It is tempting to read it, then, as suggestive of the relationship between Little and Montgomery. The novel is the story of the rebellious, discontented Meg, a dreamy child who has difficulties in school, particularly in writing. Meg also has problems with her grandmother, who has recently come to live with the family.

A significant turning point in their relationship occurs when Grandma reads *Anne of Ingleside* to Meg one night when her mother is out – and then, coming to the end of the chapter and Meg's bedtime, Grandma goes on reading, because it seems as if Anne is dying and she realizes that it would be too hard for Meg if she stopped. Meg is surprised when she realizes that Grandma is as absorbed in Anne's story as Meg herself is. When Jean Little was ten years old, she recounts elsewhere, her own grandmother stopped reading aloud one night at the end of this very chapter.[36] Little writes that, miserably fearful that Anne was about to die, she snuck out of bed and, for the only time in her life, committed the crime of "reading ahead" – only then to be smitten with terrible guilt over her transgression. This scene in *Spring Begins in March*, read with a knowledge of the biographical episode behind it, clearly reveals the power that Little feels in Montgomery's writing.

But the novel is about how to work out a harmonious relationship with a sometimes formidable female predecessor – a negotiation that occurs in the novel through reading and writing. What really transforms Meg's feelings about her grandmother is reading her grandmother's childhood diary and discovering that her feelings, as a girl, were much like Meg's own. And Meg finds her own voice as a writer (after struggling with writing for years) by learning from her grandmother's simple, natural girlhood voice. She learns so successfully that, toward the end of the novel, Meg's older sister Sal announces that Meg is "a budding genius."[37] *Spring Begins in March* suggests that the struggle with powerful, redoubtable literary grandmothers can best be resolved through sympathetic reading and understanding. If the granddaughter can read the grandmother in this way, the novel suggests, the seemingly ferocious grandmother can help the granddaughter find her own writerly voice.

Yet Little's novels also often allude to and reshape Montgomery's plots, and in doing so they implicitly criticize the idealism of the original novels. Little's most important act of revision has to do with Montgomery's representation of war. Two of Little's novels, *Listen for the Singing* (1977) and *Brothers Far from Home* (2003), allude extensively to Montgomery's *Rilla of Ingleside* but enact some important revisionary twists. Little's historical position is obviously very different from Montgomery's: writing *Rilla of Ingleside* in 1921 it was possible for Montgomery to hope that the First World War, the "Great War," had indeed been the war to end all wars, in a way that no-one writing in the 1970s or the first decade of the twenty-first century could. In *Listen for the Singing* (1977), a novel of the Second World War, Little echoes Montgomery, but she shows war to be more bungled and less heroic than it is in *Rilla*, and the emotions it leaves in those who survive are depicted as messier, less pure.

Like *Rilla of Ingleside*, Little's novel is about a younger sister who watches her brother agonize over his cowardice and then finally enlist and go off to war. *Listen for the Singing* is about Anna Solden and her family, who fled from Germany to Canada in the early 1930s. Now it is 1939 and Canada is at war with Germany. The Solden family members encounter suspicion and hostility because of their German origins, and Rudi, Anna's older brother, is particularly troubled. Only Anna, like Rilla sympathizing with Walter, seems to notice that her older brother is worried that he is a coward and to understand that he is agonizing over whether he should enlist. Rudi has an even more vivid sense than Walter Blythe does of the humanity of the enemy, because Rudi remembers German boys he played with in childhood and knows that they are now in the opposing army.

Like Walter, Rudi ultimately enlists, and his younger sister waits and worries. Unlike Walter, though, Rudi does not die heroically. Instead, he is grievously wounded, blinded in an accident on board ship, long before he ever sees action, when cleaning fluid splashes into his eyes. The accident is banal and ugly, impossible to see in heroic terms. When Anna was younger, Rudi (not a perfect older brother like Walter) teased her mercilessly about her clumsiness and stupidity, before the family realized that she was nearly blind. At the novel's end, Anna helps Rudi cope with his blindness and find hope. But the emotional resonance of Rudi's terrible war injury is complicated. Has Rudi blinded himself through his own clumsiness? Does Anna in any part of her feel that this is a just comeuppance? Anna's relationship with her brother is more emotionally tangled than Rilla's with Walter. And the novel has none of Montgomery's sense that a better era is coming, painfully bought with the sacrifices of war. Instead, for Little, the mutilations and losses of war are ugly, brutal, meaningless.

Little returns again to *Rilla* in *Brothers Far from Home: The World War I Diary of Eliza Bates* (2003).[38] *Brothers Far from Home* comments on Montgomery's fiction in many ways, some of them comical (Little's protagonist is very opposed to elocution: "I secretly think," observes Eliza, that poems "don't need all that hand waving and clutching at the heart").[39] Other aspects of Little's implicit commentary on Montgomery are more serious. Montgomery represents pacifists, through the character of "Whiskers-on-the-moon," as absurd and evil: she even implicitly endorses Norman Douglass's physical assault. But Eliza's own minister father is himself a pacifist, although he has sons at the front. He prays for all who are suffering and yearns for both sides to come to their senses and end the war, infuriating many members of his congregation. In an echo of Walter's experience in *Rilla of Ingleside*, Eliza's father says that one of the church Elders would "hand me a white feather if he did not know they would not take me."[40] And like Little's earlier novel, *Brothers Far from Home* insists on facing the ugliness of war. The family next door to Eliza has a son who was gassed, and Eliza watches him suffer terrible neurological and psychological consequences and even attempt suicide. One of Eliza's brothers, Jack, comes home horribly disfigured, his face burned so badly that Eliza screams when she first sees him in the middle of the night, thinking he is a monster.[41]

Most tellingly, in *Brothers Far from Home*, Jean Little explicitly reworks the story of Walter's Blythe's heroic rescue of another soldier. Walter dashes back from the trenches to save a wounded comrade, fallen in No-Man's-Land[42] and is awarded the DC Distinguished Service medal. Soon afterward, he dies at Courcelette. Eliza, like Rilla Blythe, loses her beloved brother in the war. But there is nothing uplifting about Hugo's death. Like Walter, Hugo dashes back to help a wounded man out of the line of fire. The soldiers have been ordered not to turn back, but the wounded man is the father of a young baby. Hugo is shot while attempting the rescue – shot and killed by a Canadian officer because he disobeyed orders.[43] In this startling act of allusion and revision, Jean Little at once honours Montgomery and retells her story, insisting on the hideous senselessness of war.

Little's references to Montgomery, then, are not merely homage, although they are partly homage. Nor are they primarily agonistic, as in the father-son struggles Bloom describes. Little's fiction suggests that reading and responding to the work of a writer of Montgomery's stature, despite their common position as Canadians and as female children's authors, is a complex process, a delicate balance between celebration and revision. Little celebrates Montgomery's fiction, alluding to it in novel after novel. But her acts of allusion are also revisionary. In particular, Little insists on reworking Montgomery's idealism, and on depicting (to her way of thinking) a more realistic world: one in which all humans are faulty, even loving feelings are messy, and war is unredeemably brutal and grotesque.

Jean Little has anticipated me in writing admiringly about Canadian author Julie Johnston, *Adam and Eve and Pinch-Me* (1994), and the allusions to and reworking of the story of *Anne of Green Gables* in Johnston's novel. *Adam and Eve and Pinch-Me* is a gripping and poignant book narrated by fifteen-year-old, red-headed Sara Moone, a long-unloved and unwanted foster child, who has come to live with the Huddlestons at their farm in Ambrose, Ontario. Sara, Little writes, "is the girl Anne Shirley would have been if L.M. Montgomery had made her the true product of the love-starved childhood Anne herself describes ... The wounds [Anne] has sustained have left her mercifully unscarred and she, idiotically when you think of her previous experiences, runs to meet life with irrepressible hope. Sara Moone, on the other hand, is guarded, hostile, cold, and extremely angry."[44] Little does not intend to suggest that one book is better than the other: she describes each heroine as "a product of her time" and of a radically different vision of childhood.

Little's comments about the parallels between Johnston's novel and L.M. Montgomery's (or, as I would put it, about the revisions of Montgomery's novel in Johnston's) are astute and convincing. I'd only like to add that *Adam and Eve and Pinch-Me* is also permeated with allusions to L.M. Montgomery's Emily novels. Like Emily, Sara is an orphan taken in by others, and like Emily she is a writer. Emily writes tirelessly to her dead father on old letter bills, hiding them from anyone else's eyes by secreting them on the board underneath an old sofa in the attic. Sara too writes for no living eyes, but her mode of writing is even more cut off from the world. Johnston's novel takes the form of the words Sara types compulsively and relentlessly into a computer, a computer with no printer (and no Internet access). Sara writes not even to her memory of a person but to a silent, disconnected machine. But each girl's literary privacy is rudely violated – Emily's by prying, self-righteous Aunt Elizabeth and Sara's by her disturbed and disturbing foster brother Nick, whose invasion is almost sexual. ("I know you inside out," he gloats.[45]) Yet in each case the violation allows the respective girl to progress toward being the writer she is becoming at the novel's end.

Even Sara *Moone*'s name is very reminiscent of Emily *Starr*'s. Angry, introverted Sara Moone ("with the E tacked on for ballast," as Sara observes, in a sentence Anne Shirley might appreciate) has none of Emily Starr's celestial, starry-eyed impulses. She is, as Little observes, scarred, isolated, and damaged. But as Sara begins to be drawn into the human family, her nature changes, as Johnston subtly hints through her changing descriptions of the moon to which Sara Moone inevitably likens herself. Early in the novel, Sara describes the moon as "a mean little curved blade slung low in the darkening sky."[46] But at the novel's end, curled up with her insistently loving younger foster brother, she watches the full moon and finds it comforting. "Frogs sang beneath it ... Something that was supposed to be in place was, in fact, in place. Josh leaned his head against me, and I didn't move away."[47] Julie Johnston's *Adam and Eve and Pinch-Me* reworks L.M. Montgomery's vision. But it is deeply shaped by the work of Montgomery; so deeply that, without Montgomery's influence, this startling and beautiful novel could not have taken shape as it did.

I'll end by turning to Kit Pearson, who writes, in the biography posted on her Web page, that it was at the age of thirteen, when she finished reading L.M. Montgomery's *Emily of New Moon*, that she decided to become a writer. "That book has had an amazing influence – in fact, all three Emily books [have] – on writers in Canada," she has said in interviews.[48] "What is it about that book?"[49] In one interview she even expresses a worry that her novels are too much like those of Montgomery, because she has so deeply internalized Montgomery's fiction, as well as other books she read in childhood.

The books of Pearson's that show the greatest similarities in plot to Montgomery's are her compelling Guests of War trilogy, in which two British children, Nora and Gavin, come to Canada during the Second World War to escape the bombings. One interviewer, Jane Flick, commented, "I was struck by an echo of Montgomery's *Anne* in Nora's situation in [Pearson's] *The Sky is Falling* as Nora learns that the Ogilvies want only a boy but are willing to take her as well as Gavin."[50]

Yet for me, where Pearson's novels resonate the most with Montgomery's, and particularly with Montgomery's *Emily* books, is in their intense emphasis on the inner life of children. After Emily Starr's loving father dies and she is left to fit into a world governed by often unsympathetic grownups, her imaginative life becomes more inward and hidden. Pearson's novels show her to be exceptionally drawn to exploring children's inner lives: her novels convincingly represent both

children's individual secret thoughts and feelings and the dynamics between children that take place out of view of adults. In Pearson's first
novel, *The Daring Game* (1986), Eliza, her protagonist, is away at boarding school for the first time and away from her loving parents, "two
people who knew her intimately and always had her welfare in mind."[51]
At the boarding school, the exterior regulation is stricter than at home
but "there were too many students for anyone in charge to be able to
know the inner state of any one girl."[52] It is exhilarating, Eliza discovers,
to be away from her parents' loving attention because now, she realizes,
"no one was responsible for her inside but herself."[53] She has the kind of
deep, inner, imaginative freedom that Emily Starr also has when separ-
ated from a loving parent.

But Kit Pearson's *Awake and Dreaming* (1996) is her most thorough
investigation of the inner life of a child and its relationship to the writing of fiction. It also contains some telling allusions to L.M. Montgomery's *Emily* books. As *Awake and Dreaming* begins, Theo, a dreamy,
neglected nine-year-old, is living in poverty in Vancouver with her
young, careless mother. The novel centres on Theo's relationship with
a ghost – the ghost of a writer who lived in Victoria years before, who
died young before having a chance to write the novel she most dreamed
of writing. The ghost sees Theo being shuttled off to live with an aunt
in Victoria and projects a happy story about her, which Theo then par-
tially lives out until the story begins to fade. As the novel comes to a
climax, Theo meets Cecily, the ghost, in a graveyard, and talks with her
several times. Between their conversations, when Theo's fate is being
decided by her mother and aunt, Theo eavesdrops in a manner reminiscent of Montgomery's newly orphaned Emily Starr, who hides under
the table in order to overhear her relatives discuss what is to be done
with her. "Theo slid out of the apartment but after she closed the door
she opened it a crack and crouched by it. She wasn't going to miss hearing them decide her future."[54]

At the end of the novel, it appears that Theo is going to resume living
with her irresponsible mother. Cecily sympathizes with Theo in her
relative powerlessness, but tells her: "when you're young you have to
cope the best you can with what adults do with your life. But remember,
they can only control your outer life. Your inner life – your core – is still
your own."[55] She also encourages Theo to see her suffering as material
for later narrative and to use her imagination to escape suffering: "Writ-

ers are both awake and dreaming ... you can force yourself to see people at a distance, like someone in a story ... Or you can make up something better and escape to it."[56] And she tells Theo to watch for something that sounds very much like what Montgomery's Emily Starr calls "the flash": "if you watch carefully, there are always what I call shining moments, even in hard times – moments of sheer joy, when you're just glad to be alive."[57] Emily's "the flash" is little enough to offer Theo or any suffering, powerless child who may be reading the book, but it is all that a writer can offer beyond aesthetic experience – recognition of her pain and encouragement to hope and to seize happiness.

Through Cecily and Theo, Pearson projects an ideal model of literary influence, an ideal model for the relationship between (in particular) children's writers of different generations. It is a relationship of affirmation, continuity, and completion, a relationship very different from Harold Bloom's agonistic struggle. In Pearson's novel, the writer of an earlier era speaks sympathetically and appealingly to the suffering child of a future generation, a child who will grow up to complete the earlier writer's incomplete work. As the novel ends, Theo pauses by Cecily's grave and touches the carving on the gravestone: "She smoothed the marble pages of the book with her palms, as if she were pressing it firmly open. 'I won't forget,' she whispered."[58] Through the open book, this final image in *Awake and Dreaming* suggests, with living hands warm on the marble pages of the past – through reading and writing – writers of different generations reach out to one another. It is an apt image for the ideal form of literary influence. This, Pearson indicates, is, in the best circumstances, what the work of one writer, a writer such as L.M. Montgomery, can mean to another – or to many others. As Pearson asks, what *is* it about those books?

NOTES

1   Hunter, *As Ever, Booky*, 343.
2   Ibid., 343. I would like to thank Benjamin Lefebvre for drawing my attention to some of the works I discuss in this essay. Raymond Jones and Jon Stott's volume *Canadian Children's Books* also proved an invaluable resource as I worked on this material.
3   Bloom, *Anxiety of Influence*, 5.

4  Gilbert and Gubar, *The Madwoman in the Attic*, 47.
5  For those who see relationships between women writers as largely affirmative, see Joanne Diehl, Mary Washington, Jane Marcus, Elizabeth Abel, Rachel Du-Plessis, Annette Kolodny, Nancy Paxton. For discussions of the tensions as well as the affirmations in relationships between women writers see Susan Meyer, Betsy Erkkila, and Andrew Brown.
6  Wynne-Jones, "The Anne Rehearsals," 105.
7  Ibid., 111.
8  Ibid., 105.
9  Ibid., 103.
10  Ibid., 104.
11  Ibid., 113.
12  Ibid.
13  Heilbron, "Bernice (Thurman) Hunter," 163–4.
14  Ibid.
15  Ibid. Jones in this volume further discusses class in Montgomery's writing and in the language of *Anne of Green Gables*.
16  Heilbron, "Bernice (Thurman) Hunter," 163–4.
17  Hunter, *Inspirations*, 88.
18  Hunter, *As Ever, Booky*, 349. Interestingly, Mary Frances Coady, in her *Lucy Maud and Me* (1999), a children's biography of Montgomery in fictional form, also has her Mrs Macdonald insist to a young girl that she should let nothing deprive her of an education. Laura, the girl protagonist, gives up her temporary dream of staying with her grandfather to keep house for him.
19  Ibid., 350.
20  Ibid.
21  Ibid., 361.
22  Ibid., 433.
23  Ibid., 452.
24  Ibid., 482.
25  Ibid., 477.
26  Matas, *Turned Away*, 126.
27  Ibid., 34.
28  Montgomery, *Anne of Green Gables*, 217.
29  Collins-Gearing's article in this volume notes the reference to the peddler as a jarring reminder of the book's colonialist context.
30  Little, *Dancing Through the Snow*, 21; Montgomery, *Emily of New Moon*, 39.
31  Montgomery, *Emily of New Moon*, 147.
32  Little, *The Belonging Place*, 67.
33  Ibid., *Brothers Far from Home*, 78.
34  Quoted in Little, "But What about Jane?" 79.
35  Little, "But What about Jane?" 80.

36  Ibid., 71.
37  Ibid., *Spring Begins in March*, 147.
38  For an interview with Jean Little in which she compares the way she kept her diaries (more than forty years of which are now housed in the University of Guelph archives) to Montgomery's, see Vowles, "From the Archives."
39  Little, *Brothers Far from Home*, 77.
40  Ibid., 68.
41  Ibid., 167.
42  Montgomery, *Rilla of Ingleside*, 166.
43  Little, *Brothers Far from Home*, 97.
44  Ibid, "Julie Johnston," 34.
45  Johnston, *Adam and Eve and Pinch-Me*, 155.
46  Ibid., 13.
47  Ibid., 168.
48  Flick, "'Writing Is the Deepest Pleasure,'" 16.
49  Quoted in Jenkinson, "Kit Pearson," 66. Kit Pearson names Alice Munro, mystery writer L.R Wright, and Jane Urquhart, as well as Rosemary Sutcliff, as having been influenced by *Emily of New Moon*. American writer Madeleine L'Engle also spoke of *Emily of New Moon* as an inspirational text.
50  Flick, "'Writing Is the Deepest Pleasure,'" 16.
51  Pearson, *The Daring Game*, 38–9.
52  Ibid.
53  Ibid.
54  Ibid., *Awake and Dreaming*, 211.
55  Ibid., 215.
56  Ibid., 217.
57  Ibid., 216.
58  Ibid., 229.

## BIBLIOGRAPHY

Abel, Elizabeth. "(E)Merging Identities: The Dynamics of Female Friendship in Contemporary Fiction by Women." *Signs*, vol. 6 (1981): 414–35.

Bloom, Harold. *The Anxiety of Influence: A Theory of Poetry*. New York: Oxford University Press, 1973.

Brown, J. Andrew. "Feminine Anxiety of Influence Revisited: Alfonsina Storni and Delmira Agustini." *Revista Canadiense de Estudios Hispanicos*, vol. 23 (1999): 191–203.

Coady, Mary Frances. *Lucy Maud and Me*. Vancouver: Beach Holme Publishing, 1999.

Diehl, Joanne Feit. "'Come Slowly–Eden': An Exploration of Women Poets and Their Muse." *Signs*, vol. 3 (1978): 572–87.

DuPlessis, Rachel Blau. *Writing Beyond the Ending: Narrative Strategies of Twentieth-Century Women Writers*. Bloomington: Indiana University Press, 1985.

Erkkila, Betsy. *The Wicked Sisters: Women Poets, Literary History, and Discord*. New York: Oxford University Press, 1992.

Flick, Jane. "'Writing Is the Deepest Pleasure I Know': An Interview with Kit Pearson." *CCL: Canadian Children's Literature*, vol. 74 (1994): 16–29.

Gilbert, Sandra M., and Susan Gubar. *The Madwoman in the Attic: The Woman Writer and the Nineteenth-Century Literary Imagination*. New Haven: Yale University Press, 1979.

Heilbron, Alexandra. "Bernice (Thurman) Hunter." In *Remembering Lucy Maud Montgomery*, 160–5. Toronto: Dundurn Press, 2001.

Hunter, Bernice Thurman. *As Ever, Booky*. In Hunter, *Booky: A Trilogy*.

– *Booky: A Trilogy*. Markham, Ontario: Scholastic Canada, 1998.

– "Inspirations." *CCL: Canadian Children's Literature*, vol. 84 (1996): 87–9.

Jenkinson, Dave. "Kit Pearson: Boarding Schools, Beaches, and Bombs." *Emergency Librarian*, vol. 17 (1989): 65–9.

Jones, Raymond E., and Jon C. Stott. *Canadian Children's Books: A Critical Guide to Authors and Illustrators*. Ontario: Oxford University Press, 2000.

Johnston, Julie. *Adam and Eve and Pinch-Me*. Toronto: Lester Publishing, 1994.

Kolodny, Annette. "The Influence of Anxiety: Prolegomena to a Study of the Production of Poetry by Women." In *A Gift of Tongues: Critical Challenges in Contemporary American Poetry*, edited by Marie Harris and Kathleen Aguero, 112–41. Athens: University of Georgia Press, 1987.

Little, Jean. *The Belonging Place*. New York: Viking Penguin, 1997.

– *Brothers Far from Home: The World War I Diary of Eliza Bates*. Dear Canada Series. Markham, Ontario: Scholastic Canada, 2003.

– "But What About Jane?" *CCL: Canadian Children's Literature*, vol. 3 (1975): 77–81.

– *Dancing Through the Snow*. Toronto: Scholastic Canada, 2007.

– "Julie Johnston: An Exciting New Voice." *CCL: Canadian Children's Literature*, vol. 77 (1995): 33–8.

– *Listen for the Singing*. New York: Dutton, 1977.

– *Spring Begins in March*. Toronto: Little, Brown, 1966.

Marcus, Jane. "Thinking Back Through Our Mothers." In *New Feminist Essays on Virginia Woolf*, edited by Jane Marcus, 1–30. Lincoln: University of Nebraska Press, 1981.

Matas, Carol. *Turned Away: The World War II Diary of Devorah Bernstein*. Dear Canada Series. Markham, Ontario: Scholastic Canada, 2005.

Meyer, Susan. "Writing More Than 'Papa Lent Me This Book': Charlotte Brontë, Gilbert and Gubar, and the Heterosexual Romance of Literary History." In *Making Feminist History: The Literary Scholarship of Sandra M. Gilbert and Susan Gubar*, 135–52. New York: Garland, 1994.

Montgomery, L.M. *Anne of Green Gables*. Edited by Cecily Devereux. Peterborough, Ontario: Broadview Press, 2004.

— *Anne of Ingleside*. New York: Grosset & Dunlap, 1939.

— *Emily of New Moon*. 1925. Toronto: McClelland-Bantam, 1992.

— *Jane of Lantern Hill*. 1937. New York: Bantam, 1988.

Paxton, Nancy L. "The Story of an African Farm and the Dynamics of Woman-to-Woman Influence." *Texas Studies in Literature and Language*, vol. 30 (1988): 562–82.

Pearson, Kit. *Awake and Dreaming*. 1986. New York: Penguin, 2007.

— *The Daring Game*. New York: Penguin, 1986.

— *The Lights Go On Again*. Guests of War: Book Three. 1993. New York: Penguin, 2007.

— *Looking at the Moon*. Guests of War: Book Two. 1991. New York: Penguin, 2007.

— *The Sky Is Falling*. Guests of War: Book One. 1989. New York: Penguin, 2007.

Vowles, Andrew. "From the Archives: Dear Diary." Guelph 51 no. 6. http://www.uoguelph.ca/atguelph/07-03-28/newsarchives.shtml (accessed 20 December 2011).

Washington, Mary Helen. "These Self-Invented Women: A Theoretical Framework for a Literary History of Black Women." *Radical Teacher*, vol. 17 (1980): 3–6.

Wynne-Jones, Tim. "The Anne Rehearsals." In *Lord of the Fries and Other Stories*, 91–115. New York: D.K. Publishing, 1999.

# Writing *Before Green Gables*

BUDGE WILSON

Early in 2006 Helen Reeves phoned me from Penguin Publishers to ask if I would be willing to write a prequel to *Anne of Green Gables*. A prequel was to be part of Penguin's proposed three-book celebration of the hundredth anniversary of the publication of *Anne*. My reaction to this astonishing request was very complicated. Basically, I didn't want to do it. I had three of my own writing projects in motion, and I was loath to abandon them. I was ready and eager to move into a form of writing that was new to me – using a lot of poetic strategies – and I resented any potential barrier to that objective. Nonetheless, I felt both shocked and honoured to be asked to write this prequel, and I knew that the invitation should neither be turned down nor accepted too quickly. So I thanked Helen for her amazing suggestion, told her I needed time to think about it, and hung up. I then spent two months trying to reach a decision.

One of my most solid stumbling blocks was the question: Would L.M. Montgomery want me – or anyone else, for that matter – to write this prequel? Would I, in fact, want anyone to write a prequel to any book I had written? No, I would not. Surely Montgomery's reply would have come back with even more emphasis. Or so I thought at the time. Also, I asked myself, would I enjoy writing a book in which the central character was not my own creation? I was very uneasy about that. I knew that Anne's following was huge – although I didn't realize at the time just how enormous it was. I was aware that Montgomery's work was now taught in universities, and that university scholars would approach their subject matter with a lot more knowledge and academic intensity than would the multitudes of ten-year-old Anne fans. If I were to accept Penguin's offer, I would have to come to terms with the possibility that there might be many critics standing in the wings, waiting to tear me to pieces. This was not a simple decision.

During what were to be my two months of uncertainty, I began to reread the *Anne* books. In my own childhood, I had preferred Emily to Anne. When I was fifteen, I began to write voluminous journals – telling everything I did and thought and felt – written in large hard-covered books. They sustained me through an emotional and often stormy adolescence. I knew that those journals originated with Emily's "Jimmy books," and I relished this connection with Emily. Only much later in life did I learn that Montgomery felt the *Emily* books to be the most autobiographical of her novels.

But my preference for Emily changed. When, at the age of 79, I reread *Anne of Green Gables*, I was completely captivated by Anne – in fact, bewitched. This was a character with whom I would be happy to spend a lot of time. I was already welcoming her into my head. When, in chapter 5, "Anne's History," I read of her difficult years with the Thomas and Hammond families – the verbal abuse, the virtual slavery, the lack of schooling – and the four long months in the orphanage, which Anne later refers to as "the worst" of her early experiences, I was already starting to ask myself some piercing questions. How was it possible that this eleven-year-old child who had had such an appalling early childhood could step down from the train in Prince Edward Island as a richly formed person who was lively, cheerful, feisty, articulate, and spilling over with an unfettered imagination? Later, when I spoke of this to Elizabeth Epperly, she said, "Well – that's your puzzle." Indeed, it was. By the time I reached the end of that first *Anne* book, I had joined the huge army of Anne lovers, and I was already thinking of ways to solve the puzzle. That became my unacknowledged goal, and, after two months of heavy thinking, I guess I discovered that I couldn't let it go.

In the meantime, something else happened that may have brought me closer to a decision. I told Elizabeth Epperly (now known to me more familiarly as "Betsy") that I had often boarded at the Halifax Ladies' College during times when my mother joined my father on a number of trips involving his work. I said I always stayed in one room in a section we called "Three-and-a-Half" – an offshoot of the third floor, containing only four or five rooms. She was astonished, and told me that L.M. Montgomery had been taken to a room on what she called

"Third-and-a-Half" after recovering from the measles. She loved the room so much that she remained there for the rest of her time at the Ladies' College.

I became convinced that Montgomery and I had lived in the same room. Why was it available when she was recovering from the measles? Why was it always empty when I needed a place to stay? My answer is that it was tiny, and it was also at the end of the hall, quite far from the other girls' rooms. I remember it as being very small, very white, very bare. Few people would have chosen to live there for a whole year. But I loved that little room and still remember it vividly, although I was only eleven years old when I spent my first night there.

In *Anne of the Island*, when Anne is about to leave a room in which she has been living while attending Redmond College, she says, "I shall leave here my fancies and dreams to bless the next comer."[1] She goes on to say that she "wondered ... if when one left behind forever the room where she had joyed and suffered and laughed and wept, something of her, intangible and invisible, yet nonetheless real, did not remain behind like a voiceful memory."[2] It is not strange that I started to feel a haunting connection with Maud Montgomery.

But I didn't stop there. I started to wonder if Montgomery had – intentionally or not – based her description of Anne's room at Green Gables on the room we shared on "Third-and-a-Half." Anne refers to it often – during absences from Green Gables – as "my little white room." I remember the room I lived in as having white walls, a white bed, and a white bedspread. And I, like Anne, was eleven years old when I first saw it.

Whether because of this coincidence about the room or for some other reason, I stopped worrying about whether L.M. Montgomery would disapprove of my writing a prequel to her book. From time to time, I have wondered if she would or would not. But wondering is different from worrying, and I let that particular anxiety die. Besides, by now, Anne was firmly planted on the inside of my head, and it was clear that she wasn't planning to leave anytime soon. I called Helen Reeves, and said that yes, I would do it, although I stipulated that I must write it in my own voice. I was already thinking that I would start the book before Anne was born, in order to include possible genetic influences ...

However, apparently this had not been an open-ended invitation. I would be required to write a sample chapter. It is not an altogether simple process to create a sample chapter for a book one hasn't even started to write. But my sample chapter was to become almost exactly chapter 69 of the finished book. After I wrote it, I sent it off, sat down, and waited. Eight long weeks passed before I heard one word about that fledgling chapter. This was not a happy time for me. Within myself, I was now committed to writing *Before Green Gables*, but the green light had not yet been turned on. I was creatively stalled – unable to return to my other work because I expected news of acceptance or rejection with each passing day. Later, I was to learn that one of Montgomery's heirs had been in China – and had therefore been unable to read the chapter. But at the time, I didn't know this.

While I was waiting for the final "go-ahead" signal, I continued with my reading of the *Anne* books, thereby absorbing a lot of the necessary research without actually realizing that I was doing it.

Apart from this, I read a short biography of Montgomery, dipped in and out of her *Journals*, read her letters to *My Dear Mr. M.*, and learned much more about the life and customs of that time. As a result, Montgomery herself became more and more familiar to me. I continue to marvel at her ability to cram so much into her life: her teaching, her arduous duties to her grandmother, the writing of her many novels and poems, her speeches and recitals, the writing and editing of her voluminous journals, her vast correspondence, the balancing of her roles as mother and protective wife and church worker, the endurance of so much anxiety and depression and repressed rebellion, the mood swings – all of this with an astonishing ability to experience and radiate humour, joy, a love of beauty, a cherishing of relationships, and a hunger for a lot of fun and foolishness. Whether consciously or through a kind of spiritual osmosis, I feel that my increasing knowledge of Montgomery somehow seeped into my understanding of who Anne was.

Another recollection helped, too. When I was a small child, my father would lie down beside me every night at bedtime and tell me stories about his own childhood. He was born in 1890 – at a time not far distant from Anne's – living on a subsistence farm in Nova Scotia, one of thirteen children. He didn't know he was providing raw material for a book I would write seventy years later. I did most of my further research by picking the brains of other people. I consulted with Betsy Epperly as well as with several less professional authorities in matters of Anne's history and that of Montgomery herself. I gave my historian husband a list of about twenty questions that needed to be answered (everything from the invention of pencils and safety pins to Victorian winter footwear, and to the various sizes and uses of horse-drawn vehicles), and he supplied me with detailed information, often with pictures from the Internet. I conferred with a first cousin who had extensive knowledge about early educational practices, traditions, and equipment. Another friend brought me up to date on the development and use of electricity in Nova Scotia during Anne's lifespan. This is how I always do my research. It's easier on the eyes and the nervous system than spending long hours in archives or on the Internet.

Eventually I was told that the sample chapter had passed the test. So far, so good. But not very far. They required an outline. I was used to producing miniscule outlines for my novels – two pages in a Hilroy notebook, produced, set aside, seldom referred to. For *Before Green Gables* I provided thirty-eight typed pages, with most of the main characters at least introduced. Word came back that they (and I never really knew who "they" were) were upset because in the outline, Anne steals something. I told Helen Reeves that I didn't yet know what she would steal, and that she might feel sorry she'd done it. She might even give it back. *But she was going to steal it.* Another similar incident happened, but once again I stood my ground. Shortly after that, I was turned loose to write the book. "They" would await the first draft of the entire book, without shooting any more holes in the outline.

Finally I asked Helen Reeves, "For whom am I writing this book?" She replied, "For all the people who have read *Anne of Green Gables.*" "From nine to eighty-nine," I thought. Eighty years of readership. This was too huge a concept to manoeuvre into my plans. So I ignored it. I would simply sit down and write the story as it came out of my head and hand. Which is what I did.

I wrote the first forty chapters on a big bed in a converted and uninsulated fishhouse in a small village on Nova Scotia's South Shore. At high tide I felt as though I were in a boat, looking out the two big windows and seeing only water. Apart from the temperature, it was a perfect place to write a book. I was about a hundred feet from our main house, and totally isolated. I started in mid-October, and worked until the end of November, with two small glass heaters trying hard to keep me warm. I put the outline aside and scarcely looked at it. Then I began to write.

As with all the stories I write, I tried to let the narrative emerge without plans as to structure or depth of character. The development of these elements took place organically, like a plant – not built piece by piece as in a tower of blocks. I followed the characters where they chose to go, and let the plot unfold accordingly. I loved writing that book. It's true that I felt genuine grief when people died or when there were wrenching partings. But through it all – and there is a lot of sadness in this book – I enjoyed what I was doing. I didn't stop to analyze Anne, or to work out what she would do or say. I didn't push her. Firmly embedded in my mind, she spoke and moved around on her own, with me coming along behind, recording it.

After the end of November, my husband and I moved into Halifax. The move, Christmas preparations and activity, and many other commitments made it impossible to keep the same tidy schedule. But I kept a record of starting and stopping dates and times, and can say that the seventy-one chapters of the first draft took me seventy-one days to write. The last of the six hundred hand-written pages was written – not by design – on my eightieth birthday, on 2 May 2007.

I then had to await the arrival of the typed version of my draft. It came from Brandon, Manitoba, where Monika Sormova – who had started the job in Dartmouth – heroically deciphered my arthritic handwriting and converted it into a text I could easily read and edit. I looked forward to this part of making the book. For me, a first draft is quick, intense, exciting. But I find the editing process relaxing and peaceful – going through the pages slowly, line by line, word by word, adjusting rhythms, checking my spelling, making sure that the dialogue sounds like real speech, inserting paragraph breaks. I love this slow and satisfying process.

But the period of peacefulness was not to be. Penguin needed my edited first draft by the end of June. Over a month was cut off my original deadline; and I also had to factor in postal times between Halifax and Brandon for changes in the manuscript. It was necessary for me to produce the edit very quickly. I had to hurry.

The American publisher, Putnam, had committed to buying the rights to *Before Green Gables* – the first of our foreign sales – early in the process. However, before we in Canada got to the copy-edit and proof stage, Putnam sent word that they wanted the book to be cut by approximately a hundred pages.

This was my biggest nightmare in the making of the book. It fell to my own editor to cut the text, and I was faced with a manuscript in which I felt that some of the most crucial sections were to be removed. Writing "stet" (meaning "keep") in the margins was the quick and easy part of my job. Explaining the reasons for keeping much of the material intact was both time-consuming and agonizing. I won most of my battles, and my editor stood by my decisions. With enough time, I could have reduced the length in a way that could have pleased everyone – including me. But by then, all of us – Americans and Canadians – were racing toward printing and publishing deadlines. Putnam used my second-last manuscript for their final copy edit. Hence, there are small but important differences between the Canadian and American editions. In fact, from the day I dotted the last "i" and crossed the last "t" on my first handwritten draft, time was my enemy.

Never mind. I'm glad I wrote the book. I still sometimes wonder if L.M. Montgomery would have wanted me to write it. But the actual writing of it was deeply satisfying. Much of the fan mail I receive starts with some variation on the words, "I approached this book with misgivings, but ..." Well – I understand that. I had misgivings, too. And most of the messages end by saying that the letter-writer is going straight to the bookshelf or the library or the bookstore to read or reread *Anne of Green Gables*. This fact pleases me very much.

Writing the prequel, surviving some of the deeper pitfalls, and enjoying some of the unexpected results of the project have certainly enriched my life. Helen Reeves was always an insightful and understanding friend and editor. It was an honour to receive the warm welcome from Montgomery's family, and to co-operate with them in this venture. Thanks also go to Sally Keefe Cohen and Marian Hebb for their ongoing assistance. I'm grateful to my publisher for making all those experiences possible.

But there were other enormous benefits for me from writing *Before Green Gables*. I discovered that I had a hunger to learn more and more about the writer of all those many *Anne* books. I wanted to really know the person who created such amazing stories. I longed to understand the inner life of a woman who could invent a character like Anne – so vibrant and real that she has become a literary icon. In the writing of my own book, my knowledge about the creator of *Anne of Green Gables* triggered an odd and tenuous triangle for me, made up of Maud, Anne, and me. How or why this helped me in my own writing is a mystery. But I feel that we were all part of one another, in a way that defies reason. Learning more about L.M. Montgomery – her life, her thoughts, her joys and suffering – has been for me as interesting and valuable as rediscovering Anne. And that particular journey is far from complete.

## NOTES

1  Montgomery, *Anne of the Island*, 296.
2  Ibid., 297.

## BIBLIOGRAPHY

Montgomery, Lucy Maud. *Anne of the Island*. Toronto: Ryerson Press, 1949.
Wilson, Budge. *Before Green Gables*. Toronto: Viking Canada, 2008

# Author Biographies

YOSHIKO AKAMATSU (PhD; professor, Notre Dame Seishin University, Okayama, Japan) is a scholar of John Donne and Emily Dickinson, but she has been interested in L.M. Montgomery since childhood. She translated Montgomery's collection of short stories, *Akin to Anne: Tales of Other Orphans* (1989), into Japanese and continues her study of Montgomery's works. In 1999 she contributed "Japanese Readings of *Anne of Green Gables*" to *L.M. Montgomery and Canadian Culture*. She was cultural advisor for the Japanese anime "The Emily Series" (2007). Her chapter, "*Anne of Green Gables* as a Girls' Story and Adolescent Novel," was published in *World Classics We Would Like to Know More About*, vol. 10: *Anne of Green Gables* (2008), and her book, *A Reading of John Donne's Rhetoric*, was published in 2009. With one exception, Akamatsu has attended every L.M. Montgomery International Conference and presented in 2008, 2010, and 2012.

DORELEY CAROLINA COLL is an associate professor of Spanish and Latin American Studies in the Department of Modern Languages at the University of Prince Edward Island. She obtained her PhD in Comparative Literature and Hispanic Studies at the University of Toronto. She is the author of several articles on Latin American contemporary literature, Cervantes (*Don Quixote*), and women writers. In 2006 she published *Epistemología subversiva: el discurso místico de Teresa de Jesús y Clarice Lispector* (Pliegos, Madrid). She emigrated to Canada with her family in 1972.

BROOKE COLLINS-GEARING grew up in Kamilaroi country in northern New South Wales. She taught Aboriginal Studies at the University of Newcastle before moving to the School of Humanities and Social

Science, where she teaches children's literature, Indigenous literature, and postcolonial literature.

**MARGARET DOODY** is an internationally recognized author, critic, and professor of Literature at Notre Dame University, Indiana, with expertise in Restoration and eighteenth-century British Literature and the history of prose fiction. She has written about L.M. Montgomery in *The Annotated Anne of Green Gables* (1997) and is the author of *Alchemists* and a series of mystery novels, entitled *Aristotle Detective*, which has been translated into many languages.

**ELIZABETH R. EPPERLY,** founder of the L.M. Montgomery Institute at the University of Prince Edward Island and former president of that university, has been a lifelong Montgomery reader. Her most recent books include *Imagining Anne: The Island Scrapbooks of L.M. Montgomery* (Penguin, 2008) and *Through Lover's Lane: L.M. Montgomery's Photography and Visual Imagination* (University of Toronto Press, 2007).

**BARBARA CARMAN GARNER** is an adjunct research professor of English and the mentorship co-ordinator in the College of the Humanities at Carleton University, where she taught from 1967 to her retirement in 2004. Garner has been active in the International Children's Literature Association (ChLA) since 1984. Garner has published on Natalis Comes and Francis Bacon, Rosemary Sutcliff, L.M. Montgomery, Canadian time-slip fantasies, and the reception history of Louis Hémon's *Maria Chapdelaine*. Current research includes L.M. Montgomery's religious beliefs as reflected in her journals, correspondence, and fiction.

**CAROLINE E. JONES** is assistant professor of English at Texas State University–San Marcos, where she teaches courses in children's literature and adolescent literature. She has published on female sexuality in children's and adolescent literature in *Children's Literature Association Quarterly, Children's Literature in Education*, and *The Lion and the Unicorn*. Her master's thesis explored the happy ending convention in L.M. Montgomery's Emily trilogy; current research projects include the roles of religion and motherhood in Montgomery's work, as well as the faces of the rebel in Suzanne Collins's Panem trilogy.

PAUL KEEN is professor of English at Carleton University. He is the author of *Literature, Commerce, and the Spectacle of Modernity, 1750–1800* (Cambridge, 2012), and *The Crisis of Literature in the 1790s: Print Culture and the Public Sphere* (Cambridge, 1999). His edited books include *The Radical Popular Press in Britain, 1817–1821* (Pickering & Chatto, 2003), *Revolutions in Romantic Literature: An Anthology of Print Culture, 1780–1832* (Broadview Press, 2004), *Bookish Histories: Books, Literature, and Commercial Modernity, 1700–1900* (with Ina Ferris, Palgrave, 2009), and *The Age of Authors: An Anthology of Eighteenth-Century Print Culture* (Broadview Press, forthcoming).

JANE LEDWELL, volume co-editor, is a writer and editor from Prince Edward Island, where she received the Award for Distinguished Contribution to the Literary Arts in 2011. She holds an MPhil from the University of Waikato, New Zealand, and has taught Island Studies and English at the University of Prince Edward Island. She contributed to *Storm and Dissonance: L.M. Montgomery and Conflict* (2008) and co-edited *Message in a Bottle: The Literature of Small Islands* (2000). She has also published a volume of poems, *Last Tomato* (2005), and recently co-authored *Elaine Harrison: I Am an Island That Dreams* (2011).

JENNIE MACDONALD received her PhD in literary studies at the University of Denver, where she focused on eighteenth-century novels and plays. Her dissertation was a critical edition of Robert Jephson's *The Count of Narbonne* (1781), the first stage adaptation of Horace Walpole's seminal Gothic novel *The Castle of Otranto* (1764). While at Denver, she served as assistant editor for *Restoration and Eighteenth-Century Theatre Research*. She recently contributed entries for the *Wiley-Blackwell Encyclopedia of British Literature 1660–1789* (forthcoming) and a chapter, "The House as Aesthetic Object in Ann Radcliffe's *The Mysteries of Udolpho*," to *The House of Fiction as the House of Life: Representations of the House from Richardson to Woolf* (Cambridge Scholar Press, 2012).

SUSAN MEYER, literary critic and children's author, is professor of English at Wellesley College. Her children's novel, *Black Radishes* (Random House 2010), about a Jewish boy in Nazi-occupied France, has won numerous awards. In addition to other honours, *Black Radishes* won the Sydney Taylor silver medal and was named a Bank Street College of Education Best Children's Book of the Year, a Boston Author's Club Highly Recommended Book, and a Massachusetts Book Award finalist in 2011. Meyer has also written two picture books, *Matthew and Tall Rabbit Go Camping* and the forthcoming *New Shoes*, a story about an African-American girl in the pre–Civil Rights South. Meyer is also the author of *Imperialism at Home: Race and Victorian Women's Fiction* (Cornell University Press), co-editor with Barbara Harman of *The New Nineteenth Century*, and author of numerous articles on nineteenth- and twentieth-century literature. Her essay on L.M. Montgomery's *Emily* novels and the turn-of-the-century Fresh Air controversy appeared in Jean Mitchell, ed, *Storm and Dissonance* (2008).

JEAN MITCHELL, volume co-editor, is an anthropologist from Prince Edward Island who teaches at the University of Prince Edward Island. A specialist in the study of gender, children, youth, and postcolonialism, she edited *Storm and Dissonance: L.M. Montgomery and Conflict* (2008) and recently published an article on police violence and youth in Vanuatu and an article on feminist anthropology. Her current research project explores missionaries and modernity in Vanuatu and Prince Edward Island.

MARY HENLEY RUBIO is university professor emeritus at the University of Guelph, where she taught Canadian, American, and children's literature for thirty-five years. With Elizabeth Hillman Waterston, also professor emeritus, she edited *The Selected Journals of L.M. Montgomery* (Vols. 1–5) between 1985 and 2004 and *The Complete Journals of L.M. Montgomery: The PEI Years, 1889–1900* (published 2012). She and Waterston also co-wrote a short biography, *L.M. Montgomery: Writing a Life*, in 1995. In 2008 Rubio completed the highly praised definitive biography, *Lucy Maud Montgomery: The Gift of Wings*, which became a finalist for Canada's largest non-fiction prize. Rubio and Waterston have collaborated on many other projects, including co-founding the academic journal, *CCL: Canadian Children's Literature* in 1975, and co-editing it with others until 2005.

GHOLAMREZA SAMIGORGANROODI received his PhD in English Literature from Sussex University, UK, in 2004. He was a professor of English in Iran for eleven years and in 2006 immigrated to Canada with his wife and daughter. He has written many articles on Persian and English literatures in academic journals, including *Modern Poetry in Translation*, and has published a book entitled *Ragged Individualism: America in the Political Drama of the 1930s* (2011). He is now professor of English at Fanshawe College in London, Ontario.

WENDY SHILTON is an associate professor at the University of Prince Edward Island and the coordinator for the University Writing Council. Her research interests are American and transatlantic literature, especially of the nineteenth century; poetic-rhetoric intersections, including literary representations of music as a cultural practice; literature and the environmental imagination; writing and rhetorical theory; writing across the curriculum; writing administration theory.

CYNTHIA SUGARS is a professor in the Department of English at the University of Ottawa, where she teaches Canadian literature. She has published widely on Canadian literature and literary criticism and is the editor of three essay collections: *Unhomely States: Theorizing English-Canadian Postcolonialism* (2004); *Home-Work: Postcolonialism, Pedagogy, and Canadian Literature* (2004),; and, with Gerry Turcotte, *Unsettled Remains: Canadian Literature and the Postcolonial Gothic* (2009). Recently, she co-edited a new two-volume historical anthology of Canadian literature with Laura Moss, entitled *Canadian Literature in English: Texts and Contexts*, published by Pearson/Penguin in 2009. She is currently editing the *Oxford Handbook of Canadian Literature* (forthcoming in 2014), and, with Herb Wylie, will be the new co-editor of the scholarly journal *Studies in Canadian Literature*, beginning in 2013.

TANFER EMIN TUNC is an associate professor in the Department of American Culture and Literature at Hacettepe University, Ankara, Turkey. She holds a PhD in American History from the State University of New York at Stony Brook and specializes in Women's Studies with an emphasis on the history of gender, sexuality and reproduction, women's writing, and cultural studies. She is the author/editor of six books and numerous book chapters, reference book entries, book reviews, and journal articles, most of which have appeared in internationally renowned publications such as *Asian Journal of Women's Studies, Foreign*

*Literature Studies, Women's History Review,* and *Journal of Women's History.* She has published extensively on women's literature, including essays and book chapters on Charlotte Perkins Gilman, Charlotte Brontë, Willa Cather, Lucille Clifton, Lillian Hellman, Ruthanne Lum McCunn, Caroline Gordon, Margaret Mitchell, Paisley Rekdal, Alice Randall, and Wendy Wasserstein, as well as the book *Feminism's Unfinished Legacy: Critiques of Gender and Racial Inequality in Contemporary American Women's Literature* (VDM, 2011).

ÅSA WARNQVIST received her PhD in literature in 2007 and holds a postdoctoral position at Stockholm University in Sweden. She has a special interest in children's literature and is the editor of the only Swedish academic journal on children's literature, *Barnboken: Journal of Children's Literature Research.* She is also a critic and former editor of children's literature in the Swedish daily newspaper *Svenska Dagbladet.* Warnqvist's postdoctoral research project "L.M. Montgomery in Sweden," largely funded by the Swedish Research Council, focuses on Montgomery's success in Sweden and her impact on Swedish readers and writers. Warnqvist has presented results from her project at several international conferences, and, together with Dr Gabriella Åhmansson, she was coordinator for the international conference "L.M. Montgomery – Writer of the World" held in Uppsala in 2009. The two scholars are currently editing a collection of essays from this conference. Warnqvist has also published several essays on Montgomery and edited a volume of Swedish reading experiences of Montgomery's fiction (published 2009). She has been a Visiting Scholar at the L.M. Montgomery Institute, University of Prince Edward Island (2011–13).

ELIZABETH HILLMAN WATERSTON is the author of *Magic Island: The Fictions of L.M. Montgomery* (2008), *Kindling Spirit: Anne of Green Gables* (1993), and many articles about Montgomery. Now professor emerita of the University of Guelph, she co-edited with Mary Rubio the five-volume *Selected Journals of L.M. Montgomery,* the recently published *Complete Journals of L.M. Montgomery: The PEI Years, 1889–1900,* the Norton Critical Edition of *Anne of Green Gables,* and five Montgomery novels in the New American Library series. In 2011 she was appointed to the Order of Ontario for her "lifetime contribution to Canadian literature and culture," as a teacher, mentor of upcoming writers, and researcher, "most authoritatively on Lucy Maud Montgomery." In 2012 she released the autobiographical *Blitzkrieg and Jitterbugs: College Life in Wartime, 1939–1942.*

BUDGE WILSON has published thirty-three books with twenty-seven foreign editions in fourteen languages – and has appeared in over ninety anthologies. Her writing has received much recognition, including twenty-one Canadian Children's Book Centre "Our Choice" awards; finalist for Commonwealth Prize (Canada and Caribbean Region); finalist for Governor General's Award (2006); being shortlisted for CBA's Libris Children's Author of the Year Award (2009); CLA's Best Children's Book Award (2009); and winner of Atlantic Independent Booksellers' Choice Award (2009). She received honorary degrees from Dalhousie University (LLD) in 2010 and Mount St. Vincent University (DHumL) in 2011. She was made a Member of the Order of Nova Scotia (2011) and was awarded the Queen Elizabeth II's Diamond Jubilee Medal (2012). Her books have been frequently read and dramatized on CBC and American and Danish Radio. Her book *Before Green Gables* appears to date in eleven countries and seven languages, with a Japanese animation, and was recognized by *Quill & Quire* as being one of the "Best Books of 2008."

# Index